Theater of State

Theater of State

A Dramaturgy of the United Nations

◆

James R. Ball III

NORTHWESTERN UNIVERSITY PRESS
EVANSTON, ILLINOIS

Northwestern University Press
www.nupress.northwestern.edu

Copyright © 2020 by Northwestern University Press.
Published 2020. All rights reserved.

Printed in the United States of America

10 9 8 7 6 5 4 3 2 1

Library of Congress Cataloging-in-Publication Data

Names: Ball, James R., III, author.
Title: Theater of state : a dramaturgy of the United Nations / James R. Ball III.
Description: Evanston : Northwestern University Press, 2019. | Includes bibliographical references.
Identifiers: LCCN 2019022509 | ISBN 9780810141117 (paperback) | ISBN 9780810141124 (cloth) | ISBN 9780810141131 (ebook)
Subjects: LCSH: Communication in politics. | Persuasion (Rhetoric)—Political aspects. | Diplomacy—Political aspects. | Theater—Political aspects.
Classification: LCC JA85 .B355 2019 | DDC 320.014—dc23
LC record available at https://lccn.loc.gov/2019022509

For my parents, Jean and Jim

CONTENTS

Acknowledgments	ix
Introduction: "Big Heart, Tiny Legs I Guess"	3
1 "Purpose Is but the Slave to Memory" *Narrative and History in the Security Council*	23
2 "To Be Seen Is to Be Doomed" *The Force of Spectatorship in UN Peacekeeping*	43
3 "The World of the Rulers Is the World of the Spectacle" *Time and Reiteration in Diplomatic Speech*	71
4 "To Receive an Impression Is to Make an Impression" *Clapping Along with the Secretary-General*	91
5 "Between One Person and Another" *Interfacing with Institutions at the International Criminal Court*	109
6 "No More Than a Piece of Paper" *The Written Word in a Theater of States*	133
Epilogue: "On Notice" and "Taking Names"	159
Notes	163
Bibliography	191
Index	205

ACKNOWLEDGMENTS

This project began while I was a graduate student in the Department of Performance Studies at New York University, where this work benefited from my encounters with many scholars. Karen Shimakawa has had the most sustained impact on the work and on my development as a scholar; I am deeply grateful for her mentorship, intellectual engagement with my work, and support. I am grateful to many others: Diana Taylor first posed to me a question that guided many of my investigations, "Why do states perform?"; Randy Martin encouraged me to lay claim to the political stakes of my arguments; Carol Martin pressed me to develop a dramaturgy of the United Nations; and Ted Ziter prompted me to ask what the United Nations' theatricality might reveal. I am also thankful for ongoing conversations with colleagues and friends made in my time at NYU, especially Pablo Assumpção Barros Costa, Biba Bell, Gelsey Bell, Lydia Brawner, Sarah Kozinn, Krista Miranda, Jessica N. Pabón-Colón, Alex Pittman, and Marcos Steuernagel.

As I began to study the United Nations, Thomas G. Weiss introduced me to Security Council Report, where I worked during much of my research. My time with Security Council Report added incalculably to my understanding of the UN, the International Criminal Court, and global conflict. I am especially thankful for conversations with Joanna Weschler, Colin Keating, Bruno Stagno Ugarte, Amanda Roberts, Shamala Kandiah Thompson, Paul Romita, Eran Sthoeger, Astrid Forberg Ryan, Nicholas Walbridge, Dahlia Morched, Laura Coquard-Wallace, and Robbin VanNewkirk.

One consequence of conducting research at the UN is that many who I must thank would prefer to remain anonymous. Nonetheless, I extend my heartfelt thanks to my anonymous interlocutors in New York, The Hague, and beyond. I also deeply appreciate the time and energies of the playwright Karen Sunde and the dramaturge Imanuel Schipper, for sitting with me for extended on-the-record interviews.

This book developed in exciting ways during my time as a visiting assistant professor in the School of Theatre, Dance, and Performance Studies at the University of Maryland, College Park. From my time there, I am especially grateful to Faedra Chatard Carpenter, Adriane Fang, Laurie Frederik, James Harding, Leigh Wilson Smiley, and Laronika Thomas. My colleagues at Texas A&M University have also contributed much to this book. I am especially thankful for the input of Harris Berger, Leonardo Cardoso, Matthew DelCiampo, David Donkor, Donnalee Dox, Kim Kattari, Elise Morrison, and Kirsten Pullen.

I have presented elements of this research at several conferences, including Performance Studies international, the Association for Theatre in Higher Education, the American Society for Theatre Research, and the Law and Society Association. The work has gained much from the input of those I have interacted with there, including Heather Nathans, Catherine Cocks, Paige McGinley, and others too numerous to name. An early version of chapter 4 appeared in *Popular Music and Public Diplomacy: Transnational and Transdisciplinary Perspectives*, edited by Mario Dunkel and Sina Nitzsche (Bielefeld: Transcript Verlag, 2018). I am deeply grateful to Mario and Sina (and all who attended the Popular Music and Public Diplomacy conference they organized) for the feedback they provided at a crucial moment in the development of this project. In addition, I am thankful for the support of Gianna Mosser at Northwestern University Press, and for the input of my anonymous readers, all of whom were invaluable in helping this book achieve its final form.

Finally, this work would have been impossible without the support of my many friends in and beyond the academy (especially Adam Kielman and Matt Clark); my parents, Jim and Jean; my sister, Meghan; and most of all my wife, Meredith Wells.

Theater of State

Figure 1. Gérard Araud (*background, right*), permanent representative of France to the UN, looks on as Vitaly I. Churkin (*foreground, left*), permanent representative of the Russian Federation to the UN, speaks to correspondents following Security Council consultations on Syria on August 2, 2012. UN Photo by Mark Garten.

Introduction

✦

"Big Heart, Tiny Legs I Guess"

A curtain rises on a simple stained-wood construction, four tall platforms forming an amphitheater evocative of the United Nations' debating forums, and outfitted with miniature microphones and country name placards, behind which each delegate—one of forty-seven brown or black dachshunds—sits or stands. Debate begins quietly, respectfully, but soon becomes heated as the delegates bark their displeasure or excitement at one another. Others are nonplussed—a few yawn, a few nap. Some delegates roam the construction, peering over its edges, though if they go too far handlers appear from interstitial spaces below to keep their representatives on task. For some, exploratory sniffs become playful tumbles, and human hands interpose themselves between the animals who have been asked to play at being diplomats. The Australian sculptor Bennett Miller's installation, *Dachshund UN*, has traveled widely in the Anglophone world since it was first exhibited in Melbourne, Australia, in 2010, making its way to Birmingham in the United Kingdom in 2012, and touring Toronto and Montreal, Canada, in 2013. The performance is a live event that has been expertly designed for mediated consumption online, and it has circulated even further on the Web in the months and years since.

This sly depiction of the United Nations Human Rights Council (a body that meets in Geneva to promote human rights norms and assess human rights situations in UN member states) offers a clear structure but no fixed script for the dachshunds that are cast anew in each locale as national representatives of the council's forty-seven member states. Press reports from each iteration attest to the variety of canine diplomatic performances (and geopolitically charged anthropomorphic interpretations) that the structure invites. In Birmingham, spectators noted that "France is rather yappy," and journalists seized on the moment when "the notably oversized United States popped up in Pakistan."[1] In Toronto, "Burkina Faso barked a lot and eventually had to be removed. Japan was on good behaviour . . . Mexico was pretty annoying. And Hungary and Bangladesh slept through the whole thing."[2] In Montreal, environmental concerns took their toll on the delegates, "some of [whom] were shivering," but they may have also contributed to closer relations between nations, as Russia was found "snuggling up to the Philippines."[3]

The event resists easy categorization. As satire it might be dismissed as a cynical riff on some low-hanging fruit; this was the course followed by one Twitter user, who opined, "Hey turns out the #DaschundUN [sic] is totally ineffective and has no consequent bearing on international law . . . just like the real UN! #rimshot."[4] Such wry detachment came easily in Sydney, Birmingham, and Montreal where the installation was exhibited in public spaces, open to passersby and the weather. However, when the piece was framed as a ticketed theatrical performance with an established running time, it asked for more attention and investment. In Toronto, the raked wooden platforms of Miller's mock-council seating mirrored the raked auditorium seating of the Harbourfront Centre's Enwave Theatre, calling on the audience to scrutinize the performance for an extended duration. This added focus troubled any easy dismissal of the frivolity of the theater or the utility of the institution.

Miller himself came to the project with reverence for both doggies and delegates. In interviews he has noted the multiple dachshunds "that were a big part of my life" and the particular resonance of his own juxtapositions: "the dachshund . . . has a physical shape that is appropriate for the UN—mainly because they have tiny 'restricted' legs and they have suitably proud expressions. Big heart, tiny legs I guess."[5]

Dachshund UN speaks volumes about the relationship between theater and international institutions like the UN. *Dachshund UN* depicts a United Nations organ, interprets it for an audience, and then reflects it back to the home institution, forming a complex of theatrical and political practices and forces that make both diplomacy and the performing arts meaningful and effective. Miller's modest commentary ("Big heart, tiny legs I guess") indicates the avenues by which institution, art, and audience can neither escape nor avoid one another. Miller's analogy between dogs and diplomats situates him as both an actor and spectator in global dramas as he figures the capacities of the UN and makes a claim for the utility of artistic intervention. *Dachshund UN* draws the attentions of many who subsequently oscillate between positions of spectator and actor: the community participants who provide the dogs, a paying audience interpreting them, and even the dogs themselves, who often act by watching one another and the curious humans who are so active around them.

Some commentators have argued that the power of *Dachshund UN* derives largely from the fact that "dogs aren't really capable of 'acting,'"[6] and that Miller's conscripted canines evade the traps of theatricality, indicting the UN in part through the authenticity of their self-presentations. While I do not doubt the power of forty-seven dachshunds to hold an audience's attention for an hour or more, I am unconvinced that *Dachshund UN* makes meaning by drawing our eyes to these pups in spite of the loaded structure they inhabit. Rather, *Dachshund UN*'s power is predicated on the structures of theatricality that inhere in public political spaces. We watch for the forms of signification made possible by placing these predictably unpredictable actors on a mock world stage.

In the twenty-first century, this is also why we watch the United Nations, however more scripted its actors prove. International institutions like the UN focus the world's attention on publicly staged spectacles of geopolitics by providing a theatrical frame that makes them legible, meaningful, and efficacious. Via this inherent theatricality, these institutions employ the forces of spectatorship that are drawn into orbit around them. International institutions crystallize a relationship between power and attention that is highly theatrical in its contours and scope. The United Nations and the International Criminal Court focus the gaze of an international community on what come to be written as errant states, dangerous populations, and individual perpetrators of violence. As a function of this global political spectatorship, the United Nations and the International Criminal Court move states, populations, and bodies across the territories of the earth and into particular configurations to act and perform in expressly theatrical modes. Theater is a material process with which diplomats and states accomplish their desired ends.

If diplomacy is theater, it is also performative. The words and gestures of diplomats—their diplomatic performative acts—make the world. And in conjuring the world, diplomats compete with theater-makers. Both tell stories that have effects and consequences, that do more than merely describe the world or some part of it. Both transform spoken or written words into concrete actions, performed by certain bodies, that have effects on other bodies. Aesthetic theater and public diplomacy are both arts of enactment that stabilize shared narratives to serve particular ends, work they can do in tandem or at odds with one another.

As performative practices grounded by the theatricality of their conventions and the spectators they require for propulsion, theater and diplomacy are mutually constitutive phenomena that emerge from a cohesive field of practices. The affinity between the two forms stretches well beyond metaphor, as Miller's casual "I guess" attests. Miller does not so much hedge the applicability of his metaphor as undermine that it is metaphor at all. In theatrically producing the link between institution and canine reinterpretation, he performatively produces the contours and capacities of an international community that is tethered to his own viewing position in the present. Standing as audience to *Dachshund UN*, Miller invites us to ask, are the dachshunds agents of parody, looking backwards at a failed project of global governance, or are they agents of aspiration, propelling us to move forward toward a world as peaceful as puppies? The work the UN is able to accomplish or not is intimately caught up with the web of meanings it inevitably takes on—"big heart, tiny legs" composes a particular vision of international community in which Miller would participate.

Our communities, and the institutions that reproduce those communities ideologically and substantially, are made in the theatrical representations of both policy-makers and artists. As such, it behooves artists, policy-makers, and scholars to develop theories and practices founded on the field shared by public political performances and aesthetic representations of the events and institutions that compose world history. When the UN proves unable to see, hear, or participate in what aesthetic dramas provide, theater opens a space for reflection, interpretation, and revision that the international system often disallows. When it does so, art can become a tool for tripping up what otherwise appear as unassailable processes. At the same time, when theater-makers underestimate the theatricality of politics, they blind themselves to the political structures in which they participate. In these cases, art serves power whether it intended to or not.

This book is a dramaturgy of international institutions. It maps the dramatic structure and cultural reach of the United Nations and the International Criminal Court. In the coming chapters I detail the theatrical efforts of world leaders, diplomats, and individual citizens to write a collective history in both policy and culture to serve as the ground for geopolitical performance. This book also provides a theory of global political spectatorship: of how the world watches itself in institutions and beyond, and of what citizens and diplomats *do* by watching. This project takes its urgency from the fact that even though global politics proceeds theatrically, interpellating individuals across the development spectrum as spectators to its machinations and gestures, the aesthetic acts of individual artists often seem powerless to intervene.

So we find an abyss between Miller's dachshunds in Toronto and the scene outside the United Nations' Security Council in New York a few weeks later, in March 2013. It was two years into Syria's deepening civil war, a crisis that regularly pitted diplomats from France, the United Kingdom, and the United States (who sided with the rebel forces) against their counterparts from Russia and China (who sided with the regime of Bashar al-Assad). In the Security Council Chamber, France had been yapping about renewed allegations that both the government of Syria and rebel forces had used chemical weapons against civilian targets in the city of Aleppo and elsewhere. At the media stakeout following consultations on March 20, 2013, Ambassador Vitaly Churkin, the permanent representative of Russia to the United Nations, had little time for allegations against a regime with which his own government was so cozy. "Of course, if the Secretary-General starts this investigation he will be free to consider . . . such exotic proposals as investigating *rumors.*" As he said this, Churkin's face and torso bulged forward to emphasize the word the French had used in an effort to rouse Secretary-General Ban Ki-moon to action.[7] The mise-en-scène of the UN brings together in one space actors who are at odds with one another, and so Gérard Araud, the permanent representative of France to the United Nations, was able to provide his exasperated rejoinder only moments later. "Now the other side of the truth," he announced as he approached the stakeout microphone, "after this fascinating reconstruction of our meeting." He went on to dispute Churkin's characterization: France and the United Kingdom had together raised the issue of *reports*, not rumors, in the Security Council, forcing the issue onto the UN's agenda (figure 1).[8]

These diplomats staged a dispute over language, quoting each other to develop their dialogue. The dynamic between Churkin and Araud illustrates the drama with which closed-door negotiations emerge into a theatrical idiom, becoming scripted or unscripted public presentations. The performance draws together in a single moment a set of forces traveling through and past the institution: other delegates looking on, journalists posing questions, national governments receiving policy recommendations, and global citizens consuming the day's news. The performance and its audience form the locus where diplomacy happens.

The theatricality of the ambassadors' verbal sparring brought differently efficacious categories of spectatorship into brief alignment with one another, and the secretary-general's subsequent activities extended these gazes to the battlefield in Syria itself. Within days, Ban Ki-moon announced his intention to launch an investigation into the use of chemical weapons in Syria. Though the mission would not be mandated to assign culpability, the subsequent obstructionism of the Syrian regime towards the inspectors indicated that its leaders understood the value of spectatorship in international relations: as the UN strove to direct the world's gaze toward a zone of conflict, Syria endeavored to keep its acts off the stage. For some time, it seemed that these tactics would be effective: throughout the summer, though wrangling over the inspectors' access continued, a stalemate in the Security Council threatened to de-theatricalize the process. Waning attention coincided with the perception among those following the war in Syria that the Security Council would not be the venue in which a peaceful resolution to the conflict would be found.

Only a threat dredged up and reiterated in a new context, and parroted and parodied by other speakers, could disrupt Syria's slide back into the geopolitical obscurity reserved for hidden atrocities. A new chemical attack on August 21 returned the issue to screens and newsprint, and the recapitulation of comments made by President Barack Obama a year earlier (that the verifiable use of chemical weapons by the Syrian government would constitute a "red line," and so precipitate military intervention) gave events renewed theatrical urgency. In the threat of military action, a head of state exercises power but also provides a performative commitment that might be invoked by citizens, media, and rivals to contrasting ends. In such a milieu, returning to the Security Council in September proved useful to both sides, a reminder of why even the militarily powerful deign to perform on the UN's stages. Syria's allies and opponents both found success in staging the adoption of Resolution 2118, which provided for the destruction of Syria's chemical weapons under the auspices of the Organization for the Prohibition of Chemical Weapons (OPCW).[9]

This brief rehearsal of the events of 2013 offers several clues to the dramaturgical logic of international institutions: the theatrical distribution of onstage and offstage roles and the forms of spectatorship that organize the use of force in world affairs. My gloss also reiterates the very work of the council, in its own reports, statements, and resolutions, to write a particular history as it proceeds: a "fascinating reconstruction" (to use Araud's words from the stakeout) in which the status of each actor transforms in each new iteration, laying the groundwork for each subsequent performance. International institutions provide the spatial, temporal, and performative structures for performances of variable magnitude, framing geopolitical dramas with short and long durations. Each individual scene detailed above (each public statement or negotiation) features its own dramatic arc and fits into larger narratives spanning ever-greater distances and time frames. The wrangling over Syria's chemical weapons becomes sensible as a drama by tying together scenes staged in New York, Washington, Damascus, Geneva, Moscow, and elsewhere. This drama also forms a constituent part of the longer saga of Syria's civil war, which itself may be nested in theatrical retellings of the Arab Spring, the War on Terror, or the history of the twenty-first century.

Drama and dramaturgy do not function here as mere metaphors or conceptual aids. Rather, taking a dramaturgical approach to international institutions serves to contextualize individual moments of performance within historical narratives that render them meaningful and efficacious. Theater provides the terms by which disparate locations of performance, diverse public utterances, and circulating sounds and images can be drawn together within a rubric that accounts for the forces captured and mobilized in public diplomacy. In diplomacy, discourse is always performative, and describing a series of events is an act with material effects; it is a way of doing politics on the world stage.

A Dramaturgy of International Institutions

In 1944, with the end of World War II approaching, representatives of the United States, the Soviet Union, the United Kingdom, and China met at the Dumbarton Oaks estate in Washington, D.C., to discuss a successor organization to the League of Nations. The league, an intergovernmental organization dedicated to maintaining peace, had been established following World War I and had been abandoned as war neared again in the late 1930s. At Dumbarton Oaks plans were debated and drafted, leading to expanded negotiations in San Francisco in April 1945 that produced a new charter for a new organization: the United Nations. The San Francisco Conference filled spaces usually reserved for stage performances with debating diplomats. Plenary sessions were held in the War Memorial Opera House, and on June 26, 1945, delegates signed the UN Charter onstage in the adjacent Veterans Auditorium.[10]

The charter scripted a United Nations system consisting of six principal organs: the Secretariat, the Security Council, the General Assembly, the Economic and Social Council, the Trusteeship Council, and the International Court of Justice. The charter arranged key actors for the postwar world on these stages. It opened UN membership to all "peace-loving states which accept the obligations" of membership in the organization.[11] At its start, the UN had 51 member states whose representatives met in the General Assembly for dialogue and debate. Owing to a slow but inexorable process of decolonization, the UN's ranks swelled in the second half of the twentieth century. A total of 76 states were meeting at the UN by 1955, a number that had nearly doubled to 144 by 1975, and that has reached 193 today.[12] These peace-loving states accept their charter obligations, but they also recognize that far from being a concerted effort towards global government, the UN has always been a place where the national sovereignty of independent states is vigorously defended.

The UN Charter's "Preamble" laid out lofty ambitions—"to save succeeding generations from the scourge of war" and "to reaffirm faith . . . in the equal rights of men and women and of nations large and small"[13]—but it also reified existing global hierarchies. The charter's authors aimed to right the perceived deficiencies of the League of Nations, such as the lack of participation by major powers like the United States.[14] Among other measures, this defect was addressed in the new organization through a veto power allotted to the five permanent members of the Security Council; these members were militarily powerful states without whom no collective effort on the part of the UN could be successful.[15] Such compromises inscribed a tension into the organization between its egalitarian premises, and the reality of what it can accomplish so long as military power remains the primary force for organizing and ordering the world.[16]

A violent world had other influences on the UN's emergent mise-en-scène. In 1967, Inis L. Claude, Jr., reminded his readers of the apocalyptic context framing the institution at its birth: "Between the Charter and the inauguration of the United Nations [in October 1945] lay the unveiling of the atomic bomb, which proved to be only the harbinger of more spectacular things to come."[17] By 1964, the five permanent members of the UN Security Council would not just wield the veto; four out of five of them would also wield nuclear weapons.

Cold War divisions largely impeded the work of the UN to address international peace and security during its first decades. Chapters VI and VII of the UN Charter (on the "Pacific Settlement of Disputes" and "Action with Respect to Threats to the Peace, Breaches of the Peace, and Acts of Aggression") direct the UN's approach to the use of force.[18] Chapter VII called for the establishment of a UN Military Staff committee to lead a standing army of troops dedicated to enforcing the Security Council's directives. This committee never materialized in the face of Soviet opposition.[19] In light of these strictures, the UN's actors improvised.

The UN deployed what would come to be known as its first peacekeeping operation, the UN Truce Supervision Organization (UNTSO), in 1948, operating under Chapter VI. In 1950, while the Soviet Union was boycotting the Security Council (to protest that the People's Republic of China had not been seated in place of the government of Taiwan), the United States led the Security Council to authorize intervention in the Korean War under Chapter VII, legitimizing the United States' effort to repel North Korea's invasion of South Korea. What now goes under the name of "UN Peacekeeping" developed via these events and subsequent ad hoc deployments: on the border between India and Pakistan, at the Suez Canal, in the Congo, and elsewhere. Without explicit instructions for peacekeeping in the charter, the second UN secretary-general, Dag Hammarskjöld, referred to the basis for such actions as "Chapter Six-and-a-Half."[20] Peacekeeping emerged as an unanticipated policy from institutional interstices where the charter permitted its actors to go off script.

The role of the secretary-general had been conceived in San Francisco as a bureaucratic and clerical position that was designed to support the work of the General Assembly and the Security Council (and thus the agendas of the states which dominated those forums).[21] Yet, the acts of diplomats like Hammarskjöld established new precedents for the role; when these actors became increasingly independent, they invited criticism and resistance from powerful states which had hoped the secretary-general would prove more meek.[22] The superpowers (i.e., the United States and the Soviet Union) may have invested in the UN as an institution that could protect their sovereign interests, but in so doing they set the stage for repertoires of action that could counteract those interests.

The progressive promise of the UN laid the ground for the affective highs and lows experienced by those who watched its work. If the UN was stymied during the Cold War, it was reinvigorated in the early 1990s. Between 1945 and 1988 the UN initiated 13 peacekeeping operations. In the years since it has authorized more than 40.[23] This expanded activity has most often been attributed to the increased collaboration between permanent members of the Security Council that was made possible by the collapse of communism in the Soviet Union. In the early 1990s, the UN seemed on the cusp of fulfilling the aspirations that had been given voice in 1945. Yet, these expectations were soon brought down to earth when the UN's responses proved inadequate to spectacular incidents of violence in Rwanda, eastern Europe, and beyond.[24] And in the first decade of the 2000s, the UN faced new crises as a U.S. administration openly hostile to the institution engaged the Security Council's mechanisms to legitimize the invasion of Iraq.[25]

The UN's purpose and limits are imagined in different ways by different constituencies. Yet, whether the UN is acting in the interests of a more equal world system or facilitating the performances of unequally stratified states, it remains a theatrical structure.[26] No matter what the intentions of the UN

Charter's authors were in reserving the veto for powerful states, the document they produced established the machinery from which would emerge counter-hegemonic efforts toward decolonization, nuclear disarmament, and global economic reform. No matter what the infelicities of the UN's founding promises may be, those same promises lessen the distance between actor and audience in global affairs. Sovereign powers find many protections at the UN, but they cannot do without its stage or the audience it arranges there; the UN may fail in its utopian promises, but few institutions offer similar spaces in which to stage such visions.

Today, the General Assembly and Security Council are the primary spaces of the UN in which the representatives of states meet to perform. The General Assembly, attended by representatives of all 193 member-states, meets regularly for open debate of any issue within the UN's purview. The Security Council's role is more narrowly defined as having "primary responsibility for the maintenance of international peace and security."[27] The Security Council has 15 members: 5 permanent members (China, France, Russia, the United Kingdom, and the United States) and 10 members elected to two-year terms. While the General Assembly makes recommendations to the Security Council, the resolutions of the Security Council are considered binding and carry the force of international law. The UN Secretariat is more an actor than a forum—headed by the secretary-general, it administers many of the UN's programs, and houses the Department of Peacekeeping Operations, which is responsible for directing the UN's peacekeeping activities.

Just as individual states are drawn to perform at or alongside the United Nations, so too do other independent institutions and organizations join with the UN to engage with diplomatic theater. These organizations include nongovernmental organizations (NGOs) and civil society groups (often formally constituted as spectators to the UN's work via their "observer" status), independent treaty-monitoring organizations like the OPCW, intergovernmental forums like the International Atomic Energy Agency, regional organizations like the European Union (EU), and international juridical mechanisms like the relatively young International Criminal Court (ICC). Though independent, many of these organizations maintain material relationships with the UN and its parts. The ICC, for example, accords certain privileges to the UN Security Council. The council can refer situations warranting investigation to the ICC, and can require the court to defer an investigation for a renewable period of twelve months. The prosecutor of the ICC also reports back to the council regularly on those situations it had referred to the court. The council exerts a direct force on what comes to be staged in the ICC's courtrooms in The Hague, and brings the prosecutor to New York for regular briefings. In this manner, the relationship between the court and the council generates theater: it requires live, embodied public performances that travel between the two spaces.

Each organ of the United Nations provides particular contours to the performances it encourages: from grand speechifying in the General Assembly, to informal oratory outside the Security Council, to the choreographies of peacekeepers, to the everyday embodied practices of legions of technocrats. The theatrical force of public diplomacy travels through these performers and between these spaces. Verbal performances in New York drive towards their material realization in the field, producing scenes along the way that invite new spectators to global dramas, that amplify or tamp down individual historical narratives, and that open geopolitical processes to public scrutiny, inviting intervention and renegotiation. This theater resists and postpones closure; it opens out into spaces beyond the UN system even as it feeds back into itself.

International institutions also appear in culture. Actors reenact the speeches of diplomats and heads of state. Plays show audiences what peacekeepers can do. Television programs find melodramas lurking behind the ICC's drab façade. And culture regularly comes to international institutions. Movie stars serve as goodwill ambassadors. Pop singers give concerts at UN headquarters. Broadway receives embassies that have traveled across town from the UN headquarters building in Manhattan.

Any given diplomatic performance inevitably cues further performances by actors elsewhere: the related performances of local politicians, the everyday performances of affected communities, and the theatrical performances of interested artists, to name just a few examples. This dramatic structure of deferral renders adequate contextualization more urgent than ever, indicating the need for a theory of global political spectatorship that can situate individuals (diplomats, politicians, citizens) in space and time as a constituent part of the historical drama of world politics: a dramaturgy of international institutions.

This dramaturgy is both a mode of spectatorship (a way of making meaning from global political spectacle) and a mode of action on the world stage (a form of individual participation in spectacularized world affairs). I privilege the terms "dramaturgy," "theater," and "theatricality" throughout this book to indicate a more specific genre than the broader catch-all term "performance" allows. "Theater" indicates the publicness of diplomatic performance, and "theatricality" points to the political relationship that emerges between stage and spectator in international institutions. "Theater" works through more precise framings than "performance," bracketing particular phenomena in space and time and in place and duration. Global political spectatorship is predicated on the theatricality of global politics, and encourages the dramaturgical acts of citizens. This dramaturgy is both a rigorously cultivated mechanism used by institutions and states and a casual and quotidian practice of individuals.

"Dramaturgy" is a notoriously slippery term, one used by academics and artists to describe a wide variety of practices, techniques, and roles.[28] Though the litheness of the concept is useful, it should not be left ambiguous. Dramaturgy is the work of creating and/or interpreting a performance; it is the work of making meaning with or from performance. It is the creative activity of artists who stage performances, and it is the analytical activity of audiences who receive performances. Framed in this way, the work of dramaturgy is the labor of connecting form and content, labor that devolves to both the artist and the audience, and thus makes an urgent question of the relationship between a spectacle and its spectators. This question bears on the space and time of performance and its reception: it asks where and when performers and spectators are placed vis-à-vis one another. Dramaturgy arranges bodies, assigns them roles, authorizes their speech, and directs them to act in particular styles, using certain gestures but not others. Dramaturgy treats performance from the perspective of those elements that structure theater: space, time, style, word, sound, movement, and so on.

My preference for the term "dramaturgy" also derives from theater's structure of historical reiteration and repetition, a structure that hinges on the relationship between the written text and embodied practice. As an aesthetic practice that has left behind traces for more than two millennia, theater is constituted by a specific historical relationship between written texts, live performances, and the consequences that ripple outward from those performances; the same relationship structures the work of diplomats in international institutions. When dramaturgy begins from a written text, it is the art of defining the relationship between what is written on the page and what a spectator sees, hears, and feels. Dramaturgy recommends itself as a practice of global political spectatorship in its emphasis on this relationship that lies at the heart of both theater and diplomacy.

As a dramaturgy of international institutions, this book is centered on the spectator that dramaturgy addresses. It aims to provide this spectator with a view of herself as a constituent part of geopolitics. If there is anything radical in the coming chapters, it does not lie in a fundamental revision of international relations theory, but in the opportunities that theater makes available to this spectator, newly positioned in a field of history and politics. Rewriting international institutions dramaturgically offers new modes of engagement between citizens, artists, and political leaders (recognizing that the divisions between these three need not be discrete) that are founded on audacious gestures; encounters in good faith; solutions that recognize the value of rehearsal and failure; and an acute awareness of the pitfalls of representation, empathy, and intervention.

To treat public political events dramaturgically is to return to a fundamental question in theater and performance studies, that of the relationship between aesthetics and politics, and the consequences of admitting, as I have done, that they share a unified field. How should we conceive the relationship between art and politics? How do the aesthetic structures of politics and the political structures of art bear on one another? While the discipline of performance studies has long claimed to be relevant to the study of local, global, historical, and contemporary political formations, sustained and rigorous efforts to theorize the fundamental relationships between artistic expression and the enactment and enforcement of public policy remain scarce. I take my first cues for such a theorization from Jacques Rancière, who offers a clear formulation of this relationship: the aesthetics of politics "is a delimitation of spaces and times, of the visible and the invisible, of speech and noise, that simultaneously determines the place and stakes of politics as a form of experience."[29] Rancière names a shared world-making capacity for art and politics, oriented toward a sensing being. At stake in the chapters that follow is this experience of an individual spectator emplaced on a unified field of aesthetics and politics, orbited by and capable of producing their own scenes of diplomatic theater.

A similar image may be found in some of the foundational texts of performance studies; for example, in the "infinity loop" drawn by Richard Schechner and Victor Turner to describe the relationship between social drama (including high-level political events) and aesthetic drama (including traditional theatrical presentations).[30] Where Rancière conceives a field into which art and politics are distributed, Schechner and Turner provide a dynamic diagram of art and politics flowing into one another. Schechner drew the loop as a sideways figure eight, the mathematical symbol for infinity, bisected along its horizontal axis by an additional line dividing the visible from the invisible contents of each field. Arrows on the loop trace the flow of content and form between what each genre puts onstage and keeps off. "The visible actions of a given social drama are informed—shaped, conditioned, guided—by underlying aesthetic principles and specific theatrical/rhetorical techniques. Reciprocally, a culture's visible aesthetic theater is informed—shaped, conditioned, guided—by underlying processes of social interaction."[31] For Schechner, comparison between political theater and staged theater reveals the inverse relationship between what each delivers to its audience and what each keeps hidden. Art and policy sublimate each other to produce their effects.

Though Turner and Schechner each speak of the spectator as they elaborate the infinity loop, the one who watches both social dramas and aesthetic dramas remains absent from the diagram. Though their figure moves, it forgets that politics takes the form of experience.[32] My dramaturgy of international institutions centers on the emplacement of a spectator on or in this loop.

Theater places us as spectators, it establishes our relationship to what we watch. I take up this conviction following Tracy C. Davis's insights into the relationship between spectatorship and theatricality.[33] To Davis, theatricality is "a process of spectatorship"[34] generated when an audience chooses "whether or not to establish a sympathetic bond"[35] with a performance, an act that enables "effects of active dissociation, or alienation, or self-reflexivity in *standing aside from* the suffering of the righteous to name and thus bring into being the self-possession of a critical stance."[36] Samuel Weber expands on the spatial effects attendant on this conjunction of spectatorship and theatricality: "Perhaps the stage can stand for a place in which one is always already placed, without ever being fully at home or definitively positioned . . . a 'being-placed' or emplacement."[37] Those who make theater place us in auditoriums and playhouses to place us in stories and histories to place us in the world. Dramaturgy is one technique that theater uses to place a spectator in a particular position, to foster a particular feeling, and to elicit a particular reaction. So too does diplomatic theater place us—physically, psychologically, and affectively. In theater and diplomacy we negotiate our relationship to politics, remaining agents who emplace and displace ourselves in turn.

When conducting my dramaturgical analyses, I am the first spectator that I place. My methodology proceeds from my emplacement as an engaged audience on the world stage, and my case studies capture performances that circulated around me: the acts of diplomats, artworks that depict institutions, and encounters between the two. In their introduction to the volume *International Politics and Performance*, Jenny Edkins and Adrian Kear bemoan an "'inter-disciplinary' approach which remains primarily interested . . . in elaborating the performance dynamics of politics . . . and the ways in which performance addresses politics and the political."[38] That volume works to bridge divisions that limit the intercourse between politics and performance (as do other recent publications in theater and performance studies).[39] My work operates in a similar vein. I do not posit the political and theatrical as two fields that cross or conjoin, but as two that overlay one another and the spectator who experiences them. In my case studies, moments when politicians go to the theater or actors visit the UN are an intensification of the co-incidence of the theatrical and the political that is especially salient in the twenty-first century.

Some scholars increasingly recognize that politics is a question of spectatorship: it is a question of *Seeing Like a State* or seeing through *The Eyes of the People*, as two recent volumes in political science have been titled.[40] In the latter, Jeffrey Edward Green suggests that "the vast majority of our political experience, whether voter or nonvoter, is not spent engaged in [explicit political] action and decision making, but rather watching and listening to others who are themselves actively engaged."[41] Green calls this situation "ocular democracy," and argues that it requires reimagining our ethical paradigms for participation in the civic sphere.[42] In turn, I argue that understanding the spectator who is the subject of global political spectatorship is the prerequisite for action in our already theatrical political world. Theater and performance studies are poised to make significant contributions to understanding a world in which who we are and what we can do as political subjects proves to be a question of spectatorship. This book provides a theory of global political spectatorship that can inform the use of performance in the public sphere, in law, and in activism.

This project began in a period of intense artistic production, as part of an interest in theater that could change the world. My fieldwork, in turn, was conducted first as an outsider to the halls of power, subsequently as a scholarly tourist to power's public spaces in New York and The Hague, and in its final manifestations as an accredited researcher reporting on the work of the UN. This transit exposed me to multiple forms of geopolitical spectatorship that are reflected in the work to follow. It also reminded me that theaters of state speak differently to spectators in different contexts.

My textual archives include the extensive transcripts kept of UN meetings and ICC proceedings and the performative documents (resolutions, treaties, etc.) produced in each venue. My audiovisual sources, the webcasts of the UN and ICC, served as both archival records of each institution's public sessions and a live stage on which diplomatic performance is disseminated to global spectators.[43] My own live observations from the public galleries of the ICC or seated with journalists and representatives of NGOs in the Security Council form another category of sources on which this study is built, as do personal interviews with artists, diplomats, and functionaries at work in each space.

Taking diplomats for dramaturges in my fieldwork, I found individuals who script and stage performances in order to impact what their audiences see, hear, and feel. In each chapter I take up two or more scenes of diplomatic theater. These scenes include the official and unofficial acts of diplomats, depictions of diplomacy on the stage or screen, and encounters between diplomats and performing artists. My dramaturgical analyses developed from my efforts to navigate this milieu. In archives, I developed my close readings of policy documents and transcripts, training my eye not just on their unique logic and style, but on the performances they scripted or captured. These I read alongside playscripts, memoirs, and essays by artists. Near and far from Turtle Bay (the Manhattan neighborhood that is home to the UN's headquarters), I also became a spectator emplaced among the variety of stages and screens on which global political spectacle plays out, and I developed forms of participant observation matched to this subjectivity. In these same arenas, I watched television, theater, and music videos. And as my contacts in New York and The Hague expanded, I fleshed out the contexts in which the performances I studied were composed or consumed, via interviews conducted on and off the record with individuals placed variously throughout political, artistic, and civic hierarchies.

This method is not, on its face, unique.[44] In fact, part of my argument is that we all conduct similar dramaturgical analyses each day as global political spectators. In this way, my dramaturgy becomes more than an organizing metaphor or conceptual framework. My dramaturgical analyses elaborate an everyday activity that is also a form of *doing* on the world stage. I do not merely read and arrange the materials that compose my case studies: I edit transcripts, reframe videos, and re-voice my interlocutors to amplify their theatricality, clarify how they perform, and indicate ways they could mean differently. Global political spectatorship consists of quotidian acts of dramaturgical analysis that impact the course of diplomacy and global governance.

In this way, my method stages the same techniques of citizen spectator intervention in global affairs that I advocate for throughout this book.

This book begins, in chapter 1, with the narrative structure of diplomacy and theater, with stories and storytelling, and with memory and history. Dramaturgy is an art of telling stories, of making coherent narratives from jumbled sources, and in that context I consider how diplomats and theater-makers compete to tell stories. I examine two cases: the Security Council grappling with Shakespeare's *Hamlet,* and Secretary of State Colin Powell at odds with David Hare's play *Stuff Happens.* In organizing many bodies to tell a story, dramaturgy highlights how theater governs the collective memories of a community: the shared stories that make shared identities and that propel collective action.

Chapter 2 examines the interrelationship of spectatorship and power. On the world stage, power is exercised by looking. The Security Council watches conflicts and sends peacekeepers to watch on its behalf. These gazes are not ancillary to the work of peacekeeping, they are the means by which the UN and its peacekeepers accomplish their mandated tasks. I investigate two peacekeeping missions to understand the relationship between spectatorship, power, and its corollary, violence. I look at UNIFIL, the UN's peacekeeping mission in Lebanon since 1978, and MONUC, the UN's peacekeeping mission in the Democratic Republic of the Congo between 1999 and 2010. I also look at two plays, Karen Sunde's *In a Kingdom by the Sea* and Lynn Nottage's *Ruined.* In each case, the structure of spectatorship opens on to dramaturgical concerns: dynamics of power and knowledge that play out on bodies in view of feeling audiences. Spectatorship delivers a violent force; it is a tool that requires more care and caution than we often allow it.

I investigate the performative and theatrical time of diplomacy in chapter 3. I follow U.S. Ambassador Samantha Power as she leads a delegation of her colleagues to the play *Fun Home* on Broadway, and I attend the theater staged by several heads of state—Muammar Qaddafi, Barack Obama, and Yoweri Museveni—in the General Assembly and Security Council. These cases elaborate the shared temporality of theater and diplomacy, a temporality that is cyclical, reiterative, and mutational. Theatrical performance cycles through established phases, reiterating their contours, and altering those phases by degrees as they pass, to make new meanings and effects in the present. Diplomats also stage and restage their scripts, they cite and quote one another, they cycle through phases, reiterate their contours, and alter them as they pass.

Chapter 3 also weighs the demands that theatricality makes of diplomats against the forms of anti-theatricality that allow so many to cynically dismiss the work of the UN. I expand this investigation of theatricality in chapter 4, looking to spectators who are emplaced or displaced at concerts of popular music staged by the UN. I consider the UN's encounters with the musicians Psy, Pharrell, and the Viva Vox Choir in events that insist on consensus, strive to make harmony, and demand our emotional investment. If dramaturgy and diplomacy are arts of emplacement, this chapter remembers that audiences might also be displaced, and in this displacement they resist the efforts of others to put them in their place.

Diplomatic theater emerges in the second half of this book as an interface between people and politics, audiences and institutions. In the figure of the interface, the distinctions between diplomatic and aesthetic theater dissolve even further: spectators act, geopolitically, whether they are watching a melodrama on stage, a police procedural in a cinema, a news broadcast on television, or a diplomat's speech that is webcast online. In chapter 5 I detail my fieldwork at the International Criminal Court in The Hague, and my experience of an institutional edge where one comes face to face with geopolitics and international law. This edge extends from the courtroom out into the world in the bodies of the court's agents and in images of the court made by others. I focus here on the court's proceedings against Jean-Pierre Bemba Gombo and Thomas Lubanga Dyilo, as well as the television program *Crossing Lines*. I find that theater as interface is also theater as horizon: a space in which images are produced that generate desires and affects with consequences beyond the realm of representation.

I conclude in chapter 6 by turning to the relationship between page and stage in diplomacy. Dramaturgy and diplomacy are arts of handling documents; dramaturges and diplomats each construct the relationship between a written text and its embodied performance. In this chapter, I watch lawyers argue over interpretation and transcription at the ICC, technocrats debate punctuation and diction in the General Assembly, and dramaturges model the collective writing exercise at the heart of a global summit. How dramaturgy treats texts has consequences for both theater and diplomacy. Dramaturgy challenges the final authority of the text, making space for disagreement, where unexpected and unanticipated meanings may erupt.

Diplomacy, like theater, oscillates between text and performance. It is an art of storytelling that seeks to harness the powers of its spectators via forms of performative and theatrical citation. But it is also a space of affective negotiation, where we interface with institutions to rewrite a world that has been scripted for us.

Narrative, spectatorship, intervention, displacement, interface, script. These terms may be found in the lexicons of dramaturges, diplomats, performers, and scholars. They indicate dramaturgy's utility to policy and administration. To recognize the dramaturgy of international institutions is to recognize the theatrical dimensions of global governance. It is to recognize that dramaturgy is a technique of power used to manage populations, and a constituent part of a global governmentality that entrenches the prevailing hierarchies of states and their peoples. But dramaturgy, in theory and practice, also asserts the collective and collaborative nature of its work. It requires both performers and spectators, and affords its tools to each. Thus, a dramaturgy of international institutions reveals a world system that is rife with fissures and vulnerabilities, a world system made by both the powerful and the weak, the enfranchised and the oppressed, the engaged and the apathetic, or the authorized and the unauthorized. A dramaturgy of international institutions governs the theater that organizes the world, but it also provides the structures with which the world pushes back. This book is organized around these structures, their uses, and their limits.

Performing in a Theater of States

In 2007, a particular question animated my scholarship and the research that produced the present volume: "Why do states perform?" Why act in public and for an audience where, as theater-makers know, so much can go wrong? There are three effects that compel states to perform at the United Nations. In the first instance, states perform to enter into relationships with one another, be those relationships friendly or antagonistic. When ambassadors announce a treaty or perform a verbal threat, these diplomatic performances reconfigure the relationships that exist between states, marking the inclusions and exclusions of contingent international communities. The Nuclear Non-Proliferation Treaty establishes particular relationships, just as the implicit threats of the nuclear arms race had before it. So too, when states perform their accession to the recommendations and activities of international institutions—as one finds when states work with the ICC or provide support to a UN peacekeeping operation—they enter into relationships with one another to particular ends. These shifting alliances fill in the negative space of a history written of events and conflicts. These relationships form a historical foundation that has consequences for diplomatic performance in the present.

These relationships indicate the second reason why states perform: to maintain a particular arrangement of power. This is why even militarily dominant states go to the Security Council before they begin their wars: in order to maintain their hegemony beyond battlefields by performing configurations of international community that abet their power. When representatives of the United States invoke certain provisions of nonproliferation and disarmament agreements in performance, they assert particular interpretations of those agreements that are favorable to their own ends. Because the ICC is able to target certain perpetrators and not others, its own performances often support a stratified and imbalanced world system. In peacekeeping, diplomatic performances that would maintain a status quo find expression in the bodies of soldiers on the ground. Frozen conflicts and the reappearance of violence in the very structures sent to ameliorate that violence attest to this static situation.

Yet, the fact that states must perform arrangements of power renders those arrangements vulnerable to counter-performances. The necessity of performance is power's Achilles heel. In a final instance, states perform to disrupt existing arrangements of power. When non-nuclear states take advantage of the UN's forums to assert their place in disarmament debates, they employ the amplified theatricality of international institutions to force new configurations of states on the world stage. When activists stage their own judgments at the ICC, or victims address those who have done them harm, they use theater to rearrange systems of power. And as state and non-state actors perform for audiences of peacekeepers, they engage theater to push against the status quo those peacekeepers would maintain. In each case, aesthetic dramas found in playhouses or on TV do not appear as merely adjacent or analogous to the theater of states; they participate directly in the work of diplomacy. Stages and screens provide their own counter-performances, offering to reconfigure the discourses in which hierarchies of states are written, to enhance or obscure the material effects of those discourses the world over, and to mobilize anew the force of spectatorship on which the work of diplomacy relies.

This book is thus addressed to three audiences, and I imagine it will be useful to each in different ways. For readers in theater and performance studies, this book offers new ways to analyze and assess political performance—whether on a Broadway stage or at a negotiating table—centered on the spectator who makes these performances meaningful and efficacious. This approach aims to extend the interdisciplinary reach of our field and the depth with which performance scholars may intervene in policy. To bridge the abyss between analyses of how politicians perform and analyses of the politics of theatrical and other artworks, we must examine the spectator who acts by watching both of them. For readers who study international relations or practice diplomacy, this book argues for the centrality of spectatorship to the work of global governance (and so the necessity of the theatricality that attends to politics). This is a perspective that can open new avenues of thought and action on issues ranging from human rights to international peace and security to climate change and beyond. Finally, for artists and activists, this book suggests that theater may be a unique point of intervention in global political spectacle, and offers dramaturgy as a technique for applying pressure to that spectacle's most distant and elusive actors. Recognizing the centrality of spectatorship to global politics—recognizing that we do so much by looking—has consequences for scholars, policy-makers, artists, activists, and citizens.

Dramaturgical analysis is a potent tool for performance studies scholars to wield. It reveals the cultural dimensions of action to policy-makers, and it can make artists' interventions stronger. Dramaturgy is not merely a technique of elucidation and elaboration, or of bringing a performance to its fullest expression. Dramaturgy and power are intimately connected. Power performs, but dramaturgy controls the contexts in which power's performance emerges and the ways it makes meaning. Theater emplaces spectators, but dramaturgy locates power.

In the more than ten years since this project began, with the rise of ethnonationalist political figures around the world, and in the wake of high-profile withdrawals from regional organizations like the European Union and attacks on intergovernmental organizations like the ICC, international institutions appear poised on the brink of renewed crises of legitimacy. Similarly, events like Brexit or the election of Donald J. Trump to the presidency of the United States have often come as a shock to progressive activists and artists, precipitating renewed reflection on the efficacy of their methods. As much as isolationist politicians in the United States would disavow the utility of the United Nations or multilateral approaches to global problems, history suggests that even regimes with antipathy towards international institutions recognize their place as a tool of state policy.

As the White House continues to deploy the tropes of reality television (with which President Trump made his name in the twenty-first century), paying renewed attention to the structures, contents, and affects shared by politics and the arts can provide profound insights into how power operates and how individual citizens might respond. The stakes of this project go well beyond questions of media manipulation, of the messaging strategies that publicists impart to their clients, of talking points, or even of fake news. Overemphasizing such frames returns to the powerful their monopoly on action, imputing to them a capacity to stabilize phenomena that are anything but stable. A dramaturgy of international institutions recognizes that performance is constituted in its capacity to misfire, that audiences return affects to those that play to them, and that meaning is produced in an intersubjective space.

In the present moment, we risk decrying the theatricality of our political spectacles as evidence of their corruption. Instead, we must recognize the opportunities that spectacularized politics provides to those who are oppressed by global inequality and violence. Where the potential of global political spectatorship is devalued, citizen spectators are disenfranchised and dispossessed. Many who study performance have long argued that spectatorship is never passive;[45] our charge should now be to recognize where and how spectatorship is used as a tool of power. If spectatorship is an action on the world stage, theater-makers and those who study performance are better poised than ever to bend this tool to progressive purposes. The UN's promises to save us from the scourge of war, to reaffirm the equal rights of all peoples, and to promote social progress may remain always unfulfilled, but the theatricality of the UN recommends itself to a world in which citizenship and spectatorship are bound together. Global political spectacles are circulated on more media, to more audiences, than ever; this book provides the first view of global governance from the perspective of a spectator so immersed.

Figure 2. U.S. Secretary of State Colin Powell briefs the Security Council on February 5, 2003. UN Photo by Mark Garten.

1

✦

"Purpose Is but the Slave to Memory"

Narrative and History in the Security Council

Hamlet is an especially dark play to perform at the United Nations. On August 4, 2014, I watched Shakespeare's Globe present the show as part of its two-year "Globe to Globe" tour. A cast of twelve played on a booth stage erected in the center of the UN's Economic and Social Council (or ECOSOC) Chamber. The dark scaffold set floated on a sea of blond wood, one theatrical architecture superimposed on another, implying the affinity of diplomacy with theater as much as it protested against their commensurability. In an official UN press conference that afternoon, the Globe's artistic director, Dominic Dromgoole, had demurred when pressed to name the ways the show would take advantage of its performance context; this buttressed my UN informants' assertions that the play had been chosen because it was universally resonant but lacked specific geopolitical relevance.[1] Yet when Fortinbras's army crossed Denmark to fight in Poland, I found it difficult not to ruminate on Russian troops in Ukraine, Americans in Iraq, or Rwandans in the Democratic Republic of the Congo. Watching Hamlet's ill-treatment of Gertrude and Ophelia, I contemplated the Security Council's ongoing efforts, since Resolution 1325, to address gender-based violence. And as the gravedigger in the play joked, I laughed a mirthless laugh at the sepulchral history that the play and the United Nations both preside over. Far from claims of universality, the play's fatalism proved particularly appropriate for world-weary observers of foreign policy, convinced of the intractability of global injustice.

I had seen the production before, two years earlier at Pace University. There, as the iambic pentameter cleared at the play's close, the corpses arrayed onstage slowly rose to dance a historically accurate jig. This theatrical resurrection offered a hopeful, quasi-carnivalesque celebration of the unity of life and death. It affirmed the triumph of the living, carried by the redemptive power of our fictions. At the UN, the same conceit evacuated hope from the proceedings—the rising corpses called attention to their dissembling. Actors playing at death coolly contrasted the specter of global violence that haunts the UN's work, inadequately treated by diplomatic antiseptics. The play, which I had hoped would bring this messy world closer to the eyes and ears of policy-makers, instead seemed to double the remove at which global bodies hold the world's catastrophes. I had invested in the play intellectually and emotionally for its potential to transmit to the highest echelons of power (the members of the Security Council were all in attendance), but it seemed that the play would miss its target and prove incapable of intervening in the space and moment of geopolitical action.

This chapter is about encounters between the Security Council and the dramas that play to, on, and in it. To consider how art can intervene in politics, I draw together competing narratives of conflict that are mobilized in the council and on the stage. I consider the memories of actors and characters, of witnesses and refugees, and of ambassadors and politicians. These memories link performance to history; they are theatrical and institutional memories that make history meaningful and drive the writing of policy. Diplomacy strives to manage operations of cultural and historical memory, but spectators maintain their own counter-memories of conflict that can open onto new affective spaces, shifting the trajectory of political action.

Hamlet in the Security Council

Not everyone in the audience shared my despondency while watching *Hamlet*. The technocrat a row in front of me with his daughter clearly had a blast, and the journalist I chatted with on my walk to the subway had been charmed to attend something other than another diplomatic briefing. Even the NGO executive I sat with had apparently been watching another drama altogether: as the house lights came up, she asked me whether I had noticed if the permanent representative of Russia, Vitaly Churkin, had left the program early. He had been sitting towards the front of the audience, along with the fourteen other members of the UN Security Council, specifically next to Mark Lyall Grant, permanent representative of the United Kingdom. For cognoscenti this was the real drama.

That August the United Kingdom had held the presidency of the Security Council, and the Globe's show was a kickoff event to draw attention to British priorities. The media spectacle expanded on similar efforts in 2013, when the British had opened their June presidency by shipping a red double-decker London bus to New York. The bus was supposed to pick up council members at Ambassador Grant's midtown Manhattan apartment and truck them down the road to UN Headquarters, but the New York Police Department pointed out that concentrating so many high-level diplomats in a large and easily identifiable target posed a security risk, so the bus was reduced to circling the driveway in the well-guarded UN compound. Britain's original plans with Shakespeare's Globe had also been derailed. When discussions began in early 2014, the target venue was the Security Council itself. Though the Security Council Chamber and the ECOSOC Chamber are located just down the hall from one another, each space activates different performance procedures. Informal Security Council conventions require unanimity among all council members when deciding what may happen in the space, and Russia refused to consent to the British plans.

The negotiations had proceeded like any others at the UN, beginning at the working level, among the first secretaries. The Russians argued that the planned venue was not appropriate: what if an emergency meeting of the Security Council was called while the space was being prepared or while the play was going on? The chamber would be inaccessible! Discussion was advanced to the ambassadorial level, but Grant and Churkin could not reconcile their positions. The Russians are consistent when it comes to performance in the Security Council—a month earlier they had put the kibosh on Netflix's plan to shoot an episode of the television program *House of Cards* there. *Foreign Policy* magazine published leaked e-mails of those discussions. In them, the Russian diplomat Mikael Agasandyan argued that "the Security Council premises should be available at any time and on short notice. Besides that, we consistently insist that the Security Council premises are not an appropriate place for filming, staging, etc."[2] In keeping with the trends in other recent Russian vetoes (on Syria) in the Security Council, China concurred with the opinion, adding that "Council members should have a rough idea on scripts for those episodes which are relating to our work."[3]

Since I was skeptical of Russia's argument that the play and players would get in the way in case of an emergency, I pressed my network of contacts in and around the UN (all requested anonymity) to see why else the Russians might have found filming and staging so inappropriate. Why did they block *Hamlet*? "Because they can," was the bluntest response I received, my interlocutor pointing to a knee-jerk contrarianism in the Russians' multilateral foreign policy—Shakespeare was collateral damage in a zero-sum game of Security Council diplomacy. Another informant put this a bit more diplomatically, saying that it was not arbitrary distemper or merciless calculation: Russia simply had "a highly conservative approach to the council in general, they go there very rarely." My contact reframed Russia's opposition as a worldview rather than a strategy, one that hesitated to take advantage of the Security Council stage.

Regardless of whether Russia's obstructionism had to do with keeping the council clear of physical impediments, with not establishing undue precedents, or with a former superpower's eroding sense of geopolitical control, there seems to be something dangerous about letting theater into the Security Council Chamber. The distaste of some at the UN for dramatic presentations often stems from a shared capacity between theater and diplomacy to manifest in bodies what otherwise appears only in text and speech. Diplomats hesitate to stage dramas because they know the work that staged narratives can do. The UN's work hinges on its unique capacity to write resolutions and other documents that script action on the world stage. Theater also does things with words, and the UN cannot brook the methodological confusion that comes from being seen so close to its aesthetic corollary. This antinomy excludes certain plays from the UN premises and discounts the most theatrical performances of diplomats as aberrations from the pragmatic work of the institution. It may also drive the occasional reluctance of artists to address diplomacy directly.

The *Hamlet* press conference had confirmed my thesis that connecting dramatic and diplomatic materialization was a bit unthinkable to those working in either field. Matthew Lee, a notorious muckraker in the UN press corps, followed up on the tour's stated goal of playing in every country on earth by asking if they would be traveling to any states not recognized by the UN. Again Dromgoole was initially evasive, before revealing that they had been to Kosovo and would love to go to Palestine. Lee's question implied the global legitimating function attached to the shared capacity of UN diplomacy and theater, and Dromgoole's hesitation confirmed an unwillingness to name it.

The interview turned to the question of "soft power," the concept in political science that culture can serve a nation's foreign policy goals without being directly instrumentalized. Dromgoole defined it as "spreading an influence throughout the world through culture rather than anything else," and refused the notion that his play was participating in a soft power project. He suggested instead, "I think we're part of a conversation . . . a conversation between us and different countries."[4] His answer seemed to forget that *Hamlet*'s centuries-old production history had long been intertwined with diplomacy. Dromgoole had already acknowledged his familiarity with this history, which was cataloged in the tour's program: "we know that [in] 1608—only five years after [*Hamlet*] was first presented—it was presented off the coast of Yemen by the crew of a ship for a collection of, sort of, Yemeni dignitaries," he told the press conference.[5] In 1607 and 1608, the crew of the *Red Dragon*, on a voyage for the East India Company, had in fact performed *Hamlet* off the coast of two different continents, first near present-day Sierra Leone and next in the Gulf of Aden, the Yemeni performance to which Dromgoole referred. Graham Holderness and Bryan Loughrey relate the diplomatic encounters in each incident, describing the first as a "landmark performance of *Hamlet* before an audience that included not only officers but a visiting African dignitary."[6]

Deployed by Dromgoole as charming trivia, the incident masks theater's place as a tool of diplomacy, an interface between individuals and world historical forces like the arrival of mercantilism in Africa and Asia. In retracing the steps of touring companies and merchant expeditions 400 years after the fact, the Globe's production inevitably performed the nation from which its embassy disembarked, mapping histories of colonialism, migration, and globalization. Featuring one Hamlet born in Nigeria (Ladi Emeruwa) and another of Pakistani descent (Naeem Hayat), as well as one Ophelia born in Hong Kong (Jennifer Leong) and another of Afro-Caribbean descent (Amanda Wilkin), the multicultural cast performed a progressive, pluralist, twenty-first-century nation, embodying the memories of human circulation and the history of empire that the tour would transcend in reiteration.[7]

Diplomacy's aversion to theater may derive from shared capacities, but it has as much to do with what theater and performance remember. Theater and diplomacy repel one another not just because they share a polarity, but also because theater remembers performance; it is a structure that refuses to allow performance to forget or be forgotten. This insight appears in *Hamlet* in the words of the Player King, who just happens to be performing a fiction within a court space that may also host the writing of policy, and whose performance is explicitly deployed as an instrument of regime change. Recall: Hamlet has enjoined a traveling theatrical company to play *The Murder of Gonzago*, a story selected for its resonance with the fratricide Hamlet would revenge, and revised so that the murderer of Hamlet's father, his uncle Claudius, will not miss the resemblance and will reveal his guilt through the outward signs he will make while watching the play as an otherwise naive spectator. Doubting the Player Queen's promises of posthumous fidelity, the Player King, in the moments before his murder, reminds her that "what we do determine oft we break. / Purpose is but the slave to memory."[8]

In this scene, a political actor (Hamlet) organizes an aesthetic performance (*The Murder of Gonzago*) that restages recent history (the murder of King Hamlet) to affectively impact a politically powerful spectator (Claudius) in order to accomplish specific policy goals (eliciting an admission of guilt for regicide). At the UN, *The Mousetrap* (as Hamlet called the performance when Claudius asked its name) was played speedily, with amplified theatricality, building a wry joke from the *mise en abyme* of a play-within-a-play-within-an-international-institution. Playing both Claudius and the Player King, the New Zealand Maori actor Rawiri Paratene generated comic energy by rapidly switching between the roles of spectator and actor. He exhausted himself in an effort that foregrounded the Player King's live performing body and King Claudius's anxious watching, and the political consequences of each. In this labor, *The Mousetrap* interrupted the smooth administration of Claudius's court by returning to its present a traumatic memory of political violence, and offered the ambassadorial audience at the UN a model for theatrical intervention in matters of state.

At the Security Council, the epigram "purpose is but the slave to memory" might be rephrased: sustained efficacious action on the world stage needs an apparatus of memory. Theater both structures and supplements the UN's institutional memory. When it first met in 1946, the Security Council developed Rules of Procedure, its working methods, but never formally adopted them—they remain provisional. There are some advantages to this arrangement. The council's working methods are quite flexible: it could put on a play in the Council Chamber even if no protocol existed for such a thing, and it could hold an emergency meeting wherever it pleased if something came up while that play was going on. But there are also some disadvantages: unwritten conventions fill in the gaps of the Rules of Procedure, rendering working methods ambiguous. Powerful states seize on this ambiguity to manipulate weaker states.

The five permanent members of the Security Council act as keepers of the council's institutional memory by virtue of their continuous presence, policing the behavior of the ten elected members who serve two-year terms. Detailing how "Institutions Remember and Forget," anthropologist Mary Douglas observes: "Institutions create shadowed places in which nothing can be seen and no questions asked. They make other areas show finely discriminated detail, which is closely scrutinized and ordered. History emerges in an unintended shape as a result of practices directed to immediate, practical ends."[9] Douglas indicates that history derives from quotidian practices designed to pragmatic ends that come to be inscribed in the institution's apparatus of memory. How an institution remembers impacts the form and content of its ongoing work, and the inclusions and exclusions that decide its politics. At the UN, this apparatus is textual; it is the transcripts that fix and inscribe performed practices that emerge in the ambiguous spaces generated by an ad hoc system and an international law built on phantasmal precedents.

The Security Council's provisional Rules of Procedure cast shadows over the places where informal conventions take root and power coalesces. The provisional Rules of Procedure require that proposed resolutions must be circulated among council members in writing, but do not say who should write them. Historically, states submitted drafts as the spirit moved them, but as the number of items on the council's agenda ballooned, this situation proved impractical and new informal practices became routine. Security Council Report dates the emergence of the current system to 2010, when issues began to be divided among various "penholders." In 2014, fifty issues had penholders attached, of which thirty-six issues were led by permanent members, primarily the P3 (France, the United Kingdom, and the United States): the United States led on 15, the United Kingdom led on 11, France led on 8, and Russia led on 2.[10]

The informal convention routinizes subsequent choreographies: according to Security Council Report, "the P3 usually agree upon a given draft among themselves and then negotiate it with China and Russia. The draft text as agreed to by the P5 is then circulated to the non-permanent members, [who are] discouraged from making meaningful amendments because this might disturb the sometimes painstakingly negotiated wording agreed to among the P5."[11] When presented as a technical issue of operational efficiency, the conventional practice becomes intractable. Tightening their grip on the pen, the P5 institutionalize their right to write the scripts that manage global affairs. As memory recedes of a period in which the elected members of the Security

Council drafted resolutions, their own capacity to perform in the council is constrained, and a repertoire of action atrophies.

Is it odd, then, that a play about the link between memory and action might be unsettling to some on the council? James Hammersmith, one of many scholars who has tackled the subject of memory in *Hamlet*, writes: "*Hamlet* is a play *about* memory, language, and the conquest of time in the significance of human action, but the play also *is* memory, language, and the significance of Hamlet's action in the transcendence of time. The play itself is the very piece of language that the play is about."[12] Hammersmith collapses together *Hamlet*'s representational and performative functions: insofar as the play asks how human action can be meaningful to history, it offers the structure of theater as an answer. We make sense of Hamlet's actions through the unity of utterance held together by *Hamlet* the play, and we can do more things with *Hamlet* down the line by removing that story to new stages and contexts. We make sense of a character's later actions by testing them against our memories of earlier actions. The play is the structure that facilitates this hermeneutic operation—Hamlet's fatalism, Laertes's furor, and Ophelia's deterioration each build affective consequences from the operations of a spectator's memory within the play's duration. On display is a live and embodied practice that can flit through the shadowed and finely detailed spaces of institutions with equal facility.

Theatrical structures maintain a series of historical acts in view in order to make meaning and to drive action—this function appears both in political spaces, like the UN, and in aesthetic spaces, like the Globe Theatre. In the UN, diplomatic theater is staged and restaged to choreograph the activities of states, and in the Globe Theatre culture generates the passions that fuel the interventions of citizens. In the ECOSOC Chamber, *Hamlet* challenges one structure of institutional memory with another. In its spatial, textual, and embodied dimensions the play confronts the Security Council with forces that can disrupt the swift coagulation of an iniquitous status quo.

Who has a right to memory in the UN's spaces? Who can wield memory on the world stage to accomplish their ends? Who remembers when Britannia ruled the seas and toured *Hamlet* to Yemen? Who remembers the Empire that leaves its trace in a cast whose heritage maps the colonies? Who remembers when an elected member circulated the first draft of a resolution? Who remembers a local conflict well enough to tell the Security Council just what happened?

Hamlet's displacement to the ECOSOC Chamber echoes the Arria-formula meeting: this is a relatively young strategy that serves to sidestep council conventions which permit only official delegations and high-level representatives of states to speak at council meetings. The practice dates to 1992, when Ambassador Diego Arria of Venezuela hoped to have the Croatian priest Fra Joko Zovko tell his story of the war in Bosnia and Herzegovina to the Security Council. When Arria was unable to formally convene the council to hear

Zovko, the meeting was relegated to the North Delegates' Lounge—the same room that served as the green room for the Globe's actors. Like *Hamlet*, an Arria-formula meeting opens onto an expansive affective field—it contains personal stories of violence and loss that are generally excluded from the usually decorous proceedings of diplomacy. Arria-formula meetings force live encounters between council members and memories of conflict—they insist on the encounter I had hoped to find at *Hamlet*.

Theater provides a compelling framework in which to locate the performances of public diplomacy precisely at the point where the work of institutions transfers from instantiation in texts to instantiation in bodies; where those who write resolutions must take notice of the live bodies their work impacts. This spectacular, animating function at the heart of the theatrical event has affective consequences: Hamlet's fatalism derives from the conflict between the promised vitality of the text brought to life, and the disempowering notion that life has been scripted by historical performative forces. Global structures of power maintain themselves through rituals that generate both the sensation that individual efforts by citizens and bureaucrats can bend the arc of history toward justice, and the sensation that the trajectory of world events cares little for those caught up in them.

In the afternoon press conference with the Globe to Globe collaborators, Rawiri Paratene dismissed the geopolitical utility of dramatic storytelling. With a gentle tone and cautious delivery, he mused:

> I guess that it would be foolish of us to go in thinking we could get the diplomats to operate better. All we can do is tell them the story and if they glean from that something that makes the Israeli representative go to the other side of the room and sit next to the Palestinian representative and maybe kiss each other on the cheek and talk and listen, that would be very nice. But that's not what we're here to do; we're here to tell a story.[13]

Paratene indicates again the mutual aversion between diplomacy and theater: what hubris to think that a well-told tale can remake the world. He names a dream of action, that theater can have immediate material effects on global politics, but he contains that dream within a pragmatic delimitation of theater's purpose and capacity, with orderly speech and geopolitical realism winning the day.

Paratene is wrong to let the realists win; even if theater cannot make the diplomats kiss, it is not a benign force when played in the halls of power. Theater is structured to make meaning from historical recollection—to activate a memorial process with affective consequences and sustain that process through a structure of reiteration that oscillates between textual and embodied media. Theater acts as a supplementary apparatus of institutional memory alongside embodied and textual UN conventions. Where theatrical forms maintain what the Security Council remembers, focusing its efforts and forces on specific targets, staged dramas channel the reciprocal force of the UN's global audience. Global civil society remembers through the theatrical structures that pervade narrative performance in multiple media. Powerful states police the stories told and written in the Security Council, but theater opens onto less predictable spaces where diplomatic spectacles can be superseded by the counter-memories that haunt global consensus, counter-memories housed in cultural products that compete with geopolitical spectacles as often as they reinforce them.

The Security Council in *Stuff Happens*

Recognizing theater's power vis-à-vis geopolitics and history may do little to mitigate the caution that Paratene expressed: theatrical intervention remains a subtle tool to put to use in contexts overwritten by the explicit use of force by constituted governing bodies. In fact, military intervention often requires diplomatic theater. War must be preceded by performances that authorize it, and war must be followed by performances that contain its effects. Theater allows the inchoate violence of more or less powerful states to be remembered and to make sense to history. Thus, the Iraq War traced an arc from President George W. Bush's first invocation of the "axis of evil" in his State of the Union address on January 29, 2002, to his infamous landing on the aircraft carrier *USS Abraham Lincoln* to announce the end of major combat operations on May 1, 2003. Where other periodizations of the Iraq War might begin with the U.S. invasion in 2003 and end with the withdrawal of U.S. troops in 2011, focusing on Bush's performances indicates that theatricality accrues to violence in an effort to produce a legitimizing frame, to contain geopolitical spectatorship, and to influence the hermeneutics by which violence gains historical meaning. Though Bush's performances may rightly be considered rituals of power, theater proves a more apt paradigm with which to consider their role in crafting and transmitting narratives to spectators. International institutions are primary settings for such diplomatic theater, where conflicts over the inscription of public memory are staged to take advantage of the broad audiences those institutions cultivate.

A series of performances at the United Nations led to the U.S. invasion. In a morning session of the Security Council on February 5, 2003, U.S. Secretary of State Colin Powell addressed the council to argue that Iraq had failed to comply with the disarmament obligations the UN had set for it, and so, as a consequence, the council should authorize U.S. military intervention in Iraq. Powell built his performance from textual archives, and his stagecraft went beyond simple oratory to include mixed media and props. From the start, he cited transcripts of previous meetings and reports. To establish Iraq's deviance from international norms, he quoted Hans Blix, executive chairman of the UN Monitoring, Verification, and Inspection Commission (UNMOVIC), and Mohamed ElBaradei, director general of the International Atomic Energy Agency (IAEA). Powell told the room full of diplomats:

> I asked for this meeting today for two purposes: first to support the core assessments made by Dr. Blix and Dr. ElBaradei. As Dr. Blix reported to the Council on 27 January, "Iraq appears not to have come to a genuine acceptance—not even today—of the disarmament that was demanded of it." And as Dr. ElBaradei reported, Iraq's declaration of 7 December "did not provide any new information relevant to certain questions that have been outstanding since 1998."[14]

Powell deftly modulated his speed and tone as he gave new voice to each man's previously transcribed words. He accelerated through Blix's interjection, "—not even today—," to emphasize the immediacy of the threats he would go on to enumerate, and their very present danger. Nearby, Blix and ElBaradei sat together, watching Powell's play. In his 2004 memoir, Blix reported, "As I listened . . . and I watched . . . I did not feel the discomfort I later realized would have been natural."[15]

To set the scene of Iraq's dissembling, Powell played audiotapes of conversations between members of Iraq's Republican Guard, and he provided translations via supertitles projected on a screen above the council. The low-fidelity audio recordings were filled with static scratches that obscured squawking voices choked into a narrow band of frequencies. These sonic artifacts had truth effects, they attested to their own authenticity, asserting that they had been found, not fabricated. Distressed and degraded, the tapes theatrically constructed their evidentiary status. When each tape concluded, Powell offered interpretation, repeating the most damning phrases used by those surveilled. "Mohamed ElBaradei is coming . . . But they are worried: 'We have this modified vehicle. What do we say if one of them sees it?' What is their concern? Their concern is that it is something they should not have, something that should not be seen."[16] Powell's close readings accumulated on and around the documentary records he staged—the tapes took their dramatic thrust from his oral art, and his interpretations became facts alongside the tapes.

Using PowerPoint, Powell next projected images of his archive. He verbally captioned the images as they appeared. Over a photograph of a mustached-man carrying binders, Powell noted, "inspectors recently found dramatic confirmation of these reports. When they searched the home of an Iraqi nuclear scientist, they uncovered roughly 2,000 pages of documents. You see them here being brought out of the home and placed in the United Nations' hands." Slides of satellite images came next. Powell modestly disclaimed, "The photos I am about to show you are sometimes hard for the average person to interpret. Indeed, hard for me . . . But as I show you these images I will explain what they mean." An aerial photograph was projected. It showed gray terrain; yellow circles and red squares highlighted points of interest (figure 2). Powell told his audience it was a munitions facility that stored chemical weapons. A close-up of the same image, still gray with yellow annotations, followed. Powell narrated again: cargo trucks arriving at a biological weapons facility and leaving a ballistic missile facility. Next was a computer rendering of "mobile production facilities of biological agents" based on the eyewitness description of a defector. Soon after, Powell played a video of an Iraqi fighter jet spraying liquid: "That is 2,000 liters of simulated anthrax that jet is spraying."[17] Moving swiftly from transcripts, to audiotapes, to images, to renderings, to video simulations—all interpreted by a live performing body—Powell's performance was an alarming use of documentary theater.

As a genre, documentary theater is defined by the verbatim texts that compose it; transcripts, interviews, testimonies, and other accounts provide its scripts. Documentary theater incorporates varied media to intervene in and interrogate the mediatized culture in which it is embedded; audiotapes, video clips, projected images, books, files, and other materials clutter its stages. Documentary theater addresses current events, history, and the theatricality of the public sphere. In the Security Council, documentary theater can also name a genre of political performance that is used to take narrative control of history's material traces.

Even as documentary theater lays claim to the authority of the real, it troubles regimes of truth.[18] Powell's production was no exception. Twenty minutes into making his case, Powell produced a small vial filled with a white substance. He lifted it to the level of his eyes and told his audience: "Less than a teaspoon of dried anthrax, a little bit—about this amount, this is just about the amount of a teaspoon—less than a teaspoonful of dried anthrax in an envelope shut down the United States Senate in 2001."[19] Though the vial he held was later reported to be only a facsimile and not in fact a bioweapon, the ambiguity of Powell's presentation typified the affective manipulations ascribed to the Bush administration by its opponents.

On *The Daily Show* that evening, satirist Ed Helms captured the typical spectator's reaction by inventing a diplomat's response: "I think the ambassador from Angola spoke for everybody when he said, 'Holy shit, dude, is that anthrax? You brought anthrax? Powell, you are a madman.' "[20] In Powell's live performance, which was broadcast to global audiences with only a brief delay, a powerful U.S. administration primed the affects that drove the American population to support an unjustified war. Powell exceeded the typical bureaucratic theater of the UN with a performance that transmitted from council stage, to television screen, to Iraqi street and that would have deadly consequences: as of August 2018, the independent monitoring group Iraq Body Count had cataloged between 181,916 and 204,133 civilian deaths from violence in Iraq since 2003.[21] If *Hamlet* depressed me in 2014, perhaps it did so by reactivating my memories of 2003.

In excluding *Hamlet* from the same space that compelled Powell to perform, the members of the Security Council ratified Ngũgĩ wa Thiong'o's thesis that "the artist and the state become not only rivals in articulating the laws, moral or formal, that regulate life in a society, but also rivals in determining the manner and circumstances of their delivery," prompting a "battle over performance space in particular."[22] In the course of occupying the same conceptual space, art and government enter into conflicts over concrete spaces. However, diplomatic theater and aesthetic theater also converge on temporal spaces: the space of memory and the texts of the historical record. In taking theater and diplomacy as facets of a cohesive field operating to produce and use history, the time frame for theatrical intervention can be extended. Ed Helms's performance replayed the events hours after they occurred, and others followed in his irreverent footsteps. Nineteen months after Powell's performance, David Hare's play *Stuff Happens* premiered at London's National Theatre to rework the history that the Bush administration wrote.

Stuff Happens meets Powell's documentary theater with its own: it restages recordings and texts from the period, adding imagined accounts to fill the spaces between them. *Stuff Happens* follows the major officials of the George W. Bush administration from his inauguration, through 9/11, into the period preceding the 2003 war in Iraq, staging internal debates and major public events. The play comes between spectators and the recent geopolitical past, inviting reconsideration of the traditional models for art's intervention in politics. Like Helms, Hare re-narrates the acts of spectators embedded in the march to war, encouraging theatrical identification to configure geopolitical spectatorship with historical consequences. In Hare's hands, Powell's play-within-a-play is not so different from Paratene's manic presentation of *The Mousetrap*: both recognize that actors and spectators combine on the world stage, and that the present is made by what we remember and how we remember it. *Stuff Happens* takes clear advantage of the theatricality of international institutions and the political powers that play in them.

Stuff Happens addresses its target directly, avoiding the metaphors, metonyms, allusions, and allegories with which so much political art plies its trade. It adheres to geopolitical spectacle by incorporating verbatim transcripts into its theatrical body. The play refuses to acknowledge divisions between politics and art, evincing the cohesive field of diplomacy and theater in the coherence of a drama built from transcripts and a playwright's craft. In writing the play, Hare intervenes after the fact to reveal and illuminate, to fill in the spaces between transcripts by imagining the cabinet meetings, working lunches, and private negotiations that were excluded from official records. In an author's note, Hare elaborates his methodology to provide a disclaimer: "Nothing in the narrative is knowingly untrue. Scenes of direct address quote people verbatim. When the doors close on the world's leaders and on their entourages, then I have used my imagination."[23]

Naturally, this risks adulterating history: Hare transgresses a bulwark that has been erected to maintain the sanctity of historical fact. Hare's irreverence may prompt skepticism: what right do artists have to pick up their pens where the transcript leaves off? Won't storytelling risk introducing poetry to try the credulity of history's spectators and mislead the masses who take fabulation for fact? Even worse, might the playwright's inventions misfire insofar as "many of the imagined conversations lack a fundamental authenticity," as June Thomas complains in her review of the show?[24]

Hardly. Hare's method recognizes that the question of the politics of aesthetics has long been prejudged for artists by politicians: an autonomous regime of art is not feasible so long as politics is itself an artful practice. Indeed, Hare's poetic license pales in comparison to Powell's. When diplomats use techniques of documentary theater to legitimize war by telling tall tales, how else could playwrights respond but by mobilizing their own arts to reveal the theatrical scaffolds elevating the powerful? In engaging historical records and refusing the boundaries of their facticity, Hare confronts the dramaturgy of politics with the dramaturgy of theater. He takes advantage of the materials that theatricalized geopolitics provides and adds to them with his own art. Hare uses theater to expand the frame in which history is captured and experienced.

This intervention into the writing of history operates on multiple, parallel tracks. In a first instance, Hare adds new voices to the record of the period, stitching counter-memories into the archive. In and among the performances of President George W. Bush, Prime Minister Tony Blair, and their cohorts, Hare intersperses monologues by individuals who have been excluded from the halls of power: an "angry" British journalist, who bemoans "the absurdity and the irrelevance . . . of discussing even . . . a historical event, an invasion already more than a year old";[25] a Palestinian academic who tells the audience, "it's about one thing: defending the interests of America's three-billion-dollar-a-year colony in the Middle East";[26] a "Brit in New York," who reflects that "on September 11, America changed. Yes, it got much stupider";[27] and an Iraqi exile who concludes that "Iraq has been crucified."[28] Where the dramaturgy of states can distract and occlude, the dramaturgy of artists often gives voice to those disenfranchised by power's acts, redeploying the excessive emotions—anger, contempt, disgust, grief—that diplomacy abhors.

Along a second track, Hare remixes the verbatim records of the period. He complicates each scene by giving lines to a series of actors who step out of character to provide contextual narration, to cite sources, and to prompt their colleagues' portrayals. With the aid of these actors, Hare condenses and expands the transcripts and records that are his raw materials, bridging the distances between distinct events. This textual surgery has temporal effects that respond to the artful manipulation of time by policy-makers. Documentary theater and diplomatic theater both modulate the experience of time in the present. Both Powell's performance with the anthrax vial and *Stuff*

Happens's recapitulation of the scene feature dynamic tempos that drive affect and action.

Powell's theatricality on February 5, 2003, built urgency from its liveness, from the intense pressure it placed on a moment that insisted action must be hasty and forthcoming. Jack Straw, the foreign secretary of the United Kingdom and a collaborator in the United States' show, followed Powell's speech to declare the session "a moment of choice for this institution, the United Nations . . . The League [of Nations] failed because it could not create actions from its words. It could not back diplomacy with a credible threat and, where necessary, the use of force."[29] Words must lead swiftly to action, debate must give way to decision, and diplomatic theater must resolve into military intervention. The theatrical and performative structure of international relations encourages the desire for immediacy, for a spectacular and climactic event that disarms a threat or fulfills its promised ends. This desire accrues equally to hawks and doves, to those who supported the war in Iraq and those who opposed it.

Theatrical intervention disappoints insofar as it does not satisfy the desire for immediate action; its effects take time. *Stuff Happens* builds temporal distance as it re-mediates its source. David Hare's play is predicated on the time it takes to perform, transcribe, and re-perform, suggesting that theatrical intervention can be neither immediate nor urgent and that it can take as its targets only memory and history. Hare intervenes at a distance to reopen the duration that Powell and Straw close, making space in history to reflect on events that insisted they required action and not debate. He provides an alternative account that disrupts the smooth history the Bush regime staged. In his author's note, Hare describes *Stuff Happens* as "a history play, which happens to centre on very recent history."[30] Doubling back to revisit fresh public memories, the play intensifies the sense of inertia that characterized the period in order to interrupt and alienate it.

The play amplifies the compressions accomplished by Powell's threats. In *Stuff Happens*, the anthrax vial performance, the clarion call to the play's climax, opens scene 21:

> *The Security Council arrives. The Foreign Ministers and their Ambassadors*
> AN ACTOR: On February 5th Powell is prevailed upon to make a presentation to the UN, using a sound-and-light show to demonstrate his case for the "imminent threat."
> *Powell sits down, then holds up a small vial of anthrax.*
> POWELL: My colleagues, every statement I make today is backed up by sources, solid sources.
> AN ACTOR: The Head of White House Communications team, Dan Bartlett, remarks:
> BARTLETT: We called it "the Powell buy-in."

POWELL: These are not assertions. What we are giving you are facts and conclusions based on solid intelligence.
AN ACTOR: Although Powell has spent the previous four days angrily throwing out much of the two-hundred-minute speech Cheney, the CIA, and the Pentagon have given him to read, he does raise the spectre of mobile laboratories to make biological agents:
POWELL: The source is an eyewitness, an Iraqi chemical engineer who supervised one of these facilities.[31]

Hare's recapitulation of the February 5 meeting compresses the time of Powell's speech, reducing it to three sound bites, each a moment when Powell emphasized the veracity of the evidence supporting his claims. Between these assertions, other times and spaces intrude: Dan Bartlett looks back on the scene from the future, and An Actor draws Powell's immediate past into the scene's present.

Soon after, time speeds up again, as Hare conflates the February 5 meeting with a subsequent meeting on February 14 in which Powell's French counterpart stole the show:

There is a flurry of excitement.
AN ACTOR: In the charged atmosphere Dominique de Villepin seizes his opportunity:
DE VILLEPIN: War is always the sanction of failure. France has never ceased to stand upright in the face of history and before mankind. In this temple of the United Nations, we are the guardians of an ideal, the guardians of a conscience.
AN ACTOR: De Villepin turns to Colin Powell:
DE VILLEPIN: This message comes to you from an old country, France, from a continent that has known wars, occupation and barbarity.[32]

With this further abbreviation of the time and duration of diplomatic theater, Hare places point and counterpoint in closer proximity in order to encourage audiences to reassess the period. Restaging the performance, Hare submits Powell's urgency to new scrutiny, inviting audiences to measure their experience of the scene against memories of 2003.

This is a doubled scene of spectatorship. Hare refracts the historical moment for an audience whose own acts of geopolitical spectatorship are now emphasized: we watch again on stage what we may have watched before on the evening news. The shortened stage time indexes the need for extended periods of reflection off stage, reflections that may have proven impossible for spectators of the initial events. In this new time-space, Hare conducts his dramaturgy: he places Powell and De Villepin in direct conversation, and he gives Hans Blix a word in edgewise. Hare's Blix points out the shoddy construction of Powell's theater: "I knew they'd cut a lot of stuff they claimed to have, and that left me thinking: if this is the best they've got, what on earth was the rest like?"[33] The insertion is a paraphrase—another compression—of four pages in Blix's 2004 memoir, *Disarming Iraq*.[34] Blix is another voice that interrupts history from the perspective of the theatrical present. On the stage, Hare's dramaturgy comes into direct contact with Powell's. This theatrical interface puts pressure on the web of relations between actors, spectators, and the histories they write.

The heterogeneous time frames deployed in the theatrical present of the play operate contrapuntally with the irreversible thrust of history cultivated by the diplomatic theater of the period. In an interview given a year after *Stuff Happens*'s premiere, Powell publicly expressed his private remorse over the February 5 Security Council meeting. Pressed by Barbara Walters, he acknowledged the unsubstantiated claims he had made and ascribed them to a failed intelligence apparatus. Of his Security Council performance, he noted: "It's a blot. I'm the one who presented it on behalf of the United States to the world, and [it] will always be a part of my record. It was painful. It's painful now."[35] Hare's play predicts this contrition in scenes in which the Secretary of State tells President Bush, "I want us to go about this in a different way,"[36] or lobbies Condoleezza Rice to support his efforts at the UN.[37] Hare's drama gets into the open events that Powell had not discussed publicly at the time the play was written. Hare's Powell and Powell's Powell are tightly integrated with one another, each a theatrical production that predicts the other. Hare builds his character from a publicly available persona, and Powell manages his place in history by doing the same work as Hare's play: revealing what was previously hidden, providing additional contexts, and offering dramaturgical interpretation. Powell and Hare each loop back to 2003 to intervene theatrically in the accelerating processes that were driving military intervention, even if these interventions cannot stop a war that is already past.

The title of Hare's play, "Stuff Happens," refers to Donald Rumsfeld's infamously callous response to reports of looting in Baghdad in the days following Saddam Hussein's fall. Rumsfeld's words indicate a moment of self-censorship, an extemporaneous revision of the more common vulgarity, "shit happens," for polite consumption in a public political scene. Hare does not hesitate to deploy scatology. His Powell breaks the fourth wall to express his frustrations as the administration he represents works at cross-purposes with his diplomatic efforts:

> What is this? What the hell is this? I've got a bunch of right-wing nutcases in the White House, I've got the treacherous French in the Security Council. I'm standing in the fucking road! And the shit is all flowing one way![38]

Powell experiences powerlessness; as he watches the diplomatic theatrics of his colleagues in Washington and New York, the spectacle in which he participates overwhelms his capacity for action by positioning him beyond its machinations; he becomes a mere spectator who resigns himself to history's thrust well before February 5, 2003.

Powell's frustration in this scene is a corollary to Hamlet's fatalism. It is an emotion shared by artists, activists, and policy-makers who find they cannot intervene in history. Framed as a tepid protagonist, caught between spectatorship and action, Powell invites identification from audiences, to see themselves in history's river of shit. The identification is twofold: to recognize the citizen's powerlessness in the technocrat, and to ponder the acts on either part that might have averted war. This is a third track on which Hare's theater intervenes, restaging geopolitical spectatorship itself as a sort of (in) action.

Accepting a cohesive field of theater and diplomacy requires abandoning the notion that art intervenes in politics in an instant as an event. Rather, spectators and spectacle configure each other in moments of variable speed, intensity, and import. Janelle Reinelt reported from *Stuff Happens*'s opening night in London: "While there may not be any new revelations, the experience of the play is stronger than any analytic account of its substance."[39] The play seems to rouse a reflective space in the duration in which it plays; Reinelt does not ask it to add to a debate or accomplish effects beyond the story it tells, but she does ascribe to it a unique power to arrest the flow of history in the moment in which the story is told. The moment of theatrical spectatorship offers a break from the forward momentum of history in which the astute spectator may recompose that history. In the moment of theatrical spectatorship that reflects geopolitical spectatorship, I am called to account for my own place on the world stage.

In a lecture he gave at a theater conference in 1978, Hare asserted, "A play is not actors, a play is not a text; a play is what happens between the stage and the audience."[40] Introducing the collection in which the talk was published, he also argued for the equivalence between stage dramas and lectures given by public political figures: "when one person speaks and is encouraged to develop his or her ideas, then it is we, the audience, who provide the challenge." Here the theatrical event demonstrates its intrinsic politics: "we provide the democracy."[41] Hare, like Reinelt, leaves the specific affective content of this exchange between spectacle and spectator ambiguous. From my own perspective, placing the Security Council on stage has effects similar to those I experienced watching *Hamlet* in the ECOSOC Chamber: I found the encounter rather depressing.

As a supplemental apparatus of memory, works like *Stuff Happens* must reckon with feelings like mine, feelings that risk refusing the spectator's complicity in the world playing out before his eyes. The spectator who shuttles between the theater of states on the world stage and the theater playing out on local stages and screens also risks losing sight of the fact that his or her acts of spectatorship reciprocally configure the institution he watches, returning desires and aspirations to it. Art and activism each develop as complex responses borne of a spectator's capacity to receive and make meaning from the theater of states, and this spectator's dramaturgy is the substance of politics.

Stuff Happens stages presidents, cabinet secretaries, diplomats, and bureaucrats not to capitalize on the distance between political spectacle and citizen spectators, but to highlight the ontological proximity of political actors and political spectators. Characters in the play seek viewing positions that can support material intervention, and their efforts interpellate theatrical spectators into the scene. Dramaturgically linking *Stuff Happens* to Colin Powell's performance in the Security Council throws the conflicts over the inscription of public memory into high relief. Recognizing the centrality of spectatorship to politics reinforces the importance of cultivating a political spectatorship that refuses to be excluded, that recognizes the spectator's constituent and constitutive role in making and using public memory.

At the end of *Stuff Happens*, Hare presents Powell at lunch with the editors of the *New York Times*:

> EDITOR: Do you think Americans would have supported this war if weapons of mass destruction had not been the issue?
> POWELL: Your question is too hypothetical to answer.
> AN ACTOR: An editor then asks:
> EDITOR: Would you personally have supported it?
> AN ACTOR: Powell smiles and reaches out his hand.
> *Powell smiles and reaches out his hand.*
> POWELL: It was good to meet you.
> *All the Actors stand like a line of inspection on either side. In silence, Powell turns and, without looking back, leaves the play.*[42]

In this final moment with Powell, Hare again implies that Powell has been the play's erstwhile tragic hero, a lone obstructionist unable to restrain the warmongers who surrounded him. Here, Hare's doubled and delayed stage directions expose the moment's theatricality and open new spaces for spectators to inhabit. Those watching the play fill the space between An Actor's narration and the Editor's speech, as well as the space between An Actor's prompting and Powell's gesture.

When theater is an instrument of power, spectatorship proves to be the insurgent force embedded in that instrument, and is able to trigger reflections that allow history to be inscribed differently. The utility of intervention as a conceptual tool for considering the influence of art in geopolitics fades as the two fields disappear into one another, replaced by dynamics of spectatorship informed by the dramaturgical analysis of political spectacle. In the shared field where public politics and the art of theater structure one another, an attuned spectator exercising conscientious spectatorship can interrupt the inscription of history. Theater can contest military violence by refusing the forward momentum of intervention when it insists we revisit, resurrect, and reinterpret the past to tell a different story about it. Theater provides an alternative institutional memory, a model for slow politics that move forward in recursive cycles inured against the urgent call to action.

The theatricality of politics is an invitation to translate spectatorship into action (as art, activism, or policy-making) in spite of the odds stacked against that proposition. The theatricality of international institutions provides a material location in which to begin that work. Its rituals are not inaccessible processes; they can be restaged, scrutinized, and disrupted. Where power takes advantage of theater's capacity to tell stories and generate feelings, it admits that its tools are not the exclusive purview of constituted authorities. The arts provide an interface between policy-makers and constituents where artists may intervene to influence interpretation, participating in making meaning from the imperturbable course of history. Insofar as purpose remains a slave to memory, a theatrical apparatus that refuses to forget promises and threats, texts and embodied practices, or the high and low arts of diplomacy, will always maintain the capacity to disconcert the theater of states.

Figure 3. A Swedish soldier with the UN Interim Force in Lebanon (UNIFIL) at an observation post on April 10, 1978. UN Photo by John Isaac.

2

✦

"To Be Seen Is to Be Doomed"

The Force of Spectatorship in UN Peacekeeping

Standing at a microphone in the center of the Economic and Social Council (ECOSOC) Chamber, the under-secretary general for communications and public information, Kiyotaka Akasaka, greeted the crowd—mostly high school students—seated around him: "Good evening ladies and gentlemen, and young students. Tonight is a special occasion and a special place, I would like to welcome you to *Battlestar Galactica*!" Excited applause rang out through the room. "My special welcome goes out to representatives from the 12 *Battlestar* Colonies: representatives from Caprica, representatives from Aerelon, representatives from Aquaria—Yes?" He glanced at his audience, unsure of the alien place names, before continuing, "and the rest of the 12 colonies."[1]

The webcast cut to a medium shot of Edward James Olmos and Mary McDonnell, who starred as Admiral Bill Adama and President Laura Roslin on the hit Sci Fi Channel series *Battlestar Galactica*. They were seated behind official UN nameplates indicating that they had come to represent "Caprica," one of the twelve fictional planets destroyed in the opening moments of the TV show. In fact, they had come to represent the show itself in a series of panel discussions between actors on the show and actors at the United Nations.[2]

Akasaka introduced Dave Howe, president of the Sci Fi Channel, who passed the mic to Whoopi Goldberg, "a huge fan of *Battlestar Galactica*." Along with Ronald D. Moore and David Eick (*Battlestar Galactica*'s creators), Goldberg, McDonnell, and Olmos moved to take new places at the base of a massive orange tapestry. "The United Nations is more than a building with fantastic curtains," Goldberg told her young audience, pausing as they laughed, "but an idea that belongs to all the people of the world."

Battlestar Galactica was a melodrama of intractable conflicts between humans and cyborgs. Airing during the most violent years of the U.S. occupation of Iraq, the show was remarkable for explicitly dramatizing many of the legal and ethical issues that emerged from the exercise of American foreign policy in the Middle East in the early twenty-first century. This televisual regurgitation attracted both viewers and critical praise while also inviting affective transmissions between spectators and spectacles. Placed in UN spaces, its artists now spoke directly to policy-makers. Goldberg enumerated four themes that the evening's conversations would tackle—human rights, children and armed conflict, terrorism, and national reconciliation—and attached art's capacity to spread ideas, values, and emotions to the UN's work: "*Battlestar Galactica* communicates these issues every week to an audience that might be largely unfamiliar with the mission of the UN while nevertheless aspiring to common goals."

As actors, writers, and producers shared their experiences on the set, and diplomats, advocates, and technocrats told stories of the UN's work, the event made its central premise clear: that what we learn from making art and what we learn from making peace may each provide insights into the other. The event suggested the UN's implicit understanding of a central tenet of theater and performance studies: that live embodied performance provides a unique epistemology.[3] As diplomats listened to the experiences of actors who had portrayed war, and actors asked diplomats what they had learned about making peace, each indicated their interest in the unique forms of knowledge made and transmitted by the performances of their counterparts.

As they took up the theme of human rights, Edward James Olmos demonstrated how an actor's way of knowing the world might offer an international institution new ways to erase the barriers dividing humankind. When a question made reference to race, he bristled: "Now the pressure comes, why did we start to use the word race as a cultural determinant? The truth is that over six hundred years ago the Caucasian 'race' decided to use it as a cultural determinant so that it would be easier for them to kill another culture. That was the total understanding: to kill one culture from another culture—you couldn't kill your own race, so you had to make them the other. And to this day—." The frustration and urgency that had been building in his voice overwhelmed his train of thought. He shifted sharply: "I spent 37 years of my adult life trying to get this word out, and now I end up well prepared, as the Admiral of the Battlestar Galactica, to say it to all of you, there is but one race and that is it." As his voice reached a crescendo, he became Admiral Bill Adama once again, impassioned and grandiloquent, in command of a heavily armed spaceship fighting to maintain the remnants of humankind in the face of their likely extinction. He shouted: "So say we all! SO SAY WE ALL! So . . . say . . . we all!" The crowd chanted along with him and as their applause died down, Whoopi Goldberg weighed in: "I love that you said it here at the UN."

Goldberg's enthusiasm marked a moment that drew together material and aspirational transmissions of feelings, ideas, and power; transmissions between a performer and his audience(s) that were also transmissions between theater and diplomacy. Goldberg seemed to hope that Adama's abilities to unite, to lead, and to make peace (the character's occasional failure to do each of these things not withstanding) might make their way into an institution that usually offers divisive, halting, and inadequate solutions to the world's problems. Her hope was not vain: Olmos's performance provides a theatrical model for the delivery of affect and effect to interested and disinterested spectators. Olmos's effort to impress upon his audience the constructedness of race—its performativity—operated through a proliferation of speech acts (requiring both his performance and their spectatorship) that prompted actor and audience to perform their unity of mind and purpose together. The scene was at once cosmopolitan and pedagogical: Olmos constructed the category of humanity to include as equals and without violence cultural and ethnic others, and he transmitted the form and content of this community to its young members via a spontaneous spectacle that was scripted and rehearsed in popular culture. He was at his most compelling as an actor in the instant he slipped into character, becoming Admiral Adama again, and then re-performing a scene that had first appeared on the television program itself.

Olmos's performance in the ECOSOC Chamber articulated a chain of associations traveling from cinema to television to institution to webcast—back and forth between live and mediated instantiations—and offering an indication of the force and vector with which cultural productions make their way into political institutions. An astute viewer of the UN webcast that day would recall the conclusion of a memorial service in an early episode of *Battlestar Galactica*, when the assembled, terrified survivors of a Cylon sneak attack weakly intoned "so say we all," their traditional end to prayer. Adama stepped forward to give a brief speech, and with the same gestures he soon had the assembled ranks chanting their determination in unison with him.[4] An even more astute viewer might be inclined to read beyond the immediate intertext to remember Olmos's Oscar-nominated turn as a math teacher single-handedly righting the institutional and civic failure of decades of inequality in public schooling in the film *Stand and Deliver* (1988). Olmos's performance at the UN indicated three dimensions in which performance functions as an epistemology: by generating, retrieving, and transmitting knowledge. Admiral Adama was an embodied knowledge developed over four seasons, a repertoire that Olmos accessed in the ECOSOC Chamber and delivered to his audience.

In this operation, the scene he played that night jarred and displaced me by reminding me that progressive ends may not always justify theatrical means. Olmos used brusque imperatives to argue for a progressive, inclusive, post-racial utopia. His speech made a case for an egalitarian and tolerant future, even as the formal qualities of his oratory—his body, tone, and verbal structures—all smacked of the intolerance of military orders. He championed certain progressive values, but delivered them to an audience of teenagers by commanding a noisy but disciplined chant. Even so, like Whoopi Goldberg, I love that he said it there at the UN, since the UN strives every day to enact precisely such a synthetic consensus. Olmos's performance was an exaggerated version of the oratory used to arrange states on the world stage, and so highlighted the shades of menace implicit in the verbal exercise of power. While Sci Fi Channel president Dave Howe had told those assembled that he was "excited to share some expertise *from* the UN," Olmos's spectacular performance indicated the utility of the expertise of artists, especially performers, *for* the institution.

As Olmos's performance reflected the UN's quotidian practices, it suggested that the parallel between the two may be more than surface resemblance: the UN may also know the world uniquely where it is embodied. Though many bodies pass through UN spaces and work on behalf of UN projects, the work of the UN is most clearly embodied in its peacekeeping missions. Peacekeeping describes a set of forces that transmit norms and ideologies, affects and desires, and hierarchies and structures from centers of power to power's fringes. Peacekeeping intervenes in the middle of the wars that once composed world history, seeking to rearrange the forces at work in conflict. Peacekeeping missions are set on their way by UN Security Council resolutions and are translated into orders to national armies, whose soldiers don blue helmets as they make their way into war zones, ameliorating or increasing the insecurity of those they encounter while producing images for global consumption.

Peacekeeping is a performance practice, born of texts, housed in bodies, and played in view of an audience. This chapter is a study of what the UN accomplishes on and with the bodies of peacekeepers and of how the UN knows itself in performance. It is also about the knowledge the UN generates in and from performance; what it learns from its own actors and from those on stage or screen. To see what the UN learns from performance, we must look to peacekeeping, to the knowledge that peacekeeping generates, and to the forces that peacekeeping transmits. These questions require that we look to the theater as well, to see how peacekeepers make their way on to stages, even if what is played there does not always transmit to the UN. Two case studies follow, each located at the intersection of a peacekeeping operation and a play. As the experience of *Hamlet* in the Security Council[5] made clear, it is not easy for the UN to go to the theater. Diplomats know that spectatorship carries obligations, and so they manage what and how they watch quite carefully. Peacekeeping operations appear in and disappear from the plays that follow, and as they do so they reveal the ways that peacekeeping—in both what it does and what it knows—is predicated on theatrical spectatorship.

Karen Sunde's play *In a Kingdom by the Sea* dramatizes the efforts of the United Nations Interim Force in Lebanon (UNIFIL) to recover a U.S. marine, Lt. Col. Hogan, who had been kidnapped by Hezbollah while working as a peacekeeper. The play is based on the true story of the kidnapping and murder of William R. Higgins between 1988 and 1990. In 1992, the *New York Observer* reported: "An attempt to stage . . . *In a Kingdom by the Sea* at the United Nations was aborted. From high in the hierarchy came the suggestion that the play might be too 'controversial' to be hosted by the United Nations Staff Writers Club."[6] Karen Sunde confirmed the story when I spoke with her in 2011, and she reflected that "somebody will always have an objection . . . if there's anything that might offend anybody, it's not to be allowed officially on the stage of the UN. I'm sure lots of things happen without that, but I think there's a principle that you have to get all parties to agree for something to happen."[7] Avoiding controversy and offense, member states appear comically anxious over the possibility that the interventions of playwrights in UN spaces could transmogrify into speech acts with the weight of international law.

Of course, the United Nations does not always find theater repellent. In a video posted to the United Nations' YouTube Channel in June 2009, Secretary-General Ban Ki-moon and the UN high commissioner for human rights, Navi Pillay, joined playwright Lynn Nottage at a performance of her Pulitzer-Prize–winning play *Ruined*. Set in a bar and brothel caught between government and rebel soldiers in the Ituri region of the Democratic Republic of the Congo (DRC), *Ruined* is a harrowing depiction of the sexual exploitation, abuse, and violence faced by a group of women who take refuge there. While Nottage described her experiences researching the play, Pillay marked her office's involvement in the production and remarked upon the production's effects: "My office, the High Commissioner for Human Rights office and Equality Now co-sponsored this play, and I think it's a very powerful play . . . It tells you, just intimately, the impact of sexual violence on women."[8] Pillay's participation in this staging of *Ruined* stands in marked contrast to the resistance aroused by *In a Kingdom by the Sea*. One theory for the Secretariat's easy embrace of Nottage's play becomes clear: the UN operations in the DRC are mentioned in it only once, and peacekeepers do not appear onstage. With a safe cordon between the play and the UN, Ban and Pillay were free to join the audience at *Ruined*, to share their horror at the atrocities the play alludes to and their empathy with the women the play depicts.

In a Kingdom by the Sea and *Ruined* each mark a missed encounter between theater and the UN; each is a theatrical effort to directly address an international institution that misfires. Where *Battlestar Galactica*'s encounter with the UN centered attention on the performing body, these plays center attention on acts of spectatorship: on what we can and cannot see, on what we choose to see or not see, and on what we do with what we see. In peacekeeping, spectatorship is also an embodied practice with its own epistemology, one necessary to the exercise of power on the world stage.

The UN Interim Force in Lebanon and *In a Kingdom by the Sea*

Peacekeeping begins as a consequence of what the Security Council sees.[9] The letters transmitted to the UN in March 1978 were succinct, but did not lack for dramatic thrust:

> 11 assassins infiltrated the Israeli coastline on Saturday afternoon . . . they then seized a bus carrying Israeli civilians, one half of them children . . . the terrorists shot indiscriminately at passing traffic, leaving more carnage in their wake . . . the bus was stopped by a roadblock with machine gun and rocket fire blazing from its windows . . . in the course of the battle which ensued, they blew up the bus, mercilessly killing many of the hostages who were still trapped inside.[10]

So wrote Pinhas Eliav, acting permanent representative of Israel, to the General Assembly and the Security Council, replaying the Coastal Road Massacre—an effort by the Palestine Liberation Organization (PLO) to undermine peace negotiations between Egypt and Israel—for institutional eyes. Though textual, the production was also theatrical and performative, and was dramatized for an audience in an effort to elicit their sympathy and stir them to action.

Ghassan Tuéni, the permanent representative of Lebanon, continued the scene two days later in his own letter detailing the start of Israel's Operation Litani, a week-long invasion of southern Lebanon:

> At midnight on 14/15 March, massive Israeli troops crossed into Lebanon . . . Israeli patrol vessels penetrated Lebanese territorial waters along the coastline from Tyre to Sidon. Furthermore, Israeli warplanes continue to fly in Lebanese air space and bombard the area . . . An undetermined number of Lebanese citizens were killed . . . large numbers of our people are leaving the south of Lebanon and going towards the north.[11]

The letter continued, asserting the lack of connection between the perpetrators of the Coastal Road Massacre and the government of Lebanon, and reiterating Lebanon's own lack of control over its southern regions, from which the massacre had been planned and launched. These letters staged the conflict between Israel and the PLO for the Security Council's institutional eyes. The descriptions in each letter were performative insofar as each was a call to action that the Security Council and the UN could not ignore. Four days after the launch of Operation Litani, the Security Council established the UN Interim Force in Lebanon (UNIFIL).

UNIFIL intervened in a conflict that predated Operation Litani and the Coastal Road Massacre. Palestinian refugees had lived in southern Lebanon since their displacement in the wars that followed the establishment of Israel in 1948.[12] In 1970 the PLO was expelled from its base of operations in Jordan, and moved to these refugee communities in Lebanon. Once there, the PLO regularly launched attacks across Israel's northern border, and its presence contributed to the outbreak of civil war in Lebanon in 1975. Approximately 2,000 people, combatants and civilians, died during Israel's Operation Litani.[13]

In his history of Israel's wars, Ahron Bregman argues that the operation was "a rehearsal for Israel's invasion [of Lebanon] of 1982."[14] The 1982 invasion precipitated the emergence of the pro-Iran political party and military group Hezbollah, and Israeli troops did not withdraw from southern Lebanon until 2000. Between and among these actors—Israel, Lebanon, the PLO, and Hezbollah—UNIFIL developed as a uniquely emplaced audience (figure 3).[15]

Peacekeepers are spectators who impact both the spaces where they are deployed and the choreographies of those they come between. The spatializing practice of peacekeepers is both theatrical and performative. Peacekeepers mark spaces in maps and reports and articulate those spaces as they patrol. This theatrical presence constructs the embodied experience of those who reside in the spaces that peacekeeping makes. As the Security Council mobilizes peacekeepers, their bodies produce new spaces in a theatrical idiom. Playing and being played for establish a distinct zone of forces that exert a gravitational pull on bodies beyond. Just as theatrical performers imbue a space with power, so too do the spatial practices of peacekeepers project the power of a group of international actors into a given space.

UNIFIL was the last UN peacekeeping operation authorized during the Cold War. Historians of the United Nations tend to think of peacekeeping operations in two broad periods: "traditional peacekeeping" during the years of the Cold War, and "next-generation peacekeeping" since the early 1990s.[16] Generally speaking, traditional peacekeeping emphasized the tasks of observing ceasefires, providing good offices to combatants to facilitate peace negotiations, the verification of compliance with treaties, and interposition—the placing of a United Nations force between belligerents to act as a buffer. Crucially, the use of force in such operations was only authorized in cases of self-defense when United Nations soldiers had clear evidence they were being targeted. Since the Cold War, UN peacekeeping operations have been much more intimately involved in issues of governance, actively working to reestablish civil order where it has been absent. Next-generation peacekeeping has involved programs to disarm and demobilize combatants, to rebuild infrastructure, and to promote the rule of law. It is also characterized by broader mandates regarding the use of force, and it has occasionally involved the engagement of United Nations peacekeepers in military exercises alongside national armies.[17]

In March 1978, in resolutions 425 and 426, the Security Council authorized a mandate for UNIFIL elaborated by the secretary-general:

(a) The Force will determine compliance with paragraph 2 of Security Council resolution 425 (1978) [which called for the cessation of Israeli military activity]

(b) The Force will confirm the withdrawal of Israeli forces, restore international peace and security and assist the Government of Lebanon in ensuring the return of its effective authority in the area.

(c) The Force will establish and maintain itself in an area of operation to be defined in the light of paragraph 2 (b) above.

(d) The Force will use its best efforts to prevent the recurrence of fighting and to ensure that its area of operation is not utilized for hostile activities of any kind.[18]

In this mandate, UNIFIL's peacekeepers were placed in southern Lebanon as a group of spectators with their bodies on the line. The mandate stressed the observational aspects of the mission (determining and confirming) and connected this activity to the peacekeepers' physical movement (establishing and maintaining). The mandate followed a logic of interposition, the principle of physically placing peacekeepers between belligerents. Interposition places bodies in particular locations and configurations to serve the cause of peace. The mandate directed UNIFIL to interpose itself between the withdrawing Israeli forces and the returning forces of the sovereign government of Lebanon.

Peacekeepers frame the territory they observe and assign positions and values to those who cross their field of view. Studies of peacekeeping occasionally consider the practice in the two registers I have been emphasizing: as spectacular or as spatializing. For example, in *Re-Envisioning Peacekeeping*, François Debrix argues that peacekeeping provides an image of activity in order to paper over the failings and inconsistencies of a cosmopolitan ideology of humanitarian intervention and democracy promotion.[19] By contrast, Paul Higate and Marsha Henry's *Insecure Spaces* elaborates the ways in which peacekeeping is a spatializing practice that performatively produces security, but can also reduce a vibrant social space to a uniform field of insecurity.[20] Both approaches indicate the need for a nuanced understanding of spectatorship as an embodied practice: the recognition that peacekeepers watch the spectacle as much as they perform it and often make spaces by looking.

Lieutenant-General Emmanuel A. Erskine of Ghana served as the first commander of UNIFIL, from 1978 to 1981. His 1989 memoir provides one account of this spectatorship in the initial period of UNIFIL's deployment. In his memoir, he names the extension of Lebanese sovereignty to Lebanon's southern border as both the mission's "ultimate goal" and its most frequently cited failure.[21] Even in failure, however, UNIFIL became integrated into the administration of southern Lebanon, and its daily activities legitimated its continued existence.[22] Indeed, this work continues: a recent report of the secretary-general on UNIFIL relates that in spring 2017 the mission had conducted "an average of over 13,500 operational activities per month, including vehicle and foot patrols, 'market walks,' checkpoints, and observation tasks," and that "UNIFIL liaison and coordination arrangements . . . remain critical."[23] In these activities peacekeepers move and watch, elaborating zones of security and insecurity by patrolling and looking. In this they are an audience: individuals who render human behavior meaningful as performance.

In peacekeeping, the UN deploys spectators to embody its gaze and to make the presence of that gaze known among the actors on the ground. Emmanuel Erskine's memoirs elaborate the multiple dimensions in which the UN observation mandates incorporate spectatorship into the work of keeping peace. When Erskine drily describes UNIFIL's initial efforts at shuttle diplomacy in 1978, he reminds his readers that "briefing each side in a dispute on what the other side is thinking has been a continuing function of peacemaking."[24] Though he does not dwell on the implications of this function, it reveals his assumption that peace can be made by establishing a comprehensive record performed with total transparency in view of an audience that can ratify it. UNIFIL observes and reports on ceasefire infractions in order to establish a third-party record by which negotiations can proceed in good faith.[25]

As his memoir proceeds, Erskine's anecdotes reveal his sophisticated understanding of the role spectatorship plays in his work; a performer's understanding that aligns him with Edward James Olmos. He considers the performances that others play for him and the audiences that he plays for. He describes Israeli forces reinforcing their positions "right under my nose . . . 100 meters from my office,"[26] a performance that signals differences between their publicly stated intentions and the reality they performed on the ground. This drives his own performance, a sound bite delivered to international media: "I finally gave the warning: should UNIFIL be unable to succeed in executing its mandate, Israel would be held responsible."[27] Acknowledging that this act got him "a good blasting" from Secretary-General Kurt Waldheim, he notes that his breach of etiquette was a calculated effort based on his conviction that "the strength of the UN largely lies in world public opinion and sympathy."[28] Peacekeepers act on the performances they see, and encourage wider audiences to do the same.

Erskine also details the ways in which others performed differently once they had UNIFIL as an audience. He relates one scenario devised by the Israel Defense Forces (IDF) for those under his command:

> On 10 September 1980 . . . Lt.-Col. J.M. Steenaert [commander of the Dutch Battalion working with UNIFIL] came to see me. He said that he had been summoned the previous day by Lt.-Col. Gary Gal, the IDF liaison officer . . . [This was] an infringement of our standard operating procedures . . . Colonel Steenaert had been with Colonel Gal for barely twenty minutes when General Rafael Eitan, IDF Chief of Staff, and General Ben Gal entered the room. This could hardly have been a coincidence and sure enough it was not. It had all been planned and possibly rehearsed.[29]

Steenaert and Erskine interpreted the interruption and subsequent meeting as an effort to gauge potential Dutch reaction were Israel to invade southern Lebanon. Positioned as theatrical spectators, the peacekeepers opened new avenues of action to the parties to the conflict. Once more, the performance prompted Erskine to seek other audiences, by sending his senior political advisor to "discuss the issue personally with Brian [Urquhart, undersecretary-general for special political affairs,] and the Secretary-General." Audiences at UNHQ "viewed the IDF's intention . . . with the utmost concern," and sprang into action to prevent a return to hostilities. "So UNIFIL did its bit by preventing 'Operation Litani 2.'"[30]

In Erskine's accounts, UNIFIL's spectatorship has material effects on the performances of national armies, and UNIFIL accomplishes its ends by conveying those performances to wider audiences. This work occurs not just in the exceptional situations I have cited from Erskine's memoir, but in the regular reporting required of each mission. In the reports produced by or about peacekeeping operations, the UN stages itself for itself, theatrically framing events to make sense of its own activities and propel subsequent action. In these cases, the efficacy of peacekeeping rests in watching and learning, and disseminating what it has seen and learned.[31]

Where reading peacekeeping as theater risks sanitizing war, transposing these activities to the stage reveals the violence that is inherent in spectatorship. Karen Sunde's play *In a Kingdom by the Sea* is based on the kidnapping and murder of Lt. Col. William R. Higgins while he served as an observer with UNIFIL in 1988, a decade after the Coastal Road Massacre (and seven years after Erskine had left the mission). In the play, Higgins becomes Hogan, a headstrong cipher for unilateral American foreign policy. The play begins with Hogan's kidnapping and ends with his murder. In between, "two actions play at once."[32] In the present, three members of UNIFIL (Tombo, the mission's Irish commander; Gabe, a Fijian corporal; and Sami, a Turkish civilian, the mission's information officer) coordinate the search for Hogan. On top of this, "the 'presence' of Hogan . . . [which is] visible only to Sami and the audience," provides the second action as he "skips time and space, 'tuning' in at will."[33] Materializing as a ghost or memory of Hogan, this presence recognizes that the work of observation involves becoming a node in the circuits of communication between armed forces: "So. Just what the hell is a Military Observer? . . . As I understand it, we investigate, liaison, make contacts."[34] In *In a Kingdom by the Sea*, the presence of peacekeepers as spectators turns private wars into publicly staged events.

Peacekeeping forces actively participate in conflict by acting as spectators to conflict. In an interview, Karen Sunde told me that she set *In a Kingdom by the Sea* in one of UNIFIL's communications centers in order to underscore these interwoven functions. "[In] that nerve center . . . their ability to operate is based on their getting information about what's going on in all their battalions . . . at the moment and how the outside political situation is affecting that."[35] *In a Kingdom by the Sea* makes evident on stage the fact that UNIFIL's observations were not subsidiary to its other activities; rather, UNIFIL acted by observing. Observation and communication were the mission's primary tools. In this way, the play materializes the relationship between theatrical spectatorship and the powers that peacekeepers wield.

Theater is a privileged medium in this context for its ability to bring together in one space various ways of looking that negotiate between layers of liveness and mediation, presence and absence. Stage directions describe the set as "a 'listening post.' . . . Clustered, as though suspended—projection screen, monitor, speakers, VCR—the means, simultaneous and fractured, by which we receive our image of events."[36] The theatrical audience watches through the audience realized onstage in the characters that make up UNIFIL via an apparatus that incorporates live performing bodies and mediated images. This sequence of spectatorial transmissions effectively models the exercise of power via observation by peacekeepers and policy-makers, inviting playgoers to consider how their own gaze participates in the same system.

Observation is a tool of power that works by collecting, codifying, and transmitting knowledge of a territory and people. In this, it is hardly benign; spectatorship carries a force that is always more or less invasive and potentially violent. When peacekeepers observe, their gaze remains on a continuum of militarized looking: observation becomes spying becomes targeting quite easily.

This relationship is at the heart of *In a Kingdom by the Sea*. Hogan's kidnapping demonstrates how little the nuanced distinctions between observation and spying mattered to certain audiences. As news of Hogan's abduction reaches the listening post, an offstage voice reads aloud the kidnappers' statement: "William Hogan, an agent of America's CIA, who is using the activities of the United Nations Observers as a cover for his dangerous role of espionage, is now in the grips of our heroic strugglers." [37] Hearing the statement, Gabe exclaims, "No! Not a spy. He's a warrior!"[38] Even while disputing that Hogan had conducted military operations, Gabe highlights Hogan's attraction to violent conflict. As war and spectatorship become inextricable, peacemaking, peacekeeping, and peace-building reveal their own paradoxical imbrication in global violence.[39] Insofar as spectatorship precedes hostilities, it may always be suspect.[40]

Sami also recognizes that even if Hogan is not a spy, his motives remain grounded in violence. In a memory layered over the communications hub, Sami accuses Hogan of being motivated by revenge: "I say Payback. Payback is why you are here."[41] Payback for the 1983 bombing of a barracks in Beirut by a group allied with Hezbollah that killed 241 U.S. and 58 French soldiers. The barracks housed soldiers with the Multinational Force in Lebanon, an intervention by the United States, France, Britain, and Italy, outside of UN auspices, to monitor a ceasefire between the PLO and Israel following the 1982 invasion in the midst of Lebanon's civil war.[42] Sami's accusation prompts Hogan to describe the blast as a scene of spectacular, retributive violence that has epistemological effects:

> Sunrise—it's . . . on Beirut, golden wash, gleaming, pastels . . . astonishing. And Sunday. the boys are nested, having a last dream, an extra half hour. (*beat*) I saw the grin. Like he was sharing a secret. Dark beard, dark blue shirt, blurred past the gate. His big truck, yellow, sitting alone in the lobby, looked silly. Then came the orange white flash, too loud to hear, glued skin to my cheekbones; wind . . . lifted the rooms, pulled out their air, set four stories down in one pile.
>
> Some boys woke with their ceiling in bed, and the floor above and its ceiling and the next, too strange to believe. They said God, oh God help me. Now I lay me down to sleep. The boys covered in ash, scattered, parts without arms, without heads, caught in trees, never woke, but were found by boys who never slept after. And the boys with head and arm hanging free, bodies crushed between slabs, dripping slow . . . red on grey ash, when they woke, those were the worst.[43]

In Hogan's monologue, Sunde elaborates a sensorium that privileges visual, sonic, and haptic registers, and that is overwhelmed by the violence it encounters. In a space of dreams and trauma, she links this sensing body to what it is able to know as it is dismembered by violence. Here, the instrument of spectacular violence appears as one sharing secret knowledge, while the soldiers, sleeping youths, unwitting representatives of structural violence, wake to this new knowledge, which is too strange to believe.

When we discussed this scene, Sunde told me:

> I don't know if you have the perspective, but that marine barracks bombing was a huge blow to our psyche. I mean, it was a tragedy for us here in the U.S., but it was completely couched in the question, "what are we doing there, anyway?" It was going into a place like this thinking we knew what to do, we knew how to handle it, we could control, even. . . . when I was first writing these plays, I was trying to say, "we don't get it, come on, wise up, let's pull back from our arrogance and learn." . . . So that's what I was thinking, and on 9/11, I watched this from the roof of where I lived, and all I could think was ok the world has changed, everything's changed, nothing's ever going to be the same. But I'm also thinking, maybe now we will learn.[44]

By layering this specifically American trauma onto the operations of UNIFIL, *In a Kingdom by the Sea* suggests ways that peacekeeping may amplify the interconnection of spectatorship, violence, and knowledge acquisition.[45]

States and populations learn from violence, violence often visited on the bodies of their citizens and soldiers. Hogan spends much of the play learning from and with violence, but Sami holds Hogan's relationship to violence against him: "Marines are trained for one thing, Col. Hogan, and it 'ain't' peace."[46] Hogan reminds Sami that each of the peacekeepers he works with began their careers as soldiers: "And because the UN asks these men not to fight, there's another quality they require . . . and that, Mister Sami, is discipline."[47] If discipline is what Hogan hopes will redeem his prying eyes from the charge of spying, the play also establishes Hogan's lack of discipline as a fatal flaw. Sami berates him for his disregard of UNIFIL's procedures: "You go into restricted areas without notification or clearance . . . Alone! You set up meetings without registering. You meet with people you have no authorization to, in places you have no authorization to be. You never do radio checks!!"[48] Hogan's lack of attention to the mission's protocols ultimately dooms him: he is kidnapped when he arranges a unilateral meeting with members of Hezbollah, and his secrecy prevents his colleagues from finding him.

Military discipline names one epistemology of peacekeeping: knowledge generated by, contained in, and transmitted through the bodies of soldiers who serve as peacekeepers. As the play draws to a close, an image of Hogan's corpse, hanged to death by his captors, is projected onstage. Laurel, Hogan's high school sweetheart, appears "*spot-lit, at a distance, on the phone.*" She observes, "As far as gruesome goes, they couldn't do better. As far as if he's dead I can't tell. All I can tell is . . . those are his toes."[49] In this concluding image, the play comes to rest on Hogan's body and draws focus to his toes, body parts dedicated to locomotion and balance. The image resonates with the story of Hogan that has emerged: that he joined UNIFIL after Laurel's son was killed in the Beirut barracks bombing as part of a personal, unilateral mission to forge peace, and that he "walked, smiling, to meet"[50] his captors. Hogan's death is a function of what he can see and what he allows others to see, of what he learns from violence and what he learns of violence. His death is also a consequence of his failure to be redisciplined by the UN. His final words in the play indicate that this failure attaches to his body: "I just need to . . . pull my skin on a little . . . differently."[51]

At the outset of our interview, Sunde articulated the core of her theatrical aesthetics in plain language: "theater exists for the community to celebrate itself, learn itself and celebrate itself."[52] Sunde intended this image quite positively, asserting that theater could be a source of intersubjective knowledge that would allow members of a community to feel good about one another. However, *In a Kingdom by the Sea* indicates that what a community learns theatrically does not only lead to celebration. Perhaps this is why it could not be allowed on to the UN's stages, where it would reveal the UN's willful blindness to peacekeeping's violence.

In a Kingdom by the Sea draws together spectatorship, violence, pedagogy, and discipline. It offers spectators an image of peacemaking as a disciplinary theater that the UN deploys to regions in conflict. The play places the eyes of its spectators in sequence with the soldiers, generals, and diplomats who act on areas of conflict via peacekeeping. As spectators navigate the play's two actions and negotiate its nonlinear storytelling, they work to discipline and master its narrative, work that attaches the playgoer to the peacekeeper. Deployed around the world, the UN's peacekeepers act to see and be seen, but also to discipline those they watch and play for: to render them calm, orderly, composed, and obedient toward international norms. Peacekeepers watch and learn, and in so doing pacify and stabilize: goals that mask the violence inherent in the means used to achieve them.

The UN Mission in the Democratic Republic of the Congo and *Ruined*

In contrast to *In a Kingdom by the Sea*, UN peacekeepers appear only once in Lynn Nottage's *Ruined*. The play begins with the arrival of Salima and Sophie at Mama Nadi's bar and brothel. Both women are seeking refuge from violence that is engulfing the eastern part of the Democratic Republic of the Congo (DRC): Salima is pregnant from rape by rebel soldiers, and Sophie suffers from a fistula. Through most of the show, the bar is a precarious refuge caught between government and rebel forces where these women and others find relative security. Sophie sings each night for an audience of miners, soldiers, and traders, all the while planning her escape from the region with Salima. As the play approaches its climax, it reverses the image of interposition as a stabilizing force.

In the play's penultimate scene, war comes to Mama Nadi's bar. Government soldiers invade the bar, searching for a rebel leader. They loot its meager earnings and violently attempt to rape Josephine, the eldest of Mama's employees. Salima stops the violence when she enters the scene with blood pooling on her dress and dripping down her legs, the result of her efforts to end her pregnancy. She collapses and dies from the self-inflicted wound. The scene ends in blackout.[53]

Lights come up again on restored calm. The stage directions indicate "the sounds of the tropical Ituri rainforest," while Sophie weeps and sings to herself. Mama stands at the door of the bar:

> (*Mama anxiously watches the road. Excited, she spots a passing truck.*)
> [. . .]
> MAMA: Dust rising.
> JOSEPHINE (*eagerly*): Who is it?

> MAMA (*excited*): I don't know. Blue helmets heading north. Hello? Hello? (*Mama seductively waves. Nothing. Disappointed, she retreats to the table.*) Damn them. How the hell are we supposed to do business? They're draining our blood.[54]

Mentioned only as they pass by, the blue helmets arrive too late to affect the violence depicted in the play, and add insult to injury by refusing to partake of either the bar's liquor or sexual services.

These scenes stage one relationship between seeing and violence in the eastern DRC in the early 2000s. They reflect a history that is partly rooted in the violence of Belgian colonialism in the region at the end of the nineteenth century.[55] In the Congo River basin, as across the continent and elsewhere, colonial administrative borders were established that "played havoc with [the] delicate cobweb of relationships" that preceded the Europeans' arrival.[56] In the 1930s, Belgium encouraged migration from its colonies in Rwanda to the Congo, establishing ethnic hierarchies that fomented resentments and tensions.[57] Mobuto Sese Seko, the military dictator who came to power a few years after the DRC won its independence in 1960, exploited and exacerbated these tensions throughout his rule, and especially as his grip on power began to slip in the 1990s.[58]

The genocide in Rwanda in 1994 provided the proximate cause of the First Congo War (1996–1997), when hundreds of thousands of refugees, including former combatants fearing reprisals, made their way from Rwanda to the eastern part of the Democratic Republic of the Congo (then known as Zaire).[59] There, elements of the defeated Rwandan government began to regroup. To address this threat, a coalition formed between Rwanda's new leadership, other African states, and anti-Mobuto rebels led by Laurent-Désiré Kabila.[60] The First Congo War ended with Mobuto deposed and Kabila installed as president in the DRC.

The Second Congo War began soon after (in 1998), when Kabila's relationship with the foreign powers that had supported him soured.[61] Rwanda, Uganda, and Burundi backed a new rebel group in the eastern DRC, the Rally for Congolese Democracy (RCD), and other rebel groups formed soon after, including the Mouvement pour la Liberation du Congo (MLC), led by Jean-Pierre Bemba. In 1999, a ceasefire was signed and the UN Security Council established the UN Organization Mission in the Democratic Republic of the Congo (MONUC).[62] Violence continued in the DRC despite the ceasefire and the peacekeeping operation. In 2001, Kabila was assassinated and succeeded by his son, Joseph. An inter-Congolese dialogue began in 2002. The Transitional Government of the Democratic Republic of the Congo came to power in 2003, marking the official end of the Second Congo War. Elections were held in 2006, which Joseph Kabila won (Jean-Pierre Bemba took second place). However, even as the political process stabilized, violence continued, especially in the east.[63]

The blue helmets' late arrival in *Ruined* suggests that the play is set in 2003 or 2004, a period when the bulk of MONUC's troops had not yet been deployed and even fewer had made their way to Ituri Province, where the violence that Nottage depicts was ongoing. MONUC mission reports (provided by the secretary-general to the Security Council) index the slow pace with which the UN put eyes on the ground. In February 2003, the secretary-general reported that MONUC had dispatched an exploratory mission to the region.[64] By May, an initial force of 720 peacekeepers had arrived.[65] Over a year later, the August 2004 report related that the strength of the Ituri Brigade had grown to roughly 4,700 personnel. [66] And in 2005 Médecins Sans Frontières released their own report on the region, titled "Nothing New in Ituri: The Violence Continues." It grimly noted that "efforts by the international community . . . did not change the status quo," especially in areas beyond the capital of Ituri, Bunia.[67]

If the scene that closes *Ruined* indicts the UN for its failure to come to the aid of Salima, Sophie, Josephine, and Mama Nadi, it also absolves the UN of any obligations it may have regarding the other forms of violence in which the peacekeepers whom Mama watches may be implicated. They are faulted not for what they do, but only for what they miss. The peacekeepers that do not appear in *Ruined* dramatize the UN's inadequate response to violence in the DRC, and Mama Nadi and her charges feel the range of its effects on their bodies. However, by limiting itself to the violence beyond MONUC's grasp, the play avoids a more complicated relationship between UN peacekeeping and sexual violence. In the August 2004 report on MONUC, the secretary-general acknowledged "serious allegations of exploitation and misconduct by MONUC civilian and military personnel in Bunia . . . including sexual exploitation of underage girls and women at the camp for internally displaced persons and other locations, consisting mainly of prostitution but also including incidents of rape."[68] The non-appearance of peacekeepers in *Ruined* may reflect their late arrival in Ituri, but it also reiterates the absence of the sexual violence committed by peacekeepers in the secretary-general's reports. Far from an aberration, the exploitation and abuse revealed in 2004 indicated widespread problems in MONUC and beyond.[69] In this light, Mama Nadi's inability to profit from MONUC is a rare unconvincing moment in a play that otherwise depicts the gendered dimensions of war quite vividly.

The distance between the soldiers at Mama's bar and the peacekeepers who passed it by seems not so great when one notes the following observation from a report prepared for the UN Development Fund for Women:

> In the DRC, members of local communities told us that peacekeepers were buying sex from young girls and that condoms were visibly scattered in the fields near UN compounds. A local woman told us that girls "just lie down in the fields for the men in full view of people as they are not allowed into the camps." In Kinshasa . . . women line up

at the hour most UN workers go home, hoping a male worker will choose them.[70]

At each turn this excerpt emphasizes the role of visibility and looking. The peacekeeper's own gaze becomes equivalent with that of the soldiers in *Ruined*, transforming vulnerable people into sexual objects.[71]

Similarly, Paul Higate reports the following exchange with a peacekeeper he interviewed in the DRC:

> PEACEKEEPER: These guys want to see what it is like.
> AUTHOR: What it is like?
> PEACEKEEPER: Sex with young girls . . . to see if it is different.
> AUTHOR: Um . . . right.
> PEACEKEEPER: Some of them [peacekeepers] have daughters who are the same age, fourteen or fifteen, and they want to know.[72]

Higate relates this conversation alongside another peacekeeper's anecdote of fighting off sexually aggressive women in local bars, and an interview with a civilian woman who "'preferred to work with a man who had a sexual outlet of [the commercial] kind,' since he was more likely to be 'controlled' in the office during the working day."[73] Where Higate focuses on the ways the peacekeepers' discourse made them blind to the exploitation and abuse they perpetrated, I am most struck, again, by what they did by seeing. In the peacekeeper's report that "these guys want *to see* what it is like," looking serves not just objectification, but the sexual violation of children justified as an effort to generate knowledge.

How is it that in deploying its peacekeepers as spectators to Ituri, ostensibly as a deterrent gaze against the gender-based and sexual violence in the region, the UN cannot see its own violence? How does it miss the forces that its own acts transmit? How too does a highly lauded playwright, turning her own gaze to the same place and period, miss the crimes committed by peacekeepers? There are reasonable answers to these questions: misconduct in MONUC followed the Department of Peacekeeping Operations' failure to imagine the likelihood of exploitation, and Nottage's own methods required that she confine her drama to the stories provided by the women she interviewed when researching the play. Or perhaps the UN's failure reflected a lack of international political will, and *Ruined* chose to focus on the worst perpetrators of sexual violence in order to advocate for the victims more effectively. But there is also a subtler answer available in *Ruined*, in the ways it expertly explores the relationship between spectatorship and violence.

The forces at work in *Ruined* appear in scenes that foreground toxic spectatorship. In the play's second scene, Sophie "plows through an upbeat dance song," while Josephine dances for a group of drunk rebel soldiers.[74] The soldiers catcall Sophie, who does not respond. When they complain to Mama, she tells one, "You want to talk to her? Behave and let me see your money." Though the soldier has spent all his currency on beer, he draws Mama's attention to his other resources: "Mama, lookie! I have this. (*Proudly displays a cloth filled with little chunks of ore*)."[75] In these opening moments the scene rapidly moves from traditional performance spectatorship, to sexualized leering, to monetized scopophilia, to the avaricious gaze of one dedicated to the extraction of natural resources. At each turn, spectatorship advances as an agent of objectification, exploitation, and violation.

At the end of the scene, these forces are weaponized. As the Lebanese merchant Mr. Harari "studies" the ruthless rebel leader Jerome Kisembe, Josephine chastises him: "Don't look so hard at a man like that." They are interrupted by Salima attempting to escape the rough treatment of a client. Mama stops her. "*Salima's eyes shoot daggers at Mama, but she reluctantly returns to the drunken soldier.*" The scene ends as Sophie and Josephine begin singing and dancing for the crowd once more, and "*Mama watches Salima like a hawk.*"[76] With their eyes, Harari spies, Salima targets, and Mama hunts. *Ruined* develops a schematic of relationships of power in the form of competing gazes, each with its own force. The scene attaches the vulnerability of its characters to the figure of spectatorship itself, posing difficult questions of complicity and action for those who watch it.

Where the UN delivers peacekeeping spectators to the DRC, plays like *Ruined* deliver the DRC to theatrical spectators in New York and elsewhere. The theatrical situation doubles the moment of exploitation and unease, as audiences quite far from the DRC also consume the performances at Mama's bar. The place of spectatorship in *Ruined* refuses easy distinctions between the gazes it depicts, avoids, and cultivates. What distances separate the theatergoer captivated by Sophie and Josephine from the leering soldier in Mama's bar? Where do an institution's blind spots and filters intersect those of an individual citizen spectator? How does the safety of the playhouse compare to the zones made secure by patrolling peacekeepers? If Nottage's characters court danger by looking at one another, and peacekeepers abet violence by looking away, what force is mobilized by a play-going audience who is otherwise disempowered by theatrical convention?

Looking and watching may risk injury to their targets, but they are also the activities that activate empathy; the degree to which a viewing subject identifies, understands, or feels compassion or sympathy for a subject viewed.[77] The extant literature on *Ruined* returns often to the play's capacity for provoking empathetic responses in its spectators. Ben Brantley hypothesizes that "people who ordinarily look away from horror stories of different wars may well find themselves bound in empathy to [these] unthinkably abused women."[78] Similarly, Robert Skloot, writing in *Genocide Studies and Prevention*, suggests that the play's success was a consequence of the "empathetic connection between audience and character [that] was successfully accomplished."[79] Binding and connecting subjects at hemispheric distances, these authors speak to the activist potential of spectatorship. To Sharon Friedman, staging these empathetic victims of violence "evoke[s] 'critical empathy,'" Wendy Hesford's term for theatrical strategies that require viewers "to consider their own '[moral] culpab[ility] for a lack of attention to—and objectification of—the suffering of others.'"[80]

These scholars propose empathy, and especially critical empathy, as an ethical way of looking that can stand as a discrete alternative to the militarized and sexualized looking of states, soldiers, and institutions. I am not convinced that the boundaries between empathy and objectification in spectatorship can hold fast. Though empathy is humanizing, making subjects of the gaze instead of objects, it maintains the asymmetry between looker and looked. In cultural spaces, especially theaters, empathy is used to promote the transgression of psychological, bodily, and political borders. Theater-makers invite their audiences to exceed their own experiences by inhabiting the experiences of others: to see what it is like to have another's mind and body and to be from a distant place.[81] Any positive view of the boundary crossings made possible by the theater must be tempered by recognition of the violations these operations resemble: the invasion of foreign lands and the abuse of alien bodies.

If critical empathy is meant to highlight an audience's culpability, in the present context that culpability extends to the forces that mobilize intervention. The absence of peacekeepers in *Ruined* implies a link between the empathetic responses of theatergoers and the possibility for constructive international responses to violence: that international forces have not been watching Mama's bar precludes a collective response born of empathy. Mobilizing empathy on stage, *Ruined* presumes that its viewers will press their governments to act. Played before UN officials, the play hopes it can transmit better than the secretary-general's reports. Drawing attention to what the world has not seen, it calls for the full force of spectatorship to bear on the women in Ituri.

But understanding peacekeeping as spectatorship should give us pause. Vulnerable populations become fixed in their victimhood to watching peacekeepers, to those who watch through the peacekeepers, and to those who watch the peacekeepers. These spectators include those who author Security Council resolutions and the mandates of peacekeeping operations, and so the continuing presence of vulnerable populations risks always legitimizing continued intervention. Policy is a function of spectatorship: what and how the council watches impacts the forces it sets in motion. Empathy points to the affects that performance knows and can transmit to others. When attached to spectatorship, empathy indicates ways in which a gaze can cross intersubjective boundaries. Such transgressions are celebrated in the theater, as that which can undo violence by encouraging compassion. But this positive view must be tempered by the recognition that when compassion drives a call for action, the forces it mobilizes risk exceeding their intended targets.

Ruined captures this ambivalence, and the despair it generates, when Sophie sings:

> A rare bird on a limb
> Sings a song heard by a few,
> A few patient and distant listeners
> Hear its sweet call,
> A sound that haunts the forest,
> . . .
> To be seen is to be doomed
> It must evade, evade capture,
> And yet the bird
> Still cries out to be heard.[82]

The song implies an ecology of seeing and hearing, in which the necessity of being seen and heard goes hand in hand with the danger it invites. The bird knows its performance may undo it, just as Sophie knows her own performances at Mama's bar may bring her doom. *Ruined* is caught in the same trap. The spectatorship of theatergoers, of peacekeepers, and of diplomats are all constituent parts of the complex of forces that direct and compose peacekeeping operations worldwide, forces that are as likely to produce violence and instability as to produce empathy and peace.

Spectatorship and Global Governmentality

Discussions of *Ruined* often center on the play's climactic moment, when Salima, bleeding to death on stage, tells the soldiers in Mama's bar, "You will not fight your battles on my body anymore."[83] I have shifted my focus to the play's subsequent moment of calm, and the brief (non)appearance of UN peacekeepers. Salima's spectacular death and the ambiguous romantic resolution of the play follow conventions of melodrama that risk containing the play's energies, especially its activist force.[84] By contrast, Mama Nadi's brief description of MONUC personnel passing by casts the UN as a vector running on a tangent past Nottage's scenes and characters. My mathematical analogy is intended to mark the peacekeepers as a quantity with a direction and a magnitude, a force in motion. In peacekeeping, the UN regulates the movement of bodies, patterning and directing them. In this manner, peacekeeping indicates the choreographic practice of international institutions; a practice in which conventional theater also participates, as its artists and audiences travel related paths.

In our interview, Karen Sunde described her travels with the UN. "When I was about to make a trip to the Middle East, [Under-Secretary-General for Political Affairs Marrack] Goulding called, wanted a meeting, and said, 'I'm

"To Be Seen Is to Be Doomed" 63

sorry Miss Sunde, we can't let you go into Lebanon.' . . . because there'd been too many Americans kidnapped right at that period."[85] Goulding's call deflected Sunde's motion, but did not arrest it: "I went anyway. Landed in Tel Aviv, went to Jerusalem, the UN Truce Supervision Organization [UNTSO], the headquarters in Jerusalem, they took me to the Golan Heights."[86] UNTSO is the UN's oldest active peacekeeping mission, established in 1948 to monitor the armistice between Egypt, Israel, Jordan, Lebanon, and Syria. UNTSO provides military observers to UNIFIL and to the UN Disengagement Observer Force (UNDOF) on the Golan Heights. With UNTSO, chaperoned by peacekeepers, Sunde carried out her own observation mission: "They would take me out to some checkpoints, so I got to see how they were operating, and I was recording all the time," taking note of their movements, "getting a sense of the mechanics of their patrols."[87] Finally, she made a last effort to encounter her subject directly, "someone was going to help me get into Lebanon," but she ultimately missed her target: "I went right up to the border with Lebanon, and did not get across."[88]

In a preface to the published edition of *Ruined*, director Kate Whoriskey described similar travels with Lynn Nottage. Whoriskey collaborated with Nottage on *Intimate Apparel* (2003) and *Fabulation, or the Re-Education of Undine* (2004) before the two worked together to develop *Ruined*. She writes:

> Lynn wanted to do a version of *Mother Courage* set in the Congo. . . . Since her days working for Amnesty International, Lynn had been disturbed by the lack of interest the international community showed for such a devastating conflict. She thought that doing an adaptation might call attention to the crisis. . . . Then, one day, Lynn called me: "I bought a ticket to Uganda," she said, "do you want to go with me?"[89]

Where Sunde's travel was deflected by skittish UN officials, Whoriskey and Nottage followed those displaced by violence, finding survivors to interview in camps across the border from the Congo in Uganda. Each set of theater-makers embodied a particular confluence of movement, information-gathering, and violence. Whoriskey described their arrival:

> One of the first people we met in Kampala was a driver who said he was willing to take us anywhere . . . First on our itinerary was the refugee camp in Arva, north of Kampala. "I am willing to take you there. I do food runs there for various NGOs, but I want to let you know the violence is increasing there." He spoke of rebels cutting off women's tongues to upset the camps. The violence was reminiscent of explorer turned colonizer Henry Morton Stanley [who] cut off the hands of anyone refusing to work. Such butchery, practiced by colonizers one hundred years earlier, seemed to influence current acts of violence in a post-colonial Congo.[90]

Her anecdote reflects spatial dynamics that peacekeeping knows well: zones of insecurity and security made by moving bodies and textured by long histories of spectacular violence that risk reinforcing atavistic stereotypes.

Sunde, Nottage, and Whoriskey each traveled the routes made available by international institutions: Sunde with peacekeepers, Nottage and Whoriskey with the support services and ancillary industries that emerge where the UN manages conflict. The labor of Nottage and Whoriskey mirrors that of their driver: he brings food to the camps, they broadcast stories from them. In this anecdote, that resonance is joined by others. When Whoriskey slips into the passive voice midway through her retelling, she erases herself as the one reminded of violence, and obscures the degree to which her own travel retraced the journeys of explorers and colonizers. Whoriskey is displaced by the unsettling history her presence remembers. Her account marks the difficulty of addressing the imbrication of activist art in international violence, much less resolving the contradictions and hazards consequent to activist art-making.

Peacekeeping is similarly compromised. Peacekeeping missions follow similar trajectories to these authors: each mission is an embodied manifestation of forces that originate in powerful states, aimed at a global periphery. Moving along this vector, peacekeeping may be intended as an effort to ameliorate imperial or colonial violence, but it cannot avoid reiterating past injustices. Artists and peacekeepers travel from secure centers to insecure fringes, bringing prying eyes and taking stories that flow to further audiences. These actors direct or deflect the force of spectatorship as it works around the globe. Peacekeeping and theater work in conjunction with one another. Framed through the vectors, flows, and forces that they organize and administer, they reveal a system of global governmentality that is predicated on spectatorship.

Peacekeeping is a global form of governmentality, a form of biopolitics and biopower that aims at "someone's body, soul, and behavior."[91] "Governmentality" is Michel Foucault's name for how power has come to think and work, especially in the practices of states and their governments. It consists of the conduct of conduct, and is, as such, a function of power aimed not at things but at relationships of force and between forces.[92] It is a form of administration that is interested not in absolute values but in relative values: in managing flows of population and the forces that affect them.[93] And it works by knowing bodies: what they contain, how they move, and what they transmit. In, through, and with the bodies of peacekeepers, the UN animates a system of global governmentality. Peacekeeping makes good subjects out of peacekeepers (Erskine's memoirs make clear the salutary effects that UNIFIL had on his troops),[94] regulates the bodies and souls of its targets (evident in MONUC's disarmament, demobilization, and reintegration campaigns),[95] and keeps aberrations out of view (such as individual peacekeepers repatriated to their home countries following their crimes of sexual exploitation and abuse).[96]

Peacekeeping is a machine that watches and acts, teaches and learns, in order to exert a governmentalizing force in specific territories and on specific populations. This is the theater the Security Council deploys in its peacekeeping operations, and through this theater global governmentality addresses populations the world over. While Foucault highlights that resistance to the conduct of conduct has its own "forms, dramaturgy, and distinct aim,"[97] he puts less emphasis on the theatrical dimensions of governmentality itself. In peacekeeping, this theatricality proves inescapable insofar as acts of spectatorship are essential to the UN's work on the world's margins. Spectatorship transmits a governmentalizing force, and the gaze of an international community participates in the conduct of conduct. What peacekeepers bring to and from the field works in concert with transmissions between peacekeeping and theater, as theatrical depictions (like *Ruined*) work to channel global will into action in centers of power, and peacekeeping performances manifest that global will for spectators at the world's margins.

In composing this chapter, I have found myself hesitating. I worry that my critique would earn me a reproach from the same Congolese woman who told Anneke Van Woudenberg, a researcher with Human Rights Watch, "Yes it is true that some girls have been raped by U.N. soldiers, but so many more have been brutally raped by other armed groups. Please focus on stopping this as it brings us so much more pain and suffering."[98] My hesitation is again a function of the fact that spectatorship is so deeply encoded in the work of peacekeeping and the systems of global governmentality of which it forms a part. A world system built on spectatorship impels me to look first at the most spectacular manifestations of violence, most often those with the statistical heft to command attention.[99] I hesitate as a function of the ideologies in which I have been trained, and the embodied practices of looking that they entail. But where I hesitate, displacing my attention from one form of violence to another, is where I recognize the need to also be sensitive to insidious manifestations of violence outside of spectacle, especially in those systems designed to ameliorate violence.

Peacekeeping, as a theater, can only address spectacular violence, and as such will always miss the systemic violence in which it is embedded. Peacekeeping can interrupt hostilities and impede belligerents, but it does so by mobilizing its own coercions. Theater seems to have similar problems, stirring emotions that pave the way for militarized solutions. As the UN's mechanisms work to fix (to make right and to make stable, to write and to secure) the political subjectivities of individuals, populations, and territories, they produce retributive forms of violence and render that violence politically legible. This may be enough to argue against continuing this arrangement; I would not go so far. My approach to *Ruined* has been to displace its climax; shifting our gazes may produce similar forms of hesitation to inform the writing of policy. Hesitating, we can see peacekeeping as a disciplinary tool, but one that materializes the global circuitry with which power acts on and through us all. This is to ask again what performance knows and how it transmits.

"I'd say it probably has to be absolutely neutral, inoffensive," Sunde told me in our interview, elaborating her interpretation of why *In a Kingdom by the Sea*'s UN run had been canceled. In response, I brought up *Battlestar Galactica*. I said, "It was easy to have science-fiction in the UN because, as science-fiction, they would assume it could not bear on real conflicts." She agreed, "Exactly, you're not pointing any fingers."

Back in the ECOSOC Chamber on March 17, 2009, a young man addressed the *Battlestar Galactica* panel:

> My question is going to pit the president against the commander perhaps for the final time, I don't know. This question is for Mary and for Edward James . . . this is a question about capital punishment . . . Was the airlock a crime?

The student's question got to the heart of the violence of states and institutions, asking the political and military leaders of the Twelve Colonies to justify their practice of jettisoning traitors and opponents from their ships to die in the void of space. The question placed in doubt the legal foundation of any use of violence by individuals, states, or institutions, and asked the actors whether their performances could resolve the dilemma.

McDonnell spoke first:

> I think it is a crime. . . . I think that my experience inside the show, and having the great opportunity to explore the condition of war and what it does to a human being and what it does to the population surrounding the positions of leadership, made me realize we are continually committing crimes in order to convince ourselves that we are right.

McDonnell tackled the question decisively, but from a perspective grounded in self-reflection. Her answer was born of her capacity to see herself within the show, to recognize her actions as part of an aesthetic simulation. "[It] was a haunting experience, and again, I would imagine that there are many people who commit these crimes who have a haunted experience from that point on." Her self-reflection hinged on a form of self-alienation derived from performance: her character was haunted, and so was she, and so, she hoped, might others be haunted. She concluded: "on a certain level I do think it's a crime. I was absolutely committed to it as Laura Roslin in the moment, because as the actor you work inside of a certain set of confines, and you have a container, and that's where you make your choices." McDonnell's container provided her distance and perspective, but it also foreclosed on the possibility that performance could generate radical solutions to the world's problems.

By contrast, Edward James Olmos made his way into his character once again, inhabiting the affects he found there. He began by recalling Adama's motivation: "We have to remember that what we were talking about in this program was the annihilation of the human species," and he highlighted the inexperience of McDonnell's Laura Roslin. He spoke of seeing former Vice President Dick Cheney criticizing the Obama administration on television, and suggested that his own work as an artist had helped turn the tide of public opinion against Cheney and his colleagues. "Many of us now are saying, because of this show, and because of people being—experiencing different really monumental moments of understanding what's going on in Iraq and Afghanistan and along the border with Mexico." Outrage at wars in the Middle East kindled his adjacent outrage at the violence in northern Mexico:

> I still don't understand why the UN has not put blue-helmeted armed forces in that region, with over 5,000 women dead in the last—since 1993. Children have been killed, and raped, and pillaged, in one city, and Mexico has the audacity to say, "We can't control it." And yet when the military started losing their captains and their sergeants and their military. And when the police started to lose theirs to the narco-traffickers, they ended up immediately dispersing 5,000 military soldiers to the region and yet—I don't— . . .

He regained his thread to conclude: "militarily, your question is—and its answer: I took care of every single military question, I don't care what the president said. I did not listen to the president when it came to military decisions. That is a mistake." He jabbed his finger at the audience, and reiterated, "That's not correct." Olmos's chain of associations indicates a lateral movement from one object of anger to another, from one source of passion to another. Switching between tracks, Olmos charges the affects he wishes to perform, bringing himself physically and emotionally to a state in which his answer will maintain the intensity he desires.

David Eick, one of the show's creators, offered commentary: "You know, you get a glimpse into the dynamics of the set when you hear Mary talk about her character as 'Laura,' and you hear Eddie talk about his character as 'I.'"

Both Mary McDonnell and Edward James Olmos learn values through performance. By performing these characters each arrives at the same conclusion: when states kill, it is crime. But each also inhabits performance differently. McDonnell is haunted as and by the character, a sort of self-alienation that allows her to remain tangential to her character and to recognize the bounded nature of performance, the confines that constitute it but that remain invisible to it. Edward James Olmos disappears into Adama again to find his angry affects and to blur his own desires with those of his character. This leads him to call for a militarized UN peacekeeping intervention in northern Mexico. McDonnell is haunted by the limits of her container, and Adama risks violence by overspilling his. McDonnell's distance from her character allows her a critical empathy that can detach from the traps of global governmentality, while Olmos reinforces and redeploys its excesses. Each is differently placed in performance, and each finds alternative viewing positions. Considering varied performance epistemologies opens new ways to consider how bodies participate in systems of global governmentality.

Peacekeeping and theater are integrated in the ways they employ spectatorship, harnessing the gaze of citizens and diplomats to a system of global governmentality that is totalizing in its effects insofar as it cannot always see the violence it produces. Revealing the centrality of spectatorship to the work of the UN in peacekeeping and beyond should expand our view of the field of forces at work in geopolitics. On the world stage, the cosmopolitan will to action born of empathy encounters governmentalist strategies of administration, and those who look to make peace meet the menace of a gaze that carries a force. These transmissions between the UN, states, their populations, theater-makers, theatergoers, and diplomats configure our world and leave no party absent. We are all spectators on the world stage, a situation that obliges us to hesitate and consider where, how, and why we look.

Figure 4. Muammar Qaddafi, Leader of the Socialist People's Libyan Arab Jamahiriya, addresses the general debate of the sixty-fourth session of the General Assembly, on September 23, 2009, while Secretary-General Ban Ki-moon, President of the Sixty-Fourth General Assembly Ali Abdussalam Treki, and Under-Secretary-General for General Assembly and Conference Management Muhammad Shaaban look on. UN Photo by Mark Garten.

3

"The World of the Rulers Is the World of the Spectacle"

Time and Reiteration in Diplomatic Speech

"Words fail me," the permanent representative of the United States to the UN, Samantha Power, told the creative team of the Broadway musical *Fun Home*. "It's going to take us longer, clearly, to recover from this amazingness than it will take you." "Us," in this case, was a group of sixteen of her colleagues at the UN, diplomats who hailed from six continents. On March 2, 2016, she brought them to the Circle in the Square Theatre to see the show and attend a talkback with its cast and crew, hosted by the actor Cynthia Nixon. "Thank you for being so amazing and for bringing all this home in a way that resolutions and statements never can," Power enthused.[1]

Despite the contrast she implied between the art of actors and the art of diplomats, the Broadway stage proves an apt analogue to the stage at Turtle Bay. Both offer gleaming, well-rehearsed productions that rarely stray from widely accepted and repeated dramatic conventions. Both also encourage formal and decorous behavior. Diplomacy and Broadway each maintain strict boundaries between actors and the audiences they require; to borrow a phrase from Guy Debord, they feature spectators "immobilized at the distorted center of the movement of the world."[2] The two scenes of diplomatic theater that compose this chapter, Power's visit to *Fun Home* in 2016 and President Barack Obama's visit to the UN in 2009, offer a view of this relationship and its performative instability.

An Unfolding Present: *Fun Home* on Broadway

Fun Home, with music by Jeanine Tesori, and book and lyrics by Lisa Kron, adapted Alison Bechdel's memoir of the same name. The play began its life as a graphic novel that revisited Bechdel's youth, her experiences coming out as a lesbian to her parents, her discovery that her father had been a closeted gay man throughout his life, and her grief when her father died in a car accident, quite possibly a suicide. Given the show's explicit queer content, press reports of the diplomats' visit made much of the fact that ambassadors from some states with poor records on lesbian, gay, bisexual, transgender, and intersex (LGBTI)[3] rights, such as Gabon, Namibia, and Russia, had attended, and that many had not realized the themes of the show before arriving.[4]

In fact, the diplomatic audience arranged by the United States combined states that shared the U.S. position on promoting LGBTI rights and those that did not. The bulk of the attendees (nine of Power's sixteen guests) were also members of the LGBT Core Group, a coordinating affiliation on LGBT issues at the UN. The remaining seven state representatives watching the play held heterogeneous views on LGBTI rights, felt varying degrees of indifference and hostility, and were selected in the hope that their position might change. The mixed composition of the audience was not an accident, but a calculated effort to demonstrate to those outside the Core Group that they would be in good company if they signed on to the group's priorities. At *Fun Home*, the United States cultivated theater's knack for generating *communitas* between independent spectators as an instrument of foreign policy, a soft power tool.[5]

During the talkback Nguyen Phuong Nga, the permanent representative of Vietnam to the United Nations, offered fuel to optimistic narratives of the capacity of the arts to change the hearts and minds of policy-makers: "I came here without any knowledge of the play . . . and yet we are here with you and we feel how you are feeling, how much suffering LGBT people have to endure. In Vietnam, it is very hard to accept that reality, but we have to accept that reality, and we have to make people happy. It's our job." Ambassador Nguyen acknowledged the transmissions the U.S. mission to the UN had hoped for in organizing the event: that the shared affective experience at the heart of the theatrical encounter would prompt new experiences of empathy that would reinvigorate progressive efforts to change social policies in global capitals; in other words, that the encounter would change the hearts and minds of diplomats so that they might bring new values home and support LGBTI rights at the UN headquarters and in resolutions of the General Assembly, the Human Rights Council, and the Security Council. The event was predicated on the use of live theater to work on the consciences of diplomats and infiltrate their official acts.

The advertising videos for *Fun Home* foregrounded the proximity between actors and audience that was enabled by the play's in-the-round staging, even as they reinscribed an absolute boundary between audience and actor. In one shot, Beth Malone, who played adult Alison, the protagonist looking back on her life, tells the camera, "You can sit right here at stage level—so close you can literally reach out and touch the actors." She extends her arm into the stage space to point at Gabriella Pizzola (Small Alison, the protagonist at nine years old), who swats her hand away, giggling, "Please don't."[6] In the theatrical encounter between *Fun Home* and Samantha Power's entourage of diplomats, the distance between stage and spectator was reduced to its barest traces, but not erased. The play promised access but remained an untouchable spectacle.

Even so, the actors who performed for the delegates insisted the divide had been bridged. Lauren Patten, who played Medium Alison, the college-aged incarnation of the protagonist, reported on her experience performing for a UN audience:

> In that scene, when I say the words, "I'm gay," . . . I felt like I was saying that speech directly to the ambassadors. It was scary, in a way, because I didn't know if they would really hear it. But talking with them after the show, it was clear that they did . . . Afterwards, there was a lot of laughter, hugging, discussion. The formality and distance I expected to feel with the ambassadors was never there.[7]

Patten confirms the effectiveness of empathy as a tool of policy, and the felicity of theater's promise that it can foster egalitarianism and promote progressive social change. Her experience provides a foil to the hypothetical exchange between Israel and Palestine that was dismissed by Rawiri Paratene in chapter 1. Patten points to the power of the live moment in which policymaker and artist meet one another, a theatrical encounter pregnant with the capacity to reorient the usual trajectories of global affairs.

The event was also designed to provide material for future scenes of diplomatic theater, as a performance that could be cited and restaged. In a speech to the Human Rights Campaign's annual Equality Convention a few days after the visit to *Fun Home*, Power described the event and quoted from the musical. Reading lines transcribed or remembered from the musical, she remediated the Broadway show from live performance, to new script, to an instrument of domestic and foreign policy when performed again. Her speech included fourteen verses of the song "Ring of Keys," a scene of recognition in which Small Alison realizes she is attracted to women; a song that ends in the repeated chorus "I know you." Power offered her own analysis of the scene's efficacy: "I think the reason that scene . . . resonates so deeply with people is that, when you watch Ali experience her first crush, you identify with her."[8] Power locates the utility of art in its capacity to prompt empathy and identification, in an affective transmission based on one's capacity to see oneself in another, but she also performs its added value as evidence of domestic promises kept and a progressive agenda moving forward.

Diplomats string together a series of such encounters, which are performative moments of diplomatic theater. These are live performances in an immediate present that are at once necessary to the smooth functioning of power and highly unstable, prone to disruption. The work of diplomacy consists of managing the flow of diplomatic performative forces as they enter into the public spaces of diplomatic theater. Diplomacy proceeds reiteratively, in scenes of citation and quotation designed to maintain and charge the force of its performatives; for example, to double down on a threat or fulfill a promise.[9] Power's speech to the Equality Convention revealed the wider orbits that the UN delegates' visit to *Fun Home* traveled. Her speech circled back to 2011, when, in his annual address to the General Debate of the UN General Assembly, U.S. President Barack Obama declared that "no country should deny people their rights because of who they love, which is why we must stand up for the rights of gays and lesbians everywhere."[10] Power then spiraled forward to the policies that would follow, to the release of a presidential memorandum that quoted the president's UN speech and directed "all agencies engaged abroad to ensure that U.S. diplomacy and foreign assistance promote and protect the human rights of LGBT persons."[11]

Power's live remarks elaborated the circuits traveled between 2011 and 2016. She described resolutions in the UN Human Rights Council that prompted the UN's first reports on LGBTI rights. She acknowledged the awkwardness of diplomacy's necessary remediations of text and speech: "I know resolutions, reports—this may sound a little wonky, a little bureaucratic." And she read aloud from the June 2015 report, sharing the UN's view of global LGBTI human rights: "the overall picture remains one of continuing, pervasive, violent abuse, harassment and discrimination."[12] Oscillating between text and speech, report and resolution, political and theatrical address, Power adds to the force of the president's initial diplomatic performative on LGBTI rights.

This effort loops between the Obama administration's military goals and the security questions that provide the Security Council with its raison d'être. From the outset, Power framed the issue in hawkish terms that emphasized the extraterritorial chauvinism of U.S. foreign policy. She summarized the view of a constituent: "No matter how much progress we were making here at home . . . as long as those places [where LGBTI persons continued to be persecuted] existed beyond our borders, real freedom and real equality would be elusive."[13] In this construction, embraced by Power in citation and performance, LGBTI rights become the instruments of a coercive foreign policy, and theatrical empathy serves to shore up the ideological rationale for armed intervention. Power made the connection evident when she continued on to "the first-ever United Nations Security Council meeting dedicated to LGBTI rights" in August 2015.[14] At this Arria-formula meeting, 13 of the 15 members of the Security Council heard from two gay men who had been subjected to persecution by ISIL (the Islamic State of Iraq and the Levant) in Iraq and Syria.[15] At the media stakeout following the closed-door session, Subhi Nahas, one of the two men, stood silently alongside Ambassador Power as press representatives posed questions to her. After fourteen minutes he was able to make his own statement, to let the world know that "LGBT people have their own voice."[16]

Watching Subhi Nahas wait patiently for the brief moments in which he would be permitted to use his own voice, the exclusions engendered by high-level diplomacy emerged to counter optimistic paeans to the radical capacity of face-to-face encounters to change the world, either in art or diplomacy. In Guy Debord's 1961 film *Critique de la separation*, as an image of the UN Security Council flashes on the screen, the narrator (Debord himself) comments on the scene: "Society broadcasts to itself its own image of its own history reduced to a superficial and static pageant of its rulers, the persons who embody the apparent inevitability of whatever happens. The world of the rulers is the world of the spectacle."[17] To Debord, the spectacle is a totalizing phenomenon in which life is mediated by images, alienating individuals from realms of authentic experience. The spectacle is economic, social, and political life experienced as a fixed image one cannot influence—a particularly bleak conception of the cohabitation of politics and aesthetics. Debord attaches these ideas to the image of the Security Council in order to capture many of the sensations associated with watching global politics: chiefly, the discouragements derived from a progression of scenes played out in the world of the rulers, announcing they are "an enormous positivity, out of reach and beyond dispute."[18]

Moving between verbal utterance, presidential memorandum, Human Rights Council resolutions and reports, and Arria-formula encounter, the diplomatic performative on LGBTI rights risks tracing a closed circuit that configures citizen spectatorship to deliver normative forces to the globe's aberrant margins. Power's pro-LGBTI rhetoric evinces its nearness to instrumentalized discourses of democracy promotion and humanitarian intervention. Policy moves between its life as text and as embodied performance, instances of diplomatic theater in which it gains mass and force. These live moments exploit the capacity of theater to transmit affects, foster identification, and promote empathy in order to pinkwash a foreign policy that returns again and again to military solutions.

Perhaps empathy is not the best way to understand *Fun Home*'s utility for either diplomacy or arts activism; instead, we should consider the two temporalities that come into conflict as Small, Medium, and adult Alison transfer from the page to the stage. In her foreword to the acting edition of the play, Lisa Kron identifies the major obstacle in adapting the graphic novel: "the book is actually a recursive meditation, circling around and around," but (she quotes Thornton Wilder) "on the stage it is always now: the personages are standing on that razor-edge between past and future."[19] Continuing, Kron reveals that the solution to the problem lay not only in her dramaturgy, but in her advice to actors and directors that the play's scenes needed to be performed in "an unfolding present" in order to maintain their urgency, power, and necessity.[20]

Kron draws readers' attention to the structure through which theater approaches the past, a structure that underscores theater's function as an apparatus of memory. Kron's efforts do not deny that historical citation is integral to the medium of theater; instead, they offer insights into how history is experienced in and by theater, and how this apparatus is felt and perceived. "Though this is a memory play, it's important to note that the past always understands itself to be the present."[21] Theater replays memories in the time and space of the present, insisting on their urgency, and invigorating history with the needs of the present.

Jeanine Tesori, Samantha Power, and Lisa Kron each elaborated elements of *Fun Home*'s relationship to time (and specifically to the time of activism and the time of diplomacy) in the conversations that developed during their talkback. Cynthia Nixon asked them, "I wonder if any of you have thoughts about, not so much the wider audience you're reaching, but actually the form in which it's reaching them. . . . having actors playing these parts and having music be a part of it, how do you think that mainlines that information [about the experiences of LGBTI persons] into people's bloodstreams?" In response to this question, the composer, ambassador, and playwright each took time to answer from the perspective of her performance medium: music, advocacy, or drama.

Jeanine Tesori built an affectively compelling image of the experience of the past in an unfolding present by extending Nixon's sanguine metaphor:

> I know more about Alison Bechdel—right down to her blood analysis. She gave me her journals from 1992, which I read, because we had to get inside her lives, and not just go from the graphic novel, which is just pen and ink, but to really understand this is not just the show: it's a family, it's a way of life. . . . When we were performing this, Lisa and I, Alison said she didn't know there was anything left in the story until she heard the lyrics and the music. It was the first time that she and her brothers cried together. It was in the back of the theater, when they realized that there was mourning left to do that had been unspoken until they heard the material that came from us.

The experience of Bechdel's family appears in Tesori's remarks as a confrontation between an unspoken past and live speech sung in the present. Tesori attaches theater's power to the ways it says, now, what had been left unsaid, then.

I have also cried each time I have seen *Fun Home*, and each time I have read the graphic novel. Inevitably, my tears well up in a climactic scene, a nighttime drive taken by Alison and her father, the last evening they spent together before his death. Though I admit to feeling empathy for Alison and sympathy for her loss, my tears that share her mourning also develop in response to a space and time held open by the narrative's unfolding present. The graphic novel makes this space apparent visually: the scene occurs in twenty-four equal-sized frames covering two full pages of the book. In each frame Alison and her father are presented in profile. In fourteen of the frames, the two are speaking aloud. Seven frames include text relaying Alison's unspoken thoughts. The remaining three are silent, devoid of text; these three dominated my experience of reading the page.[22] While the play fills these silences with music, it also maintains and heightens the experience of time that they perform. Affects adhere in the durations that theater opens for an audience.

In this duration, Samantha Power had her own epiphanies. "What I realized in watching the show is—as a good advocate, and [one] completely dedicated to pushing the cause of LGBTI rights here and abroad—what we who have not had these experiences usually encounter [is] somebody who is on the back end of an experience like this." That is, we do not encounter victims of oppression in the midst of their unfolding present: "We're not part of those moments, we're not part of the fear of disclosure. And we inherit some of those decisions." I take her to mean that decisions made in the past have ongoing effects in our unfolding present. As Power continued, she paraphrased and replayed the forms of storytelling featured in the play and in the talkback: "even hearing the stories, 'back when I told my dad, I this- and that- and everything.' And what's so powerful is life is lived forward, and yet, it's not about the box score, it's not about in the ninth inning [and] what did it look like retrospectively, it's about living forward." Power's fragmented commentary emerged as an unscripted response to the unarticulated past that the play had spoken. In the space the play opened, she recognized the disjuncture between the time of experience and the time of advocacy, and the powers that accumulate and appear in the present.

Despite their complex reflections on time and feeling, Tesori and Power also returned in their answers to conventional explanations of the play's impact. Tesori asserted the universal reach and accessibility of music, a shared internal capacity of humankind that could demonstrate sameness and encourage a consensus conceived as more or less innate: "The world is a musical, and what we have to key into is what people are singing, and more often than not we are singing the same thing." And Power echoed the form of these ideas in the context of advocacy: "The way to puncture the imagination is to tap something that goes well beyond reason . . . It's about imagining oneself, it's about imagining one's child, it's about imagining one's father." Where Tesori proclaimed the universality of music, Power insisted on the universality of family.

Responding to Cynthia Nixon's question last, Lisa Kron applauded many of Power's insights, telling her, "Ambassador Power, I think you have another career as a dramaturge." But Kron also complicated the image of universal and shared experience:

> The form of drama is that you are watching people moving forward in time. The thing that is most true, universally true, of every single person in the world that has ever lived, is that not one of us knows and can know what is going to happen. The moment of a play is the present moment. You're watching characters not know what is going to happen next.

Kron's figure conflated the opacity of the future and the opacity of other people, and in this arrangement she reframed the diplomats' work as a form of spectatorship: "Every single person in the play has a complete consciousness, and so you watch them have to interact with each other as you do at the UN. . . . We're all inside of our own consciousnesses, [and] we watch them moving forward in time, not knowing what the next person is going to do."

Kron exchanged the universality of music and the universality of family (universalities of which I am skeptical) for the universality of uncertainty (a universality I can comfortably endorse). Kron highlighted the ways in which theater, for its spectators, is in fact predicated on the unknowability of the interior psychological lives of the people who populate its stages, an uncertainty amplified by the unfolding present through which it proceeds. Kron does not deny the power and possibility of empathy here (and neither do I), but she does decouple empathy from the total and transgressive knowledge it requires. This figure allows what is unknown to remain unknown.

Though I think it is both aesthetically and politically important that Jeanine Tesori injected Alison Bechdel's blood into her music and that Samantha Power was punctured by imagining herself within the life-world of another, I find Lisa Kron's recognition that theater remains an art of surfaces to be the most useful and convincing insight into its structure and efficacy. Theater is an art of making visible and making audible, of drawing to the surface even when it appears to be plumbing the depths. Empathy is an event that occurs on theater's surface, too, and theater and diplomacy are united by the ethical demands they place on a spectator in spite of the fact that we cannot know others with the fullness that empathy demands.

A truly egalitarian diplomacy would do right by even those people it cannot imagine, who remain irredeemably other, of whom it is not certain, and with whom it cannot find common ground. Where empathy implies the necessity of agreement, drawing attention to an unfolding present makes change, transformation, and disagreement apparent. The unfolding present of diplomatic theater is a time frame that insists on the need for action, but it is also a temporality that opens a caesura in the diplomatic spectacle, a moment that may be exploited by artists and activists. Diplomatic theater proceeds in an unfolding present, channeling and charging the forces it transmits, raising them into public consciousness, and reminding spectators of the constitutive uncertainty of the promises and threats that make subjects on the world stage.

Insurrectionary Speech

Theater names the rough interface between political action and public experience—the place where the acts of policy-makers wend their way into public life. The performativity of diplomacy becomes tangible in those moments when politics meets its spectators. Both state representatives orating in the General Assembly and the Bechdel family singing at the Circle in the Square Theatre have public audiences who share the stage to participate in the ritual. The audience completes the theatrical event on Broadway and at Turtle Bay. In both the play and the geopolitical forum the audience is necessary, the source of political efficacy. Spectatorship is as much the force that can redeem political action as condemn it. The audience compels speech, but also prompts silence. This chapter provides two case studies of this figure in order to consider the relationship between the Broadway audience that renders *Fun Home* politically salient, and the audience that watches the UN proceedings at Turtle Bay and ratifies the political spectacle there. This chapter continues my investigation of theatrical time and the power of spectatorship, to find out what a spectator can do when she encounters the unfolding present of diplomacy.

Far from inaccessible (as Debord would have it), the spectacle is in fact theater's proper point of intervention in the political field. Where Debord's theories frame the spectacle's audience as one that is acted upon by world historical forces (an audience with no recourse to respond), in fact, the very theatricality of the spectacle opens durations that its audiences may interrupt. These durations are embedded in the structure of performative speech, and in the structure of theater, and so in the structure of diplomacy as well. The temporality of the speech act centers on a moment in the present that reaches back to conventions in the past (often earlier iterations of a performative) while also gesturing to certain events in the future (often further iterations of a performative). Similarly, the unfolding present of live theater feels the pull of past performances and looks forward to future action. And diplomacy also shapes the future by restaging the past in a present moment that unfolds across a vulnerable duration.

Diplomacy needs diplomatic theater and diplomatic performatives; its work proceeds by staging diplomatic performatives in diplomatic theater. States perform on the world stage by deploying and redeploying threats and promises before the audiences they intend to impact. In her investigation of threatening speech, Judith Butler reminds us that "an 'act' is not a momentary happening, but a certain nexus of temporal horizons, the condensation of an iterability that exceeds the moment it occasions."[23] Here we may locate power's Achilles heel: it lies in a moment of performance in the present that reiterates historical conventions in an effort to produce a desired future. Butler invests threats with a vulnerability borne of their performativity, and she names a radical potential to disrupt the exercise of power via the spoken word, with what she calls insurrectionary speech. "Insurrectionary speech becomes the necessary response to injurious language, a risk taken in response to being put at risk, a repetition in language that forces a change."[24] A theater of states is similarly predicated on scenes of exposure where the acts of the powerful become susceptible to rupture and deflection. Artists may exploit insurrectionary speech as a counter-hegemonic strategy for addressing the world of the rulers.

When speech acts gesture toward past utterances while projecting forward to their future reiteration, they emerge as dynamic processes. Theater often internalizes and codifies this function: plays are played to be played again, and theater history is textured by a dialectical tension between continuity and change. This cyclical time of diplomatic theater stands in stark contrast to what Debord calls the "irreversible time" of power and those who rule.[25] Theater and the performative embed cyclical temporalities in historical timelines that performatively proclaim their irreversibility. However, these same recursions must always pass before an audience in an unfolding present. Theatrical reiteration thus maintains history's continuity in gestures that are always vulnerable to those spectators who would compose history differently. The audience proves to be the essential figure: diplomatic theater awaits the insurrectionary speech that can undo it.

Cyclical Time: Obama's Disarmament Summit

I watched reports of Power's visit to *Fun Home*, and listened to tapes of the talkback, at the end of my research, after I had begun composing this book. Though the language of an unfolding present was new (and useful) to me, the dramaturgy of diplomacy in Power's scenes conformed to what I had observed from the start of my fieldwork. Seven years earlier, in 2009, I had caught my first glimpse of a world of rulers and spectacle that revealed its vulnerability to puncture in its performative structure.

On the first day of general debate at the General Assembly's 64th session, three heads of state spoke in succession. U.S. President Barack Obama noted that many around the world had "come to view America with skepticism and distrust," but he asserted that he had come to foster new engagements and rebuild a flagging international reputation.[26] The Libyan dictator Muammar Qaddafi followed with provocations: "Can we trust the Security Council or not? Can we trust the UN or not?"[27] And Yoweri Museveni, the president of Uganda since 1986, contemplated global economic inequality: "Is the present profligacy of some of the developed countries sustainable . . . or was it only possible when a tiny minority of humanity was enjoying affluence?"[28] Themes of distrust and mistrust emerged: distrust of a superpower, of a collective security arrangement, and of the capacity of states to look beyond their own narrow interests. Watching these statesmen, I found that the problems of spectacle, questions of inaccessibility and unknowability, were also constituent issues for diplomacy. On the world stage, the theatrical division between actor and intention enlarged to overdetermine the murky purposes of states.

Qaddafi and Obama were each making their first speeches to the UN as heads of state, and news organizations focused attention on the two. The *Telegraph* asked if they would meet,[29] while *Reuters* wondered if they would shake hands.[30] Each leader's engagement with the United Nations was predicated in part on the question of nuclear disarmament. Disarmament had helped recuperate Qaddafi's international image. After 34 years of his rule and 24 years on the United States' list of state sponsors of terrorism, Libya announced in December 2003 that it would abandon its nuclear program and destroy what missiles it did have. This spectacular declaration led slowly to the normalization of relations between the United States and Libya. In 2006 the United States removed Libya from its list of state sponsors of terrorism. In the years that followed, Qaddafi endeavored to recast Libya as a diplomatic leader in Africa and the Middle East, and to personally act as a peacemaker. In 2009 this activity reached an apex when Qaddafi served as president of the African Union, and made his General Assembly appearance.[31]

During his 2008 electoral campaign, Barack Obama also sought dividends from disarmament, arguing, "It's time to send a clear message to the world: America seeks a world with no nuclear weapons."[32] In April 2009, on a state visit to the Czech Republic, he reiterated his administration's interest in complete nuclear disarmament, and committed to hosting a Global Summit on Nuclear Security within the year.[33] Obama came to the UN in September 2009 to fulfill that commitment, to demonstrate and verify that his promises were not empty bluster by chairing a UN Security Council meeting on disarmament within days of the General Assembly debate. In these performances, which were efforts to construct public images and imprint public memory, and to coordinate between present and past, an inaccessible high-level geopolitical spectacle encountered the audience it required to enact the future it imagined.

In the General Assembly, Qaddafi spoke fifth, following the Assembly president (Ali Treki, Qaddafi's own ambassador), Secretary-General Ban Ki-moon, Brazilian President Luis Inácio Lula da Silva, and Obama. Rather than keep to the generally unenforced fifteen-minute time limit for speeches by heads of state, Qaddafi put on a show that lasted ninety minutes, and was broadcast around the globe by the UN webcast and various news networks. Like a seasoned monologist, he performed from handwritten notes, taking full advantage of his stage, gesticulating with his arms to underscore his remarks and saw the air around him. In an article in the *Financial Times* two days later, journalist Quentin Peel wrote of the performance: "Colonel Gaddafi got one thing right about the General Assembly: it has long been more about theater than substance."[34] This quip reveals the ways in which Qaddafi and Peel each need the other.

Qaddafi is eager to perform for those who make a living from watching the UN; he recognizes the role that diplomatic theater can play in rehabilitating

Libya's international image. In return, Peel seizes on Qaddafi's theatricality to foreclose on the possibility that it could reveal a substantive interior; Qaddafi's theatricality authorizes Peel's contempt for the performance's contents. While the speeches that open the General Assembly's session thrive on theatrical excesses that can draw the world's attention, those excesses also become the negative poles that excite the forum's harshest critics. Ironically, the imperative pressing on Qaddafi to demonstrate his engagement with the UN also led spectators to doubt his performance: called to perform, his acts were interpreted as always already inauthentic. Theatricality compels attention, but also generates cynicism, prompting Peel's interest in the scene as much as it allows him to dismiss it.

Qaddafi fully committed to the trappings of diplomatic theater. He was costumed elaborately, in brown robes accented by a black brooch in the shape of Africa. These external signifiers reinforced his public politics: his stated desire to eliminate colonial legacies and unite the African continent. Producing a pocket-sized copy of the United Nations Charter, he launched into a critique of the inequalities of representation at the UN, inequalities made concrete via the veto power allotted to permanent members of the Security Council (figure 4). Waving the small blue book around for the cameras and his audiences, Qaddafi rendered judgment on it in Arabic, and the live English interpreter struggled to keep up: "The Preamble is very tempting, and no one is objecting to the Preamble, but everything that came after that is completely in contradiction with the Preamble." Qaddafi turned left, then right, holding the document open in front of him on flat palms. "This is what we have now—this is what we are rejecting and we shall never continue it—this came to an end during the Second World War."[35]

The interpreter tripped briefly over both Qaddafi's leap of logic (from the intricacies of the charter to the historical circumstances of its production) and his physical choreography: Qaddafi next lifted the charter vertically, its binding facing the audience. His movements became more precise as he brought his hands together, then twisted them, tearing into the Charter's cover and pages a breach approximately an inch in length, before letting go with his right hand, palm open to his audience, to return the charter to his podium. Qaddafi's gesture was small, but significant. He physically performed his contempt for the hierarchy of states that had been enshrined in the UN Charter by giving a Security Council veto to five powerful states. Even so, as a dictator in power for forty-one years arguing for extending suffrage beyond a certain elite, Qaddafi produced a disingenuous scene, displaying the worst sort of political dissembling.[36]

Qaddafi paused for a moment to flip through his notes, providing an opportunity for spectators to take stock. The webcast cut to two U.S. delegates looking on, who appeared as the diplomatic equivalent of *The Muppet Show*'s Statler and Waldorf, making no bones about their dislike for the scene. One delegate seemed caught between bemusement and boredom, while the other gestured in exasperation with his right hand, rolling it through the space in front of him, as if imploring Qaddafi to keep things moving. He followed this gesture by looking left and right to register whether or not his reaction was shared by other spectators before the webcast returned to its primary subject and Qaddafi finished his thought: "The Preamble says that nations are equal whether they are small or big. Are we equal in the permanent seats? No, we are not equals, and the Preamble says that all nations are equal whether they are small or big." The charter came back out, held up for all to see. "The veto is against the Charter. The permanent seats are against the Charter. We do not accept it and we do not acknowledge it."[37]

Qaddafi's performance staged dissensus in a vulgar aspect: the dictator's drag, his contempt for procedure, and his arguments blind to their own hypocrisy all weighed against his reasonable argument for Security Council reform. His performance appeared to confirm accusations that diplomatic spectacles waste time and energy, yet Qaddafi also provoked active spectatorship that called attention to the encounter between citizens and despots. Tracy Davis notes: "With theatricality spectators are aware of their own . . . acting—allowing a reaction to a spectacle that may not be commensurate with their own sense of themselves . . . Theatricality [is] a process of spectatorship."[38] Theatricality marks the moment in which performer and audience constitute one another, colluding to make meaning and material from what they otherwise reject as inauthentic.

To assert that a performance is theatrically bogus and lacks substance does not refuse the performer's lie so much as it refuses the theatrical event in total. It refuses the use of live performance as an integral component of politics, excluding sincerity and conviction along with duplicitous grandstanding. In casting off Qaddafi's performance, onlookers like the U.S. delegates or Quentin Peel demonstrate that they are implicated in the hypocrisy they claim to expose. By betraying the secret that public political events such as a meeting of the UN General Assembly are in fact "only" so much theater, Qaddafi's elaborate performance calls the entire event into question. If this theater is without substance, how does that reflect on its audiences? Why have they come to New York, and what do they hope to accomplish?

Theatricality is the UN's condition of possibility; it makes the reiterated rituals of international relations concrete for global audiences. Theatricality exposes hidden political processes to public inspection, inviting interrogation and contestation. Luckily, power requires theatricality as much as it requires secrecy. At the UN, states stage diplomatic performatives to wield power theatrically, investing it in particular resolutions or statements. States contest power theatrically as well, as those same statements are negotiated, refused, or adopted in full view of a public. In performance, international actors become the location at which theatricality and secrecy are balanced, where appearances are managed and sincerity is assessed. In tearing the charter, Qaddafi drew together text, speech, and action in an unfolding present—beyond an illustration of the repudiation he offered in words, his gesture engaged the charter as a text with physical consequences.

The UN Charter is the founding utterance on which all the theater at Turtle Bay is based. The preamble, that part which Qaddafi found very tempting, reads: "We the Peoples of the United Nations, Determined to save succeeding generations from the scourge of war . . . [and] to reaffirm . . . the equal rights of men and women and of nations large and small . . . have resolved to combine our efforts to accomplish these aims."[39] The preamble is an inceptive diplomatic performative, a founding promise of peace and the equality of states that set the United Nations on its way. Qaddafi performs the infelicity of the UN's promise of equality and peace, staging the ways in which that promise misfired. Qaddafi intervenes theatrically in a status quo that has given up on the founding idealism of the organization, and in doing so he transmits discomforting emotions to his audience, reminding them that they are also actors, and that their stage is strewn with many such broken promises. Qaddafi amplifies the theatricality of the General Assembly to the point that it begins to destabilize the performative foundations of diplomacy's rituals of power—reasserting the final right of a public audience to ratify the acts of states.[40] Qaddafi's show returns the contingency and unpredictability of live performance to a central scene of international relations, calling attention to a global system that requires performance, and the excess that performance entails, to maintain its policies.

The next day, Qaddafi did not attend the 6,191st meeting of the UN Security Council, which was devoted to "the maintenance of international peace and security; [and] nuclear non-proliferation and nuclear disarmament." This was a summit of heads of state, and the first meeting of the Security Council to be chaired by a sitting U.S. president, and Qaddafi had been expected to make an encore there. But of the fifteen states that composed the Security Council that month, only Libya was represented at the meeting by its permanent representative to the United Nations and not a president, prime minister, or other highest-level representative.

The UN Security Council is housed in a rectangular room with no central focus. A mural by the Norwegian artist Per Krogh dominates the rear wall. It depicts a phoenix rising from the ashes of the Second World War, from a brown and gray abstraction that visually doubles the horseshoe-shaped table at which the Security Council conducts its business, and the rings of delegate seating that radiate out from it. Increasingly, I have come to read the mural through Walter Benjamin's interpretation (in his "Theses on the Philosophy of History") of Paul Klee's print *Angelus Novus*:

> This is how one pictures the angel of history. His face is turned toward the past. Where we perceive a chain of events, he sees one single catastrophe which keeps piling wreckage upon wreckage and hurls it in front of his feet . . . but a storm is blowing from Paradise . . . This

storm irresistibly propels him into the future to which his back is turned, while the pile of debris before him grows skyward. This storm is what we call progress.[41]

With Benjamin and Klee superimposed on Krogh, the phoenix, a figure of rebirth, becomes an emblem of irreversible time, chained to the fatal propulsion of history.[42] Fixed to the wall where it emerges from the catastrophe of history, it forever keeps its back to the optimistic images of progress that Krogh has arranged behind it. The mural's perspectival logic maintains its utopian promises at a shimmering distance well beyond the Council Chamber, reinforcing the pessimist's conviction that the single catastrophe of history cannot be interrupted by performance or performatives. At the horseshoe table, each representative is equally visible to each other representative, implying that when faced with a crisis, the delegates should be able to speak to one another directly. But this rarely occurs; events in the Security Council remain tightly scripted and static. Like the fifty-year-old mural, predetermined debates in the Security Council reinforce the disempowering sensations of spectacle. Neither the phoenix nor I may intervene in what plays out before us.

Like Qaddafi, Obama was obligated to perform at the UN in order to demonstrate his commitment to multilateral foreign policy and the international community. He needed to manage the distrust he had cited, compelling emotional investments in his leadership, but he also needed to wield foreign policy by managing where and how diplomatic commitments appear on the world stage. While serving as president of the Security Council he sat at the head of the table, flanked to his right by Secretary of State Hillary Clinton, and to his left by Samantha Power's predecessor as U.S. ambassador, Susan Rice. Following some opening remarks, President Obama moved directly to a vote on draft resolution 1887—a previously circulated, edited, and agreed-upon text. He solemnly intoned: "In accordance with the understanding reached in the Council's prior consultations, the Security Council will take action on the draft resolution before it prior to hearing statements from the Secretary-General and Council members. Accordingly, I shall put the draft resolution to the vote now. Will those in favor of the draft resolution contained in document S/2009/473 please raise their hand?" The fifteen representatives present raised their hands. An aide leaned over Obama's shoulder to make a note. Rice and Clinton beamed their approval behind the president. Obama continued: "The results of the voting is as follows: the draft resolution is received, unanimously, fifteen votes in favor."[43]

Resolution 1887 begins by invoking and reiterating previous performative commitments to nuclear nonproliferation and disarmament, and it recycles former presidential statements and resolutions. Its paragraphs begin with performative action verbs: "reaffirming" and "recalling" precedent statements, the resolution renews their force, centering the diplomatic performative on acts of reiteration that stitch the resolution into an ostensibly unbroken chain of Security Council actions. In the operational paragraphs—those paragraphs that direct the activities of United Nations organs, member states, and occasionally individual actors—reiteration gives way to the resolution's new promises. The cyclical structure of performative speech counterintuitively lends the resolution its sense of irreversibility. In the resolution's first three operational paragraphs, the Security Council

1. *Emphasizes* that a situation of non-compliance with non-proliferation obligations shall be brought to the attention of the Security Council, which will determine if that situation constitutes a threat to international peace and security;
2. *Calls upon* States Parties to the [Non-Proliferation Treaty (NPT)] to comply fully with all their obligations and fulfill their commitments under the treaty, [and]
3. *Notes* that enjoyment of the benefits of the NPT by a State Party can be assured only by its compliance with the obligations thereunder;[44]

Staging the Non-Proliferation Treaty in this manner, Resolution 1887 foregrounds non-nuclear weapons states' promises not to seek nuclear weapons over the benefits to those same states the treaty also provides. Those benefits are further promises made by nuclear and non-nuclear weapons states' alike, namely promises "to facilitate . . . the fullest possible exchange of equipment, materials and scientific and technological information for the peaceful uses of energy . . . [and] to pursue negotiations in good faith on effective measures relating . . . to nuclear disarmament"[45] Resolution 1887 is a promise about these promises, a series of verbal layers maintaining a commitment but leveraging the distances implicit in performativity and theatricality to keep parts of that commitment at arm's length.

In authoring Resolution 1887, the United States sought to take advantage of diplomatic performative promising as an instrument of national policy, but also demonstrated it was wary of the fact that diplomatic performatives can constrain the activities of those who utter them. The resolution takes into account the perlocutionary effects of the matrix of threats and promises that makes subjects on the world stage. By not emphasizing the benefits the treaty promises to those who meet their non-proliferation obligations, the resolution keeps those promises at a distance. Doing so, these elements of the Non-Proliferation Treaty that have not been so felicitously pursued could be kept out of public consciousness, while the force of the promise by non-nuclear powers to abstain from developing such weapons could be brought to bear on specific international actors. Keeping the promises to facilitate the exchange of nuclear expertise and to pursue negotiations on disarmament at bay manages the public appearance of their infelicity, a theatrical effort to control the life of each promise in present public memory. Here again, diplomatic theater appears as an apparatus of memory placed in the service of particular policy goals. However, the theatrical requirements of public diplomacy illuminate the gaps and fissures in the spectacular edifices built by the performances of powerful states. Promises are vulnerable to both the statecraft of diplomats and the stagecraft of artists.

Where repetition threatens to denude the resolution of its meaning or efficacy—to channel a singular interpretation and effect—it also reopens a theatrical event that is contingent on performative structures where established relations become fluid and malleable, where insurrectionary performance becomes possible. The re-performance required by the resolution delivers its original commitments to new audiences even as its authors work to deemphasize those commitments in their theater. Promises require witnesses who can hold states or individuals accountable for their commitments. The power afforded to the spectator also asserts itself in this moment. States perform to hail a wide public as spectators that can authorize the states' acts and mitigate their failures, but this operation is not certain. In both Samantha Power's citation of *Fun Home* and Qaddafi's citation of the UN Charter, theater and history intersect before an audience who must decide the import and efficacy of political performance: whether human rights abuses warrant military intervention, and whether the promise of equality warrants nuclear disarmament.

Certain audiences were arrayed onstage at the adoption of Resolution 1887: the fourteen other members of the Security Council. Most were satisfied with the mise-en-scène that the United States had developed, and they reiterated their tepid commitments to nonproliferation regimes. Austria, Vietnam, and Burkina Faso recommitted themselves to the resolution; China and Japan reaffirmed their existing nuclear policies; and Gordon Brown, the prime minister of the United Kingdom, came closest to making a new promise by pledging to reduce his nation's fleet of four ballistic missile submarines to three by the mid-2020s, contingent on the findings of an upcoming National Security Committee report. Yoweri Museveni was the only person to go off script, declaring that he would not read his prepared statement. He highlighted the brokenness of the promises on offer: "it is clear that the possession of nuclear weapons is the main cause of other countries wanting to acquire them. It is not logical to say that a few of us should possess nuclear weapons and others should not."[46] Museveni reasserted the logic of the Non-Proliferation Treaty, in which, again, non-nuclear states give up nuclear weapons programs in exchange for (a) negotiations in good faith towards general and complete disarmament by the nuclear powers (the promise of disarmament), and (b) access to nuclear power for peaceful purposes.

Diplomatic promises inscribe a right (in the case of the Non-Proliferation Treaty, the right to nuclear energy as a concession to the commons), but they also require the performance of a claim to that right. Museveni's performance enacted such a claim—in the face of a diplomatic consensus threatening the noncompliant with sanctions, he laid claim to the promises made to the compliant, promises that remained unfulfilled. Museveni concluded his comments by dwelling on this final promise. Speaking in English, with none of Qaddafi's bodily flourishes or vocal dynamics, and with his demeanor somber and earnest, Museveni said:

> I would like to inform the Security Council that Africa is interested not in nuclear weapons, but in nuclear energy. The reason for our interest in nuclear energy is that all the rivers in Africa have a potential total hydropower capacity of approximately 300,000 megawatts. In Africa, we expect to have a population of 1.3 billion by 2020. The United States, with its population of only 300 million people, currently uses 1 million megawatts . . . Even if all the sites on African rivers were developed, we would not have enough electricity to sustain our population, unless, of course, it were scientifically proved that Africans do not need electricity.

The room broke cautiously into laughter, as if those assembled were unsure they had heard a joke, and Museveni paused to let the response build and subside before concluding: "However, if one does not come to this absurd conclusion, it is clear that Africa will have to use all energy sources available, including nuclear energy."[47]

Museveni is hardly a paragon of progressive values or democratic government. He has been president of Uganda for three decades and has been a vocal proponent of anti-gay laws.[48] Uganda did not join the visiting mission to *Fun Home,* and the history of U.S. military support to Uganda suggests the limits of President Obama's memorandum on promoting LGBTI rights abroad. By 2014, approximately 300 U.S. military personnel and advisors had been deployed to Uganda, more than to any other African state.[49] Ostensibly tasked with supporting missions to defeat Joseph Kony's Lord's Resistance Army and maintain security in Somalia (where Uganda is a major troop contributor to AMISOM, the African Union peacekeeping mission in that country), their presence nonetheless prompted *Foreign Policy* magazine to ask, "Is the US military propping up Uganda's 'elected' autocrat?"[50]

Like Qaddafi, the details of Museveni's rule undermine the dissensus he would stage. However, his joke is exceptional, an example of insurrectionary speech designed to reorient the disarmament debate. Museveni's joke trades on the political uses that science can be put to, and sharpens its wit on the historical complicity of certain sciences with racist colonial projects. Museveni's counter-performance intervenes in the duration opened by the resolution's proliferating diplomatic performative promises. Configured as audience by more powerful states, he intervenes as actor on a performative ground that cares little for office or hierarchy. He defies questions of authenticity and sincerity by mobilizing "sly civility"[51] and the double-voiced ambiguities of a joke to discomfort the operations of a powerful state performing its power on the world stage.

The day after the summit, Obama, French President Nicolas Sarkozy, and British Prime Minister Gordon Brown staged a third act of the drama, publicly bringing evidence of Iran's noncompliance with the Non-Proliferation Treaty to the International Atomic Energy Agency. They thereby centered the disarmament debate squarely on the notion, as Gordon Brown put it during their announcement, that "Iran's nuclear program is the most urgent proliferation challenge that the world faces today."[52] Declassifying intelligence gathered by spies and satellites, the P3 revealed Iranian efforts to construct a secret nuclear enrichment plant. New UN sanctions against Iran would pass the Security Council the following June. In their diplomatic theater, both Obama and Museveni constructed the recursive history of the Non-Proliferation Treaty in an unfolding present in order to ask it to enact a performative future. With Museveni's performance, a cyclical time that would reassert historical rights entered into conflict with the irreversible time of Obama's performance that would continue to exert pressure on foes to come.

In scenes of live performance, the written and unwritten conventions that regulate interstate relations are made to appear and disappear from the views of diplomats and citizens—a dramaturgy that is crucial to the exercise of power. The theater of states is not merely the management of public images or ham-fisted efforts to persuade; it is the efficacious arranging of past, present, and future in order to situate and exploit the subjects the state requires to accomplish its ends. States are well practiced at using theater to do things in this way—to mobilize populations to war, to encourage austerity and privation, to construct the inclusions and exclusions that make a nation—and so little seems capable of interrupting their polished performances. Yet in their rough theatricality, scenes like those of Museveni and Qaddafi attest that diplomatic theater is not a monolithic spectacle of "the ruling order discours[ing] endlessly upon itself in an uninterrupted monologue of self-praise."[53] Though the rulers have sovereign privileges on the world stage that are unavailable to their spectator subjects, their acts offer evidence that the unfolding present of diplomatic theater is the moment to interrupt power as it performs.

The powerful perform in a theater of states to emplace spectators in an effort to keep their potential for intervention at a distance. Theatricality in international institutions emerges in a twofold figure to accomplish these ends, either by establishing traditional theatrical distances between spectator and stage, or by inducing spectators to reject theatrical excess. But theatricality also indicates the integral nature of the spectator who completes the theatrical scene, without whom the spectacle cannot signify. Diplomatic theater proceeds through an unfolding present that invites insurrectionary speech. States perform for an audience, and as they engage that audience they reveal the delicacy of the history they construct and the power they perform.

Figure 5. Pharrell Williams at the General Assembly during the special event on the occasion of the International Day of Happiness, March 20, 2015. UN Photo by Loey Felipe.

4

"To Receive an Impression Is to Make an Impression"

Clapping Along with the Secretary-General

On October 23, 2012, the Korean pop singer Park-Jae Sang, better known by his stage name Psy, visited the secretary-general at UN headquarters in New York. As camera shutters clicked, Psy joked that the press now had before them the first and second most famous Koreans in the world. Ban Ki-moon ribbed in return, "You are so cool—I hope that you can end global warming." Noting the 560 million people who had watched Psy's music video, "Gangnam Style," on YouTube, the secretary-general admitted his role as a highly placed spectator: "I myself have been counted there several times." The two men seemed mutually awed, each a big fan of the other. Each recognized the role played by the other on a world stage that stretches from the halls of the UN to music video channels on YouTube. Each also served as an embassy of the Republic of Korea, bringing prestige to the nation by virtue of his entry into a cosmopolitan political, cultural, and economic order. Psy shook his head in modest embarrassment at the notion that the secretary-general would be part of *his* audience: "Wow," Psy confessed, "for all Koreans, you know, he is the guy in . . . everyone's heart . . . even to think that he knows me is, like, so touching right now."[1] As each man oscillated between the roles of spectator and performer, each amazed by the other's celebrity, they softened the usual gravitas of high-level diplomacy.

The secretary-general facilitates spectatorship. His most explicit power is enshrined in the UN Charter's Article 99: "The Secretary-General may bring to the attention of the Security Council any matter which in his opinion may threaten the maintenance of international peace and security."[2] The charter calls on the secretary-general to act as a global spectator, harmonizing the viewing positions of powerful states with those of lowly citizens. He stages the surveillant gaze that global governmentality requires, exposing it to the audiences that public diplomacy cultivates. As a highly placed spectator, the secretary-general models spectatorship for these audiences, providing an image of where and how to look, and of what to do with the powers reserved for those who watch. Psy's visit with Ban magnified this dimension of his work, revealing energies mobilized and politics enacted when the secretary-general orients the attentions of diplomats and citizens.

At the end of their time together, despite his earlier protestations of embarrassment and following the goading of journalists and photographers, the secretary-general deigned to dance Gangnam Style—Psy's signature move—with the pop star. Ban watched Psy closely. He followed Psy's lead to cross his hands at the wrist and loosely bounced his fists like a jockey plying a horse's reins. Psy brought more of his body into the performance: his torso rose and fell with the rhythm of his bouncing hands, but he maintained a measure of decorum by keeping his legs planted instead of trotting like a horse as the dance usually requires.[3] Marcus Tan suggests that "Psy's asinine dance is an embodiment of unadulterated child behavior; it is hollow of signification, and perhaps it is in the dance's space of absent meaning and sheer silliness—the relief of responsibility—that the song finds global appeal."[4] The dance is supremely silly, and that silliness hangs oddly on the secretary-general; the relief of responsibility feels out of place when afforded to a world leader. Embarrassment also attends closely to the dance, which is apparent in Ban Ki-moon's comportment (excitement and reluctance in equal measure) throughout an event that was punctuated with awkward silences. If Ban was embarrassed, so might we be, cringing in a second-order scene of aversion, *fremdschämen* in German, where watching a participant spectator can engender uneasiness.

When the secretary-general danced Gangnam Style with Psy, I laughed at their silliness, but I also found myself dislocated. I am not alone: this clip has prompted more debate among my colleagues than any other scene of diplomatic theater I have studied and shared. When I have shown it at conferences, in invited lectures, or in informal meetings, invariably some of my interlocutors enjoy the pair's antics, while others are disturbed by the scene. Some delight in the secretary-general's willingness to play, while others find their dance off-putting. Rarely have I found an audience that reacts indifferently to the clip. What do spectators experience when they encounter diplomatic theater? What is felt where politics meet publics?

I ascribe my discomfort watching Ban and Psy dance to the peculiarity of my viewing position: to my critical gaze that sees in Gangnam Style one more dismal parody of the forms of consensus to which the UN aspires. Though I have not been able to locate a certifiable heredity, the Gangnam Style dance appears to be part of a long tradition of equine dance crazes, from the "galop" in nineteenth-century Europe, to Chubby Checker's 1961 chart-topper "Pony Time," to Cliff Noble's 1968 hit "The Horse," and extending to the rapper Silentó's recent imperative to "Watch Me" Whip and Nae Nae. Taken together, these dances offer a rough map of the social worlds imagined by popular music. The dances provide bodily and gestural terms for negotiating one's place among other humans in a contingent community. The dances indicate how individuals are placed and displaced by live performance; how spectatorship operates to put people in particular places.

The galop, a speedy dance related to the waltz, assimilates individuals into an undifferentiated whole. In an 1839 copperplate engraving by Johann Christian Schoeller, Parisians dance to a galop composed by Johann Strauss: the ring of dancers blends together, and even a couple who has tripped and fallen remains caught in the mass.[5] In the twentieth century, the Pony dance, popularized by Chubby Checker's "Pony Time," uses an individualized movement vocabulary that maintains some vestiges of social dance. Though the dancers do not touch, they face one another and react to one another, passing energy between them as they trot, tug on imaginary reins, and occasionally spin an imaginary lasso.[6] Similar choreography—in which dancers face one another in couples but avoid contact—can be seen in the video of young people dancing to Cliff Nobles's "The Horse." This dance expands the space between dancers that is already apparent in the Pony: dancers bend at the waist as though leaning over their mounts, and so the couples give each other even more room in order to avoid cracking their skulls.[7] Each dance unifies the participants, but also increases the distances that separate them.

Nearly fifty years later, Gangnam Style and the Whip and Nae Nae each continue the trend, abandoning the couples altogether in favor of an individualized choreography designed for visual consumption rather than participatory engagement. The dancers dance alone—high-stepping, manipulating reins, and whipping imaginary mounts—on display and atomized, heralding their willing and enthusiastic submission to an externally imposed order that keeps them apart as it brings them together. The social recedes in these horse dances: they are happy, exuberant, and silly, but to arrive at these effects they replace coordination between partners with a regulated, individual bodily discipline. Though each dancer ostensibly represents the rider in each dance, each ultimately resembles the horse, who can only regain agency by bucking its master off.

When the secretary-general danced Gangnam Style with Psy, their gallop quickly disintegrated. Laughing, the two men abandoned their bouncing wrists and fell together. A moment of bodily contact and mutual support emerged. It was a messy gesture born of shared embarrassment: Psy doubled over and grasped at Ban's arm, and Ban transposed his energy into a more dignified clasp behind the back. The secretary-general was generous without being overly personal, staging a new arrangement of bodies built from discomfort. Awkward stumbling resolved into assured grace. The affective displacement engendered by the appearance of a silly dance in a serious institutional space was met here by a choreographic displacement that reasserted the elegance of care and contact between persons. Ban's performance suggests the sensitive politics that may be constructed from performances that misfire at the UN. Where the expected relationship between spectator and spectacle falls apart, it induces participants to rebuild their social worlds differently.

Ban's participation in this scene is an example of what the musicologist Christopher Small calls "musicking": an expanded category that includes any instance of performing or listening to music. The term emphasizes that music is not something we receive, but something we do. Musicking draws attention to the ways we act when music is near, and to the relationships articulated in and around musical performance and audition. Small's concepts are often invoked to make romantic claims for music's capacity to forge community; claims like those Jeanine Tesori made about music's universal reach in chapter 3 of this book. Ironically, though Small argues optimistically that music is a ritual that bonds people by celebrating their unique social worlds, he also refuses the notion that this effect is achieved through the transmission of emotions via performance. He writes:

> What is the place of the emotions in music? . . . Common sense leads me to ask why people should devote so much of their lives and resources to the communication of emotions . . . and why, for that matter, listeners should be interested in having them communicated to them. After all, we all have plenty of emotions of our own without having to feel other people's.[8]

This glib argument against identifying the emotional transmissions that music engenders with its purpose pulses with charming antisocial cynicism. Small dismisses the transfer of feelings between individuals that so many name as the means and ends of art, indicating his exhaustion with the usual terms used to imagine a better world made in performance.

Small's skepticism offers a useful frame for reconsidering the use of music in diplomacy, especially in international institutions. Musical programs have often appeared at the UN, and music has long offered a set of handy metaphors to theories of international relations. In an early effort to theorize the work of the UN as performance, the Irish diplomat Conor Cruise O'Brien wrote that a resolution of the General Assembly "has the force of law in the same sense as has a sacred song: it provides spiritual encouragement and comfort and induces a sense of collective righteousness and of the legitimacy of a common endeavor."[9] O'Brien's formulation requires a spectator: the UN's sacred songs are addressed to global citizens in an effort to activate positive feelings regarding our species' shared humanity and purpose. However, a hypothetical spectator facing the spectacle of global politics and interpellated as a happy global citizen by the UN is a spectator who may have plenty of emotions of her own without having to feel other people's.

In what follows, I will locate this spectator in musicking events staged by the UN that misfired: public diplomacy efforts that deployed popular music in order to produce warm feelings and political action, but that ended infelicitously. I've been drawn to these for the counterintuitive moments of aversion they produced: instances of discomfort, distaste, and dislike that emerged from engagements between diplomats, pop singers, and citizens in the place of intended sensations of pleasure and belonging. The idiosyncratic refusal of identification with UN spectacle serves efforts to think through alternative forms of affinity and organization. When spectators refuse to be organized according to the designs of states and institutions, they demonstrate the perviousness of performances of power.

International Happiness Day

In 1972, the king of Bhutan proposed a new indicator of national development, Gross National Happiness, or GNH, to be measured alongside indicators like Gross Domestic Product.[10] GNH looks beyond what money can buy in the administration of the state by focusing regulative and legislative attention on four pillars: Sustainable and Equitable Socio-Economic Development, Conservation of the Environment, Preservation and Promotion of Culture, and Good Governance.[11] In Bhutan, a Gross National Happiness Commission is charged with mainstreaming these principles into national policies, orienting the apparatus of government towards the subjective well-being of citizens, monitoring their affective lives in regular nationwide surveys.[12] Internationally, GNH has also become an ideological export, a form of diplomatic cultural capital for Bhutan on the world stage. In an effort to advance the cause of happiness, Bhutan placed the issue on the UN's agenda in 2011 through Resolution 65/309, and a year later the General Assembly unanimously adopted Resolution 66/281, also penned by Bhutan, proclaiming March 20 the International Day of Happiness. The resolution also emphasized the secretary-general's important duties vis-à-vis global spectatorship. Its final operational paragraph *"requests* the Secretary-General to bring the present resolution to the attention of all Member States, organizations of the United Nations system, and civil society organizations for appropriate observance."[13]

International Happiness Day is hardly a distraction for the Secretariat: it provides an anchor for spectacles designed to encourage global citizens to sign on to UN priorities on issues like climate change and poverty eradication. Happiness also functions as a performative promise, as Sara Ahmed details in *The Promise of Happiness*, that "gives us a specific image of the future," suggesting that "happiness lies ahead of us, at least if we do the right thing."[14] As a promise, happiness organizes and intensifies the energies of those to whom it is addressed, potentially modifying their behavior. At the UN, the promise of happiness becomes one more diplomatic performative working to interpellate states and citizens as good subjects on the world stage. The UN's happiness agenda indicates the strong affinity between the matrix of diplomatic performatives enabling and constraining action on the world stage and the global governmentality evident in more martial figures like peacekeeping.

For the third observance of International Happiness Day, Secretary-General Ban Ki-moon released a brief video advertising programs run by the Secretariat in cooperation with groups like the UN Foundation, a nongovernmental organization founded by Ted Turner to "connect people, ideas and resources to help the United Nations solve global problems."[15] In the video, the secretary-general stands in front of a wall of neon pink flat-screen monitors, imploring spectators to "be happy" in different languages, while the best-selling song of 2014, pop star Pharrell Williams's "Happy," plays in the background. The video launched multiple programs planned for 2015, including the #HappySoundsLike Campaign, a collaboration with the streaming music platform Mix Radio, in which the public was invited to nominate songs to a global happiness playlist; an educational event in the General Assembly featuring Pharrell in conversation with environmental activists Philippe Cousteau and Sylvia Earle; and Happy Party, another Pharrell and UN Foundation coproduction, with support from Google, in which the world's citizens were invited to upload images to make animated GIFs of themselves dancing along to Pharrell's ubiquitous hit, "Happy," yet again.

At first glance, Pharrell's pervasive presence appears to be a product of the happy accident that Gross National Happiness found global purchase in the same period when his song "Happy" was climbing the charts. Extended reflection suggests an even deeper affinity between a discourse of happiness that is anti-consumerist on its face and a heavily commercialized popular music market. Even if some economists are stymied by a "Happy Planet Index" that ranks the United States in 150th place—"behind Burkina Faso," as *Foreign Policy* magazine reported in 2009[16]—it is not hard to be suspicious of the Gross National Happiness concept on the grounds that it rewrites the terms with which populations are governed and managed while doing little to alter the structures of power underwriting the hierarchical distribution of states and peoples in the twenty-first century.

As was evident in the 2015 programs, implementing the secretary-general's Happiness Day mandate has required significant corporate sponsorship and has been largely facilitated by an NGO (Turner's UN Foundation) whose mission is to coordinate partnerships between the public and private sectors. These partnerships entrench a twenty-first-century neoliberal political order that prefers marketplace solutions when addressing civic issues. Where the raw measurement of wealth and production gives way to delicate assessments of individual and collective happiness, one still finds a market logic refining its tools for the conduct of conduct.[17] Like peacekeeping, Gross National Happiness mobilizes indirect forces that are essential to the biopolitical administration of global populations. Gross National Happiness risks intensifying a global governmentality that sustains and obscures inequality, exploitation, and oppression by reiterating and extending neoliberal economic structures. Even if the circulation of global capital is absent from an ideal theory of Gross National Happiness, neoliberal structures prove adept at incorporating the happiness discourse and infiltrating its material expressions. As a producer, songwriter, and performer with his own clothing lines and fragrances, who ranked number 78 on *Forbes* magazine's 2015 list of the world's highest-paid celebrities, Pharrell Williams embodies this contradiction.

While Gross National Happiness can be a positive and disruptive force in the field of economic and development policy, its implementation inevitably proves ambivalent where it becomes attached to the exercise of power via regimes of governmentality. Discourses of happiness proceed through the construction of a particular future; when such discourses are mobilized by institutions, those futures are limited by the frames and structures that similarly restrict the institution. Institutionalized happiness is a technique of governance that proceeds by colonizing the emotions of those it addresses. It is soft power at its most soft, and so perhaps also at its most powerful.[18] These operations center on the secretary-general, who is charged with managing the attentions of states and civil society, and orienting them towards appropriate observances. This is a difficult obligation for the secretary-general. Because they are prone to misfire, the secretary-general's efforts to facilitate global spectatorship produce ambivalent spaces at the interface between the institution and individual citizens. Though the Secretariat seeks pleasurable engagements with its constituents, these spaces are just as often characterized by sensations of discomfort, unease, and revulsion. These can be generative of alternative political formations. Where diplomats mobilize performance on the world stage to emplace a spectator, in that spectator's reactions she may refuse to be placed.

Each of the Secretariat's 2015 Happiness Day observances prompts my unease, but perhaps none so much as the Happy Party website produced in collaboration between Pharrell, Google, and the UN Foundation.[19] On the web page, a visitor scrolls from an orange-yellow splash page to an endless sea of animated GIFs of people dancing, each uploaded by other visitors. I find that the Happy Party website becomes increasingly unsettling the longer I browse it. The site's looping music reduces Pharrell's "Happy" to melody and rhythm, absenting the singer's voice to invite participation in performances that affirm the sentiment on offer: visitors are called to fill the space the lyrics have left behind. Without voice and lyrics only one index of the performing body remains, the clapping hands which refer one back to the song's eschewed verbal content: the repeated chorus of imperatives commanding the audience to "clap along if you feel like a room without a roof . . . clap along if you feel like happiness is the truth . . . clap along if you know what happiness is to you . . . clap along if you feel like that's what you wanna do."[20] What these orders lack in severity, they make up for with a presumed social pressure evinced by the many exercises in excessive participation that proliferated around the song and of which the Happy Party website was emblematic. The parade of animated GIFs collected for the event amplifies the uncanny effects of the Happy Party: though many of the GIFs feature people in groups, suggesting the scenes of sociality that Happy Party produced locally, the overwhelming visual motif of the page is a uniform grid of squares in which the strobe-like rhythm of the shifting frames of each GIF unifies globally diffuse dancers. Participants are atomized, they participate to be codified and arranged, and assimilated uniformly under the banner of happiness. Though they seem to be having fun, I recoil from this scene of affective administration and refuse to be placed among them.

The UN Foundation and *National Geographic* magazine also brought Pharrell into the General Assembly Hall on Happiness Day, to participate in an educational event on climate change. Greeting the crowd of assembled youths, he drily observed, "So this is fun."[21] His mild affect and ambiguous intonation seemed to epitomize the wry response engendered by institutional efforts to inorganically command fun, from corporate team-building exercises to high-school pep rallies. Pharrell performed cool detachment, but I am not sure he was insincere: this might, in fact, have been fun. In contradistinction to the canned and reduced track playing on the Happy Party website or Ban Ki-moon's own overproduced Happiness Day message, Pharrell's live appearance opened a moment of radical indeterminacy in which performer and spectator navigated and negotiated their relationships with one another and with the international community they formed as the evening progressed. Hegemonic forces require that those they address return only docile affects. As such, spontaneous individual and collective action can prove deeply unsettling in the General Assembly.

Maher Nasser, director of the Outreach Division for the UN's Department of Public Information, opened the event with a call for participation that had clear limits: "Please use your cell phones. You can tweet, use social media. You can dance, but not on the tables."[22] As Nasser attempted to organize the presenters for a photograph to which the audience would form a backdrop, the music video of "Happy" began playing in the General Assembly Hall. The crowd of students and invited guests left their seats to make their way to the General Assembly dais, staying off the tables. On his own initiative, Pharrell descended into the crowd, which now became a sea of smartphones pressing forward for a selfie with the celebrity (figure 5). The webcast of the event cut between images of the music video and the growing chaos in the Assembly Hall, and after a minute Nasser could be heard again, booming over the song to entreat the crowd to "Please don't push, there are children who might get suffocated."[23] The song was cut off and security guards pulled Pharrell and others back to the safety of the stage, from which they could exit the disorder.

Two groups of spectators looked on one another at this event: a group of youths who transported the energy and conventions of a pop concert into the assembly hall, and an institution's security apparatus that watched them uneasily. The surging, self-organized crowd proved inappropriate, perhaps even subversive, in the serious diplomatic space of the General Assembly, and the representatives of authority on the stage recoiled. While the disorder may have posed an immediate safety hazard to those present, it also posed an implicit threat to an institution striving to bring order to the world. A third spectator was also watching: I smirked at the ironic chaos streamed to me online, which seemed to ape the more consequential forms of crowd control for which the UN is often responsible in refugee camps or around demilitarized zones. Scholar, students, and security guards—spectators all—we performatively materialized our relationship to an international order in the ways we watched.

Performance spaces are designed with the implicit unity of the audience they collect in mind. Auditoriums of all sorts cue those who enter them to act in particular ways, whether they are onstage or not. To be a spectator is to recognize certain rules of etiquette shared with the other spectators with which one is emplaced, and to admit that this shared etiquette indicates the collective affinity of a coherent community.[24] Space, spectatorship, and expectation combine to make the power of crowds legible; these are the grounds on which the crowds' inchoate responses (whether voluntary or involuntary) take on ritual meanings. The General Assembly hall also activates expectations of behavior, whether it is playing host to a diplomatic or to a musical performance. During its usual sessions, one expects dull speeches that are only occasionally interrupted by scenes of Nikita Khrushchev brandishing his shoe at the General Assembly podium in 1960, or Jamil Baroody throwing a punch at the General Assembly president in 1973, or Chaim Herzog tearing up a resolution equating Zionism with racism in 1975.[25] These theatrically excessive performative acts only take on meaning by virtue of their departure from the orderly norms of diplomacy.

Bringing musical performance into the General Assembly intensifies the norms governing audience behavior. How one acts and reacts to performance takes on added performative force in institutional spaces. These added forces subvert the presumption of audience unity by rendering it a performative promise rather than a manifest reality; something to be made that is always at risk of failure. UN diplomats call on music to establish the collective kinship of all people as a desired horizon, organizing these auditors into a unity that is reflected again in the concert of instruments or voices they watch. When alternative organizations emerge, such as the self-organized audience threatening to suffocate Pharrell, they demonstrate the contingency and instability of the proposition. Deployed to generate affects (like happiness) that can foster community bonds, musical performance at the UN in fact opens a time and space that put pressure on the processes that construct our social worlds.

New Year's Concert of the 67th Session of the General Assembly

When introducing Serbia's Viva Vox Choir in January 2013, Ban Ki-moon credited former Secretary-General Dag Hammarskjöld with innovating the tradition of musical performance at the UN in the 1950s. Ban spoke at a concert that had been organized by the permanent mission of Serbia to the UN to celebrate the Eastern Orthodox New Year. Serbia explicitly framed the event as a gesture of peace carried by elements intrinsic to the music presented. Turning to the performers, Ban noted, "Tonight's performance should give us hope. The Viva Vox choir sings a cappella. This style more than any other showcases the human voice. Voices can be used . . . to divide and oppress, or if they are used well, they can be used to heal and uplift, and harmonize."[26] Ban invoked a popular musical metaphor in diplomacy by deploying conceptual links between the harmony of voices or instruments, the harmony of the soul or spheres, and the harmony of nations or peoples. While contemporary scholarship has proven adept at deconstructing this musical metaphor, challenging the assumptions of universality that undergird it and the stable community it implies,[27] it remains a potent shorthand for policy-makers.

Speaking next, Vuk Jeremić, the permanent representative of Serbia to the UN and the president of the General Assembly that year, continued Ban's theme: "Great music can cut across every boundary and touch every soul. It transcends differences. Irrespective of where we come from, it binds us together as human beings."[28] In their combined oratory, Ban and Jeremić indicated their attachment to an ideal of music that unites a community, performatively enacting common kinship among their auditors. Yet each diplomat also noted that voices can oppress, that music transgresses political boundaries, and that sound penetrates the human body. If music forges community, it does so by mobilizing forces that are equally capable of dividing, destabilizing, and degrading the subjects on which they act.

The Viva Vox concert in the General Assembly made clear the contradictions inherent in the UN's cosmopolitan promises; when melodies and lyrics prove contrapuntal, they imply the abyss separating aspirations towards global peace and the reality of competing nationalisms in international institutions. The Viva Vox Choir, according to their website, was formed in 2005 by a group of high school graduates and their former teacher and conductor, Jasmina Lorin. The group achieved international visibility in 2011, when their a cappella rendition of the German industrial-metal band Rammstein's 1997 hit, "Du Hast," went viral online.[29] Though Viva Vox is best known for their interpretations of popular music, for their performance at the UN they added what announcer Zoran Baranac described as "a few pieces that represent their national heritage."[30] These included "Tomo Daleko," a folk song composed during World War I; the nineteenth-century folk song "Ajde Jano"; and, most controversially, Stanislav Binički's "March on the Drina," which was written to commemorate the Serbian victory in the Battle of Cer in 1914. The rest of the program included pop classics like Abba's "Mamma Mia" and Queen's "Bohemian Rhapsody"; novelty songs such as Monty Python's "Always Look on the Bright Side of Life"; and representatives of a cosmopolitan commercial-cultural order, like the Somali-Canadian rapper

K'naan's "Wavin' Flag," which had been popularized as Coca-Cola's promotional anthem for the 2010 World Cup.

Viva Vox's rendition of John Lennon's 1971 hit "Imagine" formed the thematic heart of the program; Jeremić received resounding applause when he quoted it in his opening remarks. But "Imagine" also imported some sentiments into the General Assembly hall that rest uneasily with the explicit and implicit goals of the organization. The song's melodic tranquility masks the anarchic content of its lyrics, which call on auditors to "imagine there's no countries," "imagine there's no religion," and "imagine no possessions."[31] While performing nationalist songs to celebrate the Eastern Orthodox New Year a few miles down the road from Wall Street, Viva Vox seemed unlikely to do any of the things proposed by Lennon. Perhaps this is why several of the songs they performed had a lyrical content which was quite obscure. The concert opened with "Ameno," a song composed by the new-age group Era and written in pseudo-Latin, a gibberish designed to sound vaguely religious; and they followed "Imagine" with "Baba Yetu," a 2005 composition in which the Lord's Prayer is sung in Swahili.

Finally, in "March on the Drina," the choir's encore presentation, they chose to substitute non-referential vocables for lyrics composed in 1964 that celebrate Serbia's expulsion of foreign invaders, with stark images of blood flowing and streaming near the cold waters of the Drina River. In lieu of words, the singers mimicked the martial instrumentation of drums and horns, shifting between fast and slow marching tempos. After three minutes the audience began clapping along to the driving rhythm, and the official UN webcast of the performance cut to a medium shot of Ban and Jeremić seated next to one another, clapping along as well. After a moment the cameras returned to the performers on stage, the clapping was drowned out by beatboxing, the song ended, and the room erupted in applause.

This scene precipitated a minor geopolitical incident: the day after the concert, the Congress of North American Bosniaks, a nongovernmental organization representing Bosniak communities in the United States and Canada, delivered a letter to the secretary-general condemning his participation in the evening's presentation, given that it had included the "infamous and offensive Serb nationalist song, 'March on the River Drina.'"[32] Two days later, a Bosnian-American reporter, Erol Avdović, raised the issue again during the daily noon briefing by the spokesperson for the secretary-general. He explained, "One of the songs that was performed was, as many people understood, the favorite song of the nationalist who committed some of the biggest atrocities in Bosnia, Croatia, and Kosovo. It's 'March on the Drina,' and the Secretary-General was seen applauding there." Avdović brought his flat palms together imitating a clap, but without enough force to make a sound. He continued with questions: was the secretary-general aware "of the very harsh reaction of some of the people—women—from Srebrenica that [he met with] today," and did he intend to apologize? On behalf of the secretary-general, the spokesperson responded, "We sincerely regret that people were offended by this song, which was not listed in the official program. The Secretary-General obviously was not aware what the song was about or the use that has been made of it in the past."[33]

According to testimonies collected in the U.S. State Department's "Seventh Report on War Crimes in the Former Yugoslavia," the song "March on the Drina" served during the Balkan conflict as a soundtrack for mass sexual violence. In Foča, the report asserts, Muslim "women knew the rapes would begin when ['March on the Drina'] was played over the loudspeaker of the main mosque."[34] It is not difficult to believe that the secretary-general was indeed ignorant of the song's traumatic heritage, but this does little to ameliorate the inadequacy of the claims made by those who defended the song's inclusion in the event. From announcer Zoran Baranac's introduction, framing the performance as a reorientation of a once-martial song to the project of peace, to Jeremić's later contention that the offended parties were "twisting the meaning of our musical gift,"[35] the organizers and participants in the concert demonstrated their inability to recognize the gestures and sounds that can reactivate historical traumas in the present. Where UN diplomats turn to music to sidestep the political pitfalls of words, they prove blind to the politics performed and the meanings carried by the structures those words inhabit. Once again, a live encounter between spectators and performers disconcerted the smooth administration of international relations, undermining the performance of unity, agreement, and consensus that lends so much diplomacy its normative force.

Chief among those gestures that verbose diplomats cannot account for is perhaps the sound of two hands clapping, especially those hands that clap along, which is one reason why the secretary-general proved much more the locus of offense in the incident than either Viva Vox or the Serbian mission. Steven Connor describes clapping as "a form of bodily overflow into sound"[36] that "retains its associations with violence."[37] When Ban Ki-moon claps along to a military march in a concert for peace, he reiterates the implicit intolerance of Pharrell's injunction to "clap along" and provides a bodily and sonic trigger that risks returning auditors to the Balkan conflict of the early 1990s; his hands are agents of time travel that destabilize history by reopening old wounds. Perhaps the American and Canadian Bosniak audiences focused on the secretary-general's rhythmic clapping in their complaint because of a similar sense of implicit menace amplified by the song's historical uses. On the other hand, perhaps the secretary-general's participatory spectatorship offended for the ways it transgressed hard-won political boundaries. In clapping along, an ostensibly benign gesture required by his office, Ban acquiesced to the intentional and unintentional meanings arranged onstage by Serbian diplomats and performers, and he retransmitted those contents and their affective charge through the sounds produced when his hands came together to form a rhythm.

His individual act of clapping unnerves in part by its ignorance, but in larger part by its submission to a collective. Though different people each clap in their own way, the roar of applause is the sound of a crowd overwhelming the individuals that compose it. To participate in applause is to give oneself over to that crowd, and acts of refusal often become illegible when the clamor of clapping hands indicates general consensus. Clapping hails spectators to form community with one another in a set of embodied acts, by striking hand on hand alongside others doing the same.[38] Insofar as any articulation of community also implies the necessary acts of exclusion (and perhaps expulsion) which produce that community, the clap that claps along acknowledges the short distance between an audience unified in applause and the cacophonous clapping that might be used to chase away an object of fear. Much like the promise of happiness, unison applause becomes a duty and demand that forecloses on disagreement or dissensus. So the Congress of North American Bosniaks and the Serbian mission to the United Nations entered into dispute over the contours and contents of an international community; a dispute that centered on the gestures and sounds made by the secretary-general.

Instances of audience aversion to geopolitical spectacle mark operations of international abjection; they are a visceral response to cultural and political forces that smudge the boundaries of the subject. The offended reaction of Bosniak audiences may be profitably understood at this nexus, where an individual's sense of psychological identity collides with the symbolic structures of public diplomacy, the legal ramifications of events staged in international institutions, and the aesthetic experience of spectatorship.[39] Audiences that recoil in international institutions exhibit negative reactions to the performative production of community. Abjection erupts in this space where the UN works to build or transform a global community that may not fit an individual's preexisting sense of self. In these moments, the forces circulating between scenes of diplomatic theater show their effects on and in the bodies of spectators.

Clapping itself, as a gesture, destabilizes notions of a coherent psychological subject. Steven Connor writes: "Clapping one hand on another dramatizes the fact that you are a subject and an object simultaneously, a doer and a done to; you fold yourself over yourself, you form an interface with yourself, which joins to the interface you form with others."[40] To the annihilation of the individual by the collective in applause, we may add an individualized terror of bodily and psychological boundaries losing their solidity as palm meets palm.[41] The clapping body as interface produces a sonic mesh that unites spectator and performer in shared rhythm or returned sentiment, knits together an audience in shared actions, and even incorporates bystanders (like those of us watching the video online) when the sound reaches our ears. While these effects may be inconsequential in most scenes of musicking, at the UN they reiterate the vital work of the institution (making common cause among people who are divided) and expose the potential failure of that work. Both the spectator who claps and the spectator who does not, the spectator present at the live event and the spectator watching at mediated distances, intensify the social function of musicking, prompting confrontations between individuals and the forces that bind them together.

When I watch Ban Ki-moon clap along to "March on the Drina," I recoil for different reasons than Avdović or others who were offended. When watching Ban Ki-moon I find my own gaze doubled, uncannily, teleporting me into the scene. We are both spectators, and his acts of spectatorship surrogate my own, highlighting differential experiences of power on the world stage. Here I must recoil, I must cast off my recognition, I must be unsettled and displaced in order to remain psychologically sound. The secretary-general, by clapping, imports existential dread into geopolitical spectacle, the terror of identity lost when an individual subject becomes an object of collective administration, a constituent part of a system of global governmentality that operates through spectatorship. Watching him join the clapping crowd, I become inordinately aware of the forms of social control that govern my world: I see myself and the power and limits of my own spectatorship.

Powerful states wield diplomatic theater to emplace a spectator to global politics, but that spectator's aversive responses resist these efforts and displace him or her in turn. Spectators have been uncannily doubled in each of the plays examined thus far: by King Claudius in *Hamlet*, by Colin Powell in *Stuff Happens*, by the peacekeepers of *In a Kingdom by the Sea*, by the customers in Mama Nadi's Bar in *Ruined*, and by Alison in *Fun Home*. In each work, the spectator is a privileged performer who is allowed a particular place by theatrical conventions. The secretary-general reiterates this theme on a global scale, fostering geopolitical alienation effects that rouse an otherwise compliant spectator.

The pressures of performance bear inordinately on the secretary-general. According to the authors of *The UN and Changing World Politics*, a textbook for students of political science and international relations, "the Secretary-General walks a tightrope, needing to appear independent and not simply a pawn of any or all of the [permanent members of the Security Council], but at the same time he must maintain the confidence and support of those same states."[42] The tightrope image captures the virtuosity with which the secretary-general performs for audiences at cross-purposes. The secretary-general is interposed between and acts on behalf of the Security Council, the General Assembly, and a nebulous international community, directed by them and enabling their view of the world's mysteries. Here, the secretary-general becomes "an attentive spectator of his own actions,"[43] as Conor Cruise O'Brien once described Dag Hammarskjöld. He is self-alienated like the spectator become object in the act of applause.

Ban's vulgar participation in ill-conceived diplomatic musicking generates aversion in subjects who are resistant to unreflexive invocations of unity, community, and consensus. These cascading phenomena in which liminal activity destabilizes identity, function, and meaning, imbue the instant of the secretary-general's participant spectatorship with a radical potential. As a locus for multiple forms of spectatorship on the world stage, he generates energies that fire off to global spectators, that circulate among the diplomats at Turtle Bay, or that rebound back on to the Secretariat. The secretary-general claps along and Vuk Jeremić joins him, Erol Avdović recoils, and some of us cringe. In these reactions we cast the contours of our international community, materially impacting the capacities of the institution.

The philosopher Aurel Kolnai, in his essay "The Standard Modes of Aversion: Fear, Disgust, and Hatred," lists some markers of what he deems morally disgusting:

> the *shirókaya natura* of the Russians . . . ; inconsistency and irresponsibility; what the French call *inconscience*, overspontaneity, overpersonalness, softness, and sentimentalism; above all, what the Germans call *Verlogenheit*: that is, a character organically wedded to a mental life diffusely steeped in lying, dissembling, illusion, and self-deception.[44]

Kolnai's enumerations capture the many ways in which a diplomat's magnanimity toward cultural participation might prove unsettling: in its broadness, its sentimental sincerity, and its suspect theatricality. Kolnai's emphasis on national difference is also remarkable insofar as his theory of disgust investigates the affective phenomena at the heart of scenes of abjection that make nations and states: that racialize communities and risk exploding into genocidal violence. That the secretary-general's overly generous participation in the Viva Vox concert offended Bosniak onlookers is not an example of misplaced outrage or a disproportionate response to a frivolous event: it is an integral and material moment in which international relations are negotiated in autonomous reactions and calculated responses.

In their aversive reactions, audiences express their resistance not to the egalitarian and ecological goals of Gross National Happiness or to the secretary-general's right to have a bit of silly fun, but to the broader projects of social and political administration (tethered to military violence and iniquitous economic distributions) that lie at the heart of the UN's work. These displaced spectators resist the unreflexive harmony that the UN seeks. When harmony is invoked as a goal, it is experienced as a demand.[45] This imperative has sonic, temporal, and spatial dimensions: one's voice must fit, one must be on beat, and one must remain in the place one has been assigned. Radical powers reside in those moments when the UN's participatory events misfire and bodies refuse to be placed. To find oneself out of place is to embody disagreement precisely where it has been forbidden. Where one encounters the demand to be happy or to clap along or to dance an asinine choreography, one is invited to rearrange social coordinates that are psychological, physical, and spatial. Diplomatic performance assigns coordinates to states and subjects, but it remains vulnerable to spectators who are displaced.

According to Kolnai, "it is as a disgusted self that I inscribe my quality and lineaments into the stuff of the world, and as a hating self that I set the seal of my personality on a universe reluctant and vulnerable like myself."[46] The UN's scenes of public diplomacy may mean different things to different spectators, but all transmit their effects in the moment of encounter between a performance and its audiences: in our reactions we do things with even the most banal performances. As Sara Ahmed puts it, "to receive an impression is to make an impression."[47] In both positive and negative reactions, I become inscribed in the world culturally, ideologically, and physiologically; whether I am dancing like a horse, taking a selfie, or clapping along. In watching others participate, I become alienated from the processes that organize my social life, be they explicit, like public diplomacy, or implicit, like cultural abjection. A radical constituent power thus adheres to the crowds assembled for the scripted spectacles staged by the international institutions that administer global governmentality. When the UN brings popular music into its spaces and onto its stages, even as I recoil, it unwittingly invites me to revise the scripts with which it writes the world.

Figure 6. Permanent Representative of Sudan to the UN Abdalmahmood Mohamad and Prosecutor of the ICC Luis Moreno Ocampo address the media following consultations with the Security Council, on June 5, 2009. UN Photo by Eskinder Debebe.

5

✦

"Between One Person and Another"

Interfacing with Institutions at the International Criminal Court

I watched the permanent representative of Sudan address the media stakeout, live on the UN webcast. Abdalmahmood Abdalhaleem Mohamad's remarks followed the regular briefing of the chief prosecutor of the International Criminal Court (ICC), Luis Moreno Ocampo, to the UN Security Council on the situation in Darfur, on June 5, 2009. Mohamad began, "Good day to all of you. Once again the mercenary of death and destruction, the so-called prosecutor of the International Criminal Court, is before the Security Council." His broad smile evaporated: "once again he is coming, spreading lies." As his remarks continued the camera slowly pulled away. The medium close-up of Mohamad alone expanded to a wider angle that revealed Moreno Ocampo standing mere inches away, waiting through the ambassador's invective for his turn to speak (figure 6).[1]

The scene came six years after the start of the conflict in Darfur between the government of Sudan and non-Arab rebel groups. In that time the government of Sudan, coordinating with the Janjaweed militia, had been indiscriminate in its response to rebel attacks, targeting civilian communities in addition to combatants. In 2005 Louise Arbour, the UN high commissioner for human rights, reported to the Security Council that "large scale war crimes had been committed" by the government and militias in Darfur.[2] In response the council passed Resolution 1593, referring the situation in Darfur to the ICC. On March 4, 2009, the ICC issued an arrest warrant for the president of Sudan, Omar al-Bashir, for war crimes and crimes against humanity.[3] The report, resolution, and warrant articulated formal relationships between institutions, organs, and individuals, drawing Mohamad and Moreno Ocampo on to stage in New York and prompting my eager spectatorship.

Standing alongside Moreno Ocampo, Mohamad continued: "This mercenary of destruction and death should be told very loud and clear to respect himself as a jurist and not to come as a political activist, and he should also summon the necessary courage not to intervene when a member state is speaking at the stakeout!" Moreno Ocampo kept his eyes trained on a few loose sheets of paper he shuffled in his hands. Mohamad went on: "This is an expression in no uncertain terms that he is scared of logic and that he would like to continue his . . . what should I say? Heh. His drama!" As the press began posing questions to Mohamad in English and Arabic, Moreno Ocampo looked up, scanning the room incredulously, taking in reactions, before settling his gaze on Mohamad. Moreno Ocampo's arched eyebrows framed the look he gave his adversary, adding comic energy to the scene by inviting laughter to match Mohamad's hyperbole. Several feet away the actor Mia Farrow, an advocate for Darfur and a UNICEF goodwill ambassador, also watched, taking notes and waiting to address the stakeout.

Mohamad launched a final salvo against the ICC: "This is a Court for European justice, European justice that enslaved and killed millions in Africa. We are not going to cooperate in any way with it. . . . This is an element of old colonialism, as I said, a Court of European Justice, and we are not going to cooperate with it and we are not going to be bound by it. Any questions?" A voice off camera replied from the crowd of journalists, "Yeah, a question right here. My name is General, I'm a member of the National Religious Leaders of African Ancestry that is seriously concerned about Darfur and the genocide that is going on there by your president Omar al-Bashir. . . . The Arabs have killed over—"

Mohamad cut him off: "No please, please, this should not be allowed, you are not a journalist." He began turning away from the crowd as General cited the numbers of dead in Darfur. Mohamad concluded: "The peace process will continue, it is now very promising . . . It should not be held hostage to the Prosecutor-General [*sic*] and the chorus who he used to bring, like some of the people whom I see around me. This morning I met Mia Farrow, and she told me he invited her to come to this debate. For him the issue is media and publicity. This is why he is now a real threat to peace and stability in Darfur."[4]

As Mohamad walked away from the stakeout, Moreno Ocampo approached the microphone. He spoke softly and to the point, summarizing the contents of the briefing he had given to the Security Council. He made no reference to Mohamad's epithets. Moreno Ocampo's earlier pose, presence, and gaze, which was equal parts withering and bemused, had provided his rejoinder. Confronted with Mohamad's name-calling, Moreno Ocampo disarmed him with a look. Moreno Ocampo's gaze was an impression that made an impression, that shifted the trajectory of Mohamad's diplomatic theater, displacing its reception by spectators beyond Turtle Bay. The moment crystallized the lines of sight that cross one another on the stages that international institutions make available: the institutional gaze of the UN Security Council passing through the ICC; the glances exchanged by Mohamad, Moreno Ocampo, and Farrow; and my own spectatorship, refracted by these others as I watched the webcast. The scene also indicated the destabilizing encounters that can erupt when officials meet their publics, individuals like General, and the mediums that facilitate such meetings: institutional structures, embodied encounters, and televisual spectacles.

Watching Moreno Ocampo at the UN, I was watching the Security Council extend its own gaze through the court and its prosecutor into Darfur and Sudan. Mohamad was an audience emplaced by the Security Council and ICC, and his name-calling responded to their scrutiny. The ICC's work requires spectatorship.[5] To see what has happened where crimes have been alleged, the court draws images, videos, documents, and witnesses to its premises. To see justice done the victims watch the court's proceedings in person, via broadcast, or via webcast. And to fulfill its deterrent promise, the court requires the sincere spectatorship of a broad public, building moral meaning from the administration of international criminal law. These structures assembled the chorus (General, Farrow, and myself) that had ruffled Mohamad, and exposed him to us. This chapter will follow the work of the International Criminal Court at those interfaces where it meets diplomats, lawyers, clerks, witnesses, victims, war criminals, civilians, journalists, scholars, and movie stars.[6]

Spectatorship calls attention to the thresholds at which institutions meet each other and the world. At this edge, diplomatic theater provides a permeable surface through which forces travel and where power is exercised. An impression makes an impression at the interface. This surface takes many forms: it can be a screen through which a gaze passes, a body in which diplomacy and law become action, or a virtual space mapped in the public imagination. In these zones of theatrical contestation, international institutions are felt well beyond their official organs, and so the work of an institution proves indivisible from the ways that work appears to and is embodied for its constituents. Theater provides an interface between people and politics, and in diplomatic theater an institution and its public act on one another.

The Prosecutor v. Jean-Pierre Bemba Gombo

The International Criminal Court draws a range of spectators to its proceedings: audiences who watch the court from distinct distances, who invest in the court's work with diverse intensities, and who negotiate their place in international politics and law in divergent ways. On May 12, 2011, I joined these audiences in The Hague. I arrived early at the side entrance through which the public was admitted to the court. At the time, the ICC was housed in temporary premises—an office building that had formerly belonged to the Dutch telecommunications firm KPN. The courtrooms themselves had been built in a renovated parking garage. I chatted with the one other person waiting for the court to open. He was a U.S. citizen, a court reporter who had joined the ICC some years earlier. I asked what had led him to make the move. Smiling, he told me, "the work they do here is great."

A guard unlocked the doors. Beyond security screening, the visitors' lobby was a curved concrete and cinderblock space painted white and green. Three television monitors hung on one wall. CNN International played silently on the middle screen, while those to either side of it indicated whether each courtroom was open to the public. In Courtroom Two, Trial Chamber III was examining evidence in the trial of Jean-Pierre Bemba Gombo, who was charged with two crimes against humanity and three war crimes. Bemba was the head of the Mouvement de Libération du Congo (MLC), a former rebel group, now a political party, in the Democratic Republic of the Congo (DRC). In 2002 the president of the Central African Republic (CAR), Ange-Félix Patassé, had called on Bemba and the MLC to assist his national forces to quash a coup and rebel insurrection.[7] MLC troops were accused of rape, murder, and pillaging while in the CAR in 2002–2003. Bemba was convicted of two counts of crimes against humanity and three counts of war crimes in 2016. In 2018, as I finalized this chapter, Bemba was acquitted of these charges on appeal. The bulk of this chapter treats the proceedings I attended in 2011 and Bemba's conviction in 2016; I reflect on his subsequent acquittal at the end of the chapter, in a postscript.

Taking my seat in the public gallery of Courtroom Two, I read over the court's Rules of Decorum, which are guidelines for audience etiquette at the court. Stand when the judges rise. Do not talk, eat, drink, or smoke. Do not wear offensive or provocative clothing. "Visitors are not permitted to point or gesture at anyone seated in the courtroom. Do not read newspapers, books or journals while seated in the public galleries." Active response in speech, gesture, or costume was forbidden. So too was disinterest: keep your eyes on the proceedings, but only your eyes. When visiting law students nodded off, court security firmly nudged them awake. Spectatorship at the court required attentive engagement, and indifference was tantamount to contempt.

The rules narrowed the live interface with the court in its galleries. Most days at the court, I watched the proceedings either through thick panes of glass running the length of the room or on one of two television monitors suspended above them. No sound penetrated the glass, but I listened to the voices of participants or interpreters through headphones attached to my seat. When witnesses gave testimony, they sat at a desk in the center of the room with their back to the public gallery. When testifying put a witness at risk, visual barriers were introduced to protect those in the court's charge: voices were distorted or censored, the monitors became pixelated or went blank, and curtains were lowered to obstruct my view.

On May 17, 2011, the Bemba proceeding featured the most stringent forms of witness protection I encountered at the court, short of closing the proceedings to the public entirely. Seated in the gallery, I could not peer over the witness's shoulder: venetian blinds had been drawn on the central third of the windows dividing the gallery from the courtroom, and two further cream-colored curtains extended into the courtroom from the window. These

"Between One Person and Another" 113

interrupted the line of sight between the witness and the accused. Though the accused would be provided undistorted audio and video (given his right to confront his accuser), direct visual encounter was prevented. In the galleries we saw and heard even less: on screen, the witness appeared as large shifting blocks of blue, black, white, and brown, and his voice was digitally distorted. The curtains protecting the witness had divided those of us watching: we clumped to either side of the room to better see those in the courtroom who were unobstructed. I sat nearer to the prosecutors, who were posing questions to the witness. Nearer the defense sat a group of Bemba's supporters who had been coming daily since the trial began.

Court records referred to the witness as P-63; he spoke Sango, a language indigenous to the Central African Republic; and he had already spent several days testifying. Eric Iverson, a trial lawyer from the Office of the Prosecutor, asked him whether there had been battles between Bemba's MLC forces and anti-Patassé rebels in the town of Damara. P-63 reported:

> To tell you the truth there was fighting but—but from what I saw—well, you see . . . I followed them for two or three days and I didn't see with my own eyes. I didn't see that fighting with my own eyes. I do know that . . . they would abduct people who were going by . . . They raped the women. They kidnapped and held the men and brutalized them. Sometimes they killed their hostages.[8]

I looked up at the video screens, hoping to see Bemba's reactions, since my view of him was blocked by the curtains protecting the witness. I sought evidence of guilt, or anger, or something else dramatic: involuntary bodily effects that I could invest with meaning. But the camera stayed on the distorted view of the witness, as if to keep me from prejudging Bemba on the basis of his unconscious gestures. Many have pointed to the *Bemba* proceedings and his initial conviction as historic—Bemba was the first person at the ICC convicted for his command responsibility in the commission of a war crime, and he was the first person at the ICC to be convicted for rape.[9]

"You said that the girl told you her story," Iverson asked. "What did she tell you about her experience?" P-63 responded:

> As you know, Central African girls have a certain way of doing things traditionally, and it is difficult for them in the light of this tradition to actually recount the story of a rape . . . I couldn't spend too much time with her . . . she was speaking to me, trying to hide herself so that people wouldn't notice that she was speaking to me . . . she felt she was in danger.[10]

Iverson pressed P-63 for more details: "You said that she was the victim of collective rape. What was the group that collectively raped her, if she told you?" P-63 described the military structures that made distinguishing perpetrators difficult:

> Among the Banyamulengue[11] soldiers who were on the road, the smallest ones usually are out front and the taller ones are in the back. And when the small ones who are out front actually apprehend someone, and when that person, if it happens to be a girl, is shown to their leader, then the leader immediately takes her to his residence. . . . So you cannot actually identify who the rapist is. There are very many of them, beginning with the children who are out front, all the way up to the leader, and when you talk to the girl, she cannot tell you in detail because it's such an ignominious story.[12]

Competing and complementary spatial and social relations intersected in P-63's grim testimony. P-63's descriptions of the victim's reticence to speak reiterated the disjointed access the court provided to its audiences, indicating that a cultural system that insists on a victim's silence had been displaced by a legal system that requires visibility and audibility. Meanwhile, P-63's ground-level view of the MLC's command structures provided a synecdoche for the larger hierarchy by which Bemba proved culpable to the judges of the Trial Chamber in 2016; even when one may not be able to identify an individual perpetrator, guilt falls upward, all the way up to the leader. And these compounding relations formed part of the complex geography that would permit a court in The Hague to hold an individual accountable for crimes committed by soldiers in the CAR while he was in the DRC. The dramaturgy of the courtroom, contoured by obstructed or unobstructed lines of sight and the exposure and visibility of participants, opens on to a geopolitical dramaturgy that seeps into culture, extends through social hierarchies and organizations, and crosses state borders.

Iverson addressed the bench: "Madam President, at this time we would request to go into private session." Presiding Judge Sylvia Steiner gave the order to a court officer, and my headphones went silent. Without knowing how long the private session would last, I waited and watched. One of Iverson's colleagues stood a book on his desk, his own impromptu screen to hide the evidence behind it. Later, I discussed the day's proceedings with individuals who reported on the trials for NGOs and civil society groups. One told me:

> Sometimes what isn't said can be a lot more potent than what has been announced in open court. The intermittent editing of evidence . . . relegates mass rapes back into the private domain. It goes back to the theatricality of the court, and the trial as the most public incarnation of the law itself. It's difficult enough for women in the CAR to recount the story of their violation, . . . but to actually physically turn around and edit someone's story out of that entirely may in itself be a violation.

"Between One Person and Another" *115*

In this account, the court's protective measures generate a dramaturgy with narrative effects and political consequences. The words of those who come to the court are fractured, their stories are dismembered. At the interface, competing imperatives—of justice, transparency, protection, and care—make a theater that foregrounds the ways that institutions and individuals work on one another as they construct their stories.

Watching Iverson pose questions to the witness without being able to hear him, I focused on the gentleness of his manner. Shifting between his desk and the witness stand, Iverson's movements were slowly paced, his muscles were relaxed, and his body was calm. I thought of the questions he had posed earlier: they were simple and direct without being provocative. According to a contact who had worked for the judges in the case, what I saw contrasted with the behavior of Bemba's representation:

> At the beginning of the trial [Bemba's lead attorney, Peter] Haynes was actually reprimanded a couple of times for asking very personal, invasive questions of rape victims. The judges do not like that at all. His attempt to pick holes in the testimony was not allowed. . . . It's just such a sensitive—*Bemba* in particular is very sensitive when you're dealing with horrific, mostly rape situations.

For victims and witnesses appearing at the court, international institutions are hardly impersonal bureaucracies. Rather, they are complex assemblages, and their components may be sensitive or insensitive to those they address. For victims and witnesses, the court is both the lawyer who poses gentle questions and the lawyer who mounts an invasive cross-examination; it is both the judges who prioritize the law, and the court psychologists who focus on mental well-being.[13]

Witnesses at the ICC are not prepared for their testimony by the legal team that calls them to the stand. Instead, they enter into the care of the Victims and Witnesses Unit (VWU) before they testify. In The Hague, I found that representatives of the VWU did not hesitate to use the language of the stage to describe this work. In the court, "small things become big, a function of the theater," I was told. Witnesses watched a video of the courtroom before they were taken into the space, and when time allowed they toured the courtroom itself in advance of their testimony. There, witnesses explored the courtroom to see it from multiple perspectives, including the judges' chairs and the desks reserved for the accused. Members of the VWU rehearsed with witnesses, practicing their entrance, using the microphone, taking the oath, posing and responding to mock questions, and so on. The process recognized that giving testimony was an ordeal. I was told, "Sitting in court is heavy—another effect of the theater, very tiring."

After an hour of testimony, Iverson indicated to Judge Steiner that they had reached a good stopping point. Steiner addressed P-63: "Mr. Witness, we'll have now half-an-hour, our break, in order for you to take some rest, and as well our interpreters and court reporters." Blinds descended over what remained of the windows dividing the gallery from courtroom so that the witness could exit privately. I took my leave as well, heading to the lobby via a stairwell hung with images of the court's Public Information Department at work: photographs of screenings of proceedings in the DRC, workshops with ICC representatives in the CAR, and so on. Many were similarly staged: a crowd of men and women watching a distant screen.

Back on the ground floor, a man approached me as I bought a cup of coffee from a machine. I recognized him as one of the others who had been sitting with me in the courtroom's public galleries. Drawing me into conversation, he suggested that P-63 did not appear truthful to him. I asked him what brought him to the court, and he explained, "Bemba is our leader." He was a member of the political wing of the MLC, and saw conspiracy at the court. To him, the trial of Bemba was a political prosecution organized by the president of the DRC, Joseph Kabila.[14] Asserting anti-African bias in the court's prosecutions, the man built a dissensual scene of global politics. "Africans are angry," he told me, "there is too much injustice: why are there only Africans on trial here? This is the question you must ask in your research." The real crime, he told me, was that Bemba had been held for three years and kept away from his family, who had been traumatized by the proceedings.

Several of my contacts remarked upon the ebbs and flows of the audience at the court. One reported:

> Some days it's very quiet as I am sure you've noticed; there's no one there, literally no one there. Other days it can be quite busy, [Bemba's] got a lot of supporters in Belgium who come every day. One woman I could never identify, possibly some family relative, she wears orange sunglasses, sits in the front row. She's there all the time, every Friday, or every day, she's there a lot anyway. She's the only person in the audience who interacts; she would wave to Bemba as the curtains were going down.

Another suggested that the woman was most likely Bemba's wife, Liliane Bemba, a Portuguese businesswoman who lived in Brussels with their children during the trial, commuting regularly to The Hague. My contact added: "I rather like the interaction you have in the public gallery. You can see the accused, you can see the prosecutor, you can see the interaction with the witness, and the Bemba supporters, who are there sometimes in really big numbers, the whole entourage." The crowds posed their own problems for the court, as another informant related: on "some of the bigger, more exciting days, when the gallery is packed, there will be a lot of noise, and the security officers keep everybody down." Even so, "generally there is that bulletproof glass, soundproof thing. It creates a distance." Power is exercised at this interface, by those who mass on either side of the glass, by those who look through it, and by those who manage its permeability—the judges, lawyers, and officers who choreograph its occlusions.

The following day, as I made my way to the court, I could hear music and voices amplified on a public-address system. Upon entering the public square facing the ICC building, I saw that a platform stage had been erected. More than 100 people had gathered, and a few dozen Dutch police officers manned a small cordon around the corner nearest the court. Many in the crowd held the flag of Tamil Eelam, the aspirational state of Tamil-speaking northern Sri Lanka, while others held placards featuring an image of Sri Lankan president Mahinda Rajapaksa and the text, "18 May: War Crimes Day—Arrest This War Criminal." The event marked the second anniversary of the official end of the decades-long conflict between the Sri Lankan government and the separatist Liberation Tigers of Tamil Eelam, a war which killed an estimated 100,000 people.[15] On the stage a life-size cutout image of Rajapaksa stood in a makeshift defendant's box. His hands were painted red to suggest they were covered in blood. Two cyclists, their bicycles adorned with more Tamil flags, approached. They had ridden from their home in Denmark to the court to deliver a letter imploring the prosecutor to open an investigation.

At the time, this goal struck me as somewhat misguided. Sri Lanka is not a state that is party to the Rome Statute (the treaty that established the International Criminal Court), and so what the protest asked was impossible: the prosecutor would not be able to open such an investigation of his own volition. An informant from the Office of the Prosecutor reminded me that the performance was not so neatly circumscribed:

> They may stand on our corner, but the message is directed to the Security Council, or directed to particular states, or other actors. They want to be seen in front of the ICC asking for justice. They don't expect they can get it here, but they think they can draw attention to the need for a justice solution, as opposed to a political or humanitarian solution. We're a bit of a backboard for them. They know it's not going to go in, they just want to get some bounce, you know?

The court attracts this theater to its environs, spaces primed for the emergence of people power. Even as it passes its own judgments, the court invites the verdictive acts of its audiences, who denounce abuses and stage their claims to human rights. Where my informant's interpretation emphasized theatricality's capacity to amplify a grievance, I am also drawn to the powers that might adhere where people and institution share a space. I am drawn more to their contact than their bounce.

A few days later, I saw the Bemba supporter I had spoken to on the 17th one last time. He was leading a protest in the square facing the court. A few dozen others were with him, standing at a barricade over which they had strung a banner that read "Liberez Jean-Pierre Bemba," airing their grievances in slogans chanted at the court through a megaphone. These contrasting demonstrations marked material and immaterial territories generated by the court where it encounters its publics. Each scene was driven by emotions the court had prompted—the hope for justice where there had been none, and anger at unjust incarceration—and each scene was motivated by the notion that these emotions may be redeployed to impact the court's work. At the interface power acts and may be contested, theatrically.

The ICC exhibits a vulnerable dramaturgy, one that responds to the perils faced by its participants but that also generates new forms of exposure. The dramaturgy of the court is born of the dangers incurred by those who participate in it: the sensitivity of victims risking new trauma, the precariousness of witnesses facing reprisals, the weakness of postcolonial subjects hailed by a transnational legal mechanism, and so on. The court arranges those in its charge according to their vulnerability, yet this mise-en-scène is also available to those beyond the court. In narratives and images the court mobilizes forces that do not remain its sole property. Others may stage diplomatic theater at the court and with its tools. The court's dramaturgy shields those in its care, but also opens avenues for intervention where its theater may be co-opted or transformed.

The Prosecutor v. Thomas Lubanga Dyilo

Much of the dramaturgy I observed in the *Bemba* proceeding developed following the International Criminal Court's first prosecution, that of Thomas Lubanga Dyilo. Lubanga was found guilty in 2012 of the war crimes of enlisting, conscripting, and deploying child soldiers in active hostilities during the conflicts in Ituri Province that followed the Second Congo War.[16] On January 28, 2009, prosecutors called their first witness to the stand in *Lubanga*, witness P-0298. Both witness and victim, P-0298, claimed to have been forcibly conscripted into Lubanga's Union of Congolese Patriots (UPC) as a child. Questioned by prosecutor Fatou Bensouda, his composure broke: "Now as I swore before God that I would tell the truth, the whole truth, your question puts me in a difficult position with regards to my truth, because I said that I must tell the truth . . . What I said previously did not come from me. *It came from someone else.* They taught me that over three and a half years. I don't like it. I would like to speak my mind as I swore before God and before everyone."[17]

Multiple interpretations have proliferated as to why P-0298 recanted his testimony, and most of these center on spectatorship: that the witness "may have been shaken by the crowd in the courtroom,"[18] or that "the witness was deeply perturbed that day and clearly influenced by the presence of the accused, his former Commander-in-Chief [Thomas Lubanga] whom he had to look in the eye."[19] While these explanations confirm that spectatorship can be dangerous to the court (the event precipitated the layers of witness protection I encountered in my fieldwork), they do not address the content of P-0298's revelations. In the background of the scene lurks that "someone else" who taught the witness his lines, scripting and rehearsing him for his performance. P-0298 was not referring to the services of the VWU. Rather, "someone else" was an individual hired by the Office of the Prosecutor to recruit him: the shadowy figure of the intermediary. In March 2014, the court published guidelines and a code of conduct for intermediaries. They define an intermediary as "someone who comes between one person and another."[20] Intermediaries "assist with outreach and public information activities in the field; . . . assist a party or participant to conduct investigations . . . facilitating contact with potential witnesses; . . . [and] assist (potential) victims."[21]

In fact, intermediaries had already appeared in the transcript of the proceedings on January 28, 2009. Before P-0298 testified, defense counsel Catherine Mabille related to the presiding judge, Adrian Fulford, that in the capital of Ituri Province where the UPC had operated, "a large television screen was set up for the inhabitants to follow the trial . . . the statements of the Office of the Prosecutor and Legal Representatives of Victims were broadcast. However, the screen remained switched off yesterday . . . A decision was taken not to broadcast the opening statements of the Defence."[22] Mabille's complaint implied the presence of other intermediaries who were regulating spectatorship: those who set up the screen, switched it on, and decided what to broadcast. Intermediaries reside at the intersection of the court's efforts to see what has happened on the ground in the situations it investigates and the court's efforts to present its work in turn to affected communities.[23] They are another interface through which the court acts and is acted upon.

According to the *Lubanga* judgment, prosecutors came to rely on intermediaries as an indirect consequence of the court's lack of an enforcement mechanism.[24] Bernard Lavigne, an official investigator with the Office of the Prosecutor, provided a rationale for the use of intermediaries in his own testimony. He noted that "it was almost impossible [for official investigators] to operate in the open, first of all because the ICC was expected by the population."[25] Lavigne described a precarious security situation in the regions under investigation, citing incidents in which investigators were fired upon, a broad insecurity produced by the absence of police forces, and a general perception that the court was unwelcome. Local intermediaries could travel freely and safely where prosecutors could not. Local intermediaries could also meet with witnesses when being seen with ICC officials might exacerbate their vulnerability. Lavigne asserted that intermediaries "were considered to be an integral part of the protection system,"[26] but the guidelines also make clear that they "fall within the broader category of persons 'at risk on account of the activities of the Court.'"[27]

Intermediaries operate in what Robert Cover has called "the shadow of the violence of the law itself."[28] They are at once posited as a solution to insecurity in the field and they face insecurity in their own activities. Contracted by the court, they extend the court's gaze and they protect the witnesses and victims they encounter from the threatening eyes of others. Intermediaries also amplify the inherent theatricality of legal proceedings when they embody the court's authority for local audiences or prepare witnesses to testify in The Hague. Combining the theatricality and violence of the law, intermediaries destabilize the easy transmission of information and affects to and from the court.

Intermediaries provide a body at the interface between the court and its margins, a body that serves as a vehicle for legal performance and as a locus for legal anxiety over that same. Most of the extensive discussion of intermediaries in the *Lubanga* judgment centered on the effects intermediaries had on the evidence they delivered (often for a fee) to the court. Nine witnesses presented by the prosecution during the trial as child soldiers conscripted into Thomas Lubanga's militia, who were initially identified to investigators by three intermediaries, were ultimately deemed unreliable by the judges and their testimony was largely disregarded. The judges found that "there is a risk that [intermediary] P-0143 persuaded, encouraged, or assisted witnesses to give false evidence; there are strong reasons to believe that [intermediary] P-0316 persuaded witnesses to lie . . . ; and a real possibility exists that [intermediary] P-0321 encouraged and assisted witnesses," including the prosecution's first witness, P-0298, "to give false evidence."[29] Though many children, alleged victims, were called as witnesses, their evidence did not convict Lubanga.[30] Instead, judges relied on the testimony of adult witnesses, video evidence, and documentary evidence.[31]

Witness P-0010, first contacted by intermediary 143, makes clear that while an intermediary can invalidate witness performance, video may redeem it. Though the chamber found that P-0010 was unreliable, certain elements of her testimony relating to video evidence were not considered tainted by the inconsistencies in the rest of her account.[32] According to the *Lubanga* judgment, "The witness recognized herself in a portion of a video recording as the figure standing in the centre of the screen with her hands together in front of her body . . . In one section the witness said the person on the screen was Thomas Lubanga. They were singing battle songs."[33] This video evidence foregrounded bodies in performance: posed in particular ways, entering onto and exiting from the scene, and singing songs. The images stabilized P-0010's inconsistent speech. The spectating judges wrote: "the video material, to a significant extent, 'speaks for itself' and it falls therefore (along with the account of the witness as regards its content) into a separate category" of evidence than that tainted by the tampering of intermediary 143.[34] The video rescued elements of P-0010's otherwise inauthentic performance on the stand. Intermediaries make urgent a preexisting anti-theatrical anxiety attending to the court's work, foregrounding the dangerous agency of a performing body in its encounter with the court.

In the *Lubanga* judgment, the court asked: what does credible testimony look like? Here the judges took up a favorite question of scholars of performance: how can performance be verified by astute spectators? Is a well-rehearsed performance evidence of authenticity or a marker of dissembling?[35] In one instance, the judges pointed to an investigator's testimony that the prosecution interview of a witness lasted several days and must be credible because it is "difficult to imagine that you can learn a story and memorise it and repeat in the same way over several days."[36] A contrasting construction of truth in performance appeared in Judge Odio Benito's dissent: she argued that since so much time had passed since witnesses first experienced the events, "it would be suspicious if the accounts would remain perfectly alike and unchanged. Memory is faulty."[37] On the one hand, a perfectly rehearsed performance gave credibility to the testimony, while on the other hand imperfect performance indexed the fallibility of human memory, rendering the recollections more realistic, and, by extension, more true. The inconsistency tracks along the degree of perceived theatricality in any performance of testimony: scripting and rehearsal are red flags that impugn the witness who suggests them.

Through what medium does evidence transmit to the gaze of the court, and by what medium does the image of justice emanate from the court in turn? The court holds intermediaries at arm's length: though the Guidelines tell us they are one form of the ICC's "field presence," and are part of the model of international criminal justice the court hopes to project, it adds that "they should not be called upon to undertake core functions of the Court."[38] As Haslam and Edmunds point out in their critique of the court's drive to formalize its use of intermediaries, "although they are not staff members, the perception may arise that intermediaries . . . may be seen to 'belong' to the ICC, or may be regarded by those they assist as being in some way part of the Court's official apparatus."[39] For many, intermediaries are the court, even if the court would disavow them. Intermediaries are the bodies in which certain publics see the court and through which the court sees the field. They are actors and spectators who choreograph and direct witnesses and collect and distribute videos, images, and other documents. As agents and subjects of the court, they permit others to act on and within it.

Intermediaries produce an intermedial theater, one that invites us to locate the content and quality of the court's work in where and how it touches the world, in the energies it transmits and transforms. At the court, I pressed one contact to define justice, focused as I was at the time on the law's textual life. Were I to revisit the moment, I might also ask her what justice looks or sounds like and how it might come to be embodied. She demurred, saying that justice must be defined by the victims, but she indicated the function of the law in a justice equation: "the law is intended to make a place stable, to make a community stable" so that a sense of justice and peace can emerge in that community.

In deciding the innocence or guilt of individual perpetrators, the ICC works to fix narratives at its core that might lend stability to local histories. However, the multiple media in which these histories are constructed in the courtroom and the additional media through which they transmit to global spectators betray the contingency of any historical record. Where the work of the court meets local communities, it necessarily produces theater and theatrical disputes. In these spaces the court relinquishes narrative control, and its capacity to make meaning devolves to its spectators.

At the end of the day on January 28, 2009, after witness P-0298 had left the courtroom, Judge Fulford returned to the issue the defense had raised in the morning, the question of the video broadcast that had excised their statements. Alas, Fulford reported to counsel, the interruption was

> in what is broadcast on television in the Democratic Republic of the Congo over which this court has absolutely no control . . . whether or not your speech was broadcast was a decision that was taken not by us but by someone in the Congo, whether it's in the government or in the television company or both we know not . . . Over these matters, Maître Mabille, unless you can tell us of some power of which I am unaware, we, I fear, have no control.[40]

In his repeated phrase, "no control," Fulford names what the court abandons as it extends into the world, inviting dramatic conflict at the interface between international law and individual citizen. Powerful actors must stage diplomatic theater to maintain their power, but over the instant of performance they may have no control.

In July 2012, Thomas Lubanga was sentenced to fourteen years in prison, minus the six years he had already been detained. In a commentary published by the International Justice Monitor, Olivia Bueno (of the International Refugee Rights Initiative) summarized the variety of responses the sentence prompted among those living in the Ituri region of the DRC. Though some were satisfied that Lubanga had faced justice, most fell into one of two camps: "for those who had hoped that the ICC would show itself as a force that could intimidate those who would consider committing similar crimes, the sentence seems weak," while others found the sentence too harsh given the trial's many irregularities. As one of Bueno's informants put it, "I would have let Lubanga go because seeing the process from the beginning, it began with a lot of false witnesses . . . in my opinion the process was not credible."[41] Disappointment attends to both Lubanga's supporters and detractors, to both those who see the court's intervention as a salve to wounds left by past conflicts and those who see the ICC as the latest tool with which European powers might maintain the subservience of Africa.

Where it meets the world, the court generates cultural effects that exceed its legal mandate: feelings of optimism for a world that can will away the violence of war, and disappointment over mechanisms that seem inadequate to the task; satisfaction that justice might be done, and anger that judgment may only fall on perpetrators in the global South. Optimistic and disappointed affects maintain the utility of international legal mechanisms as a horizon in which global spectators invest. International institutions appear to spectators in the bodies of their actors, and as such those institutions are not merely seen or heard, but deeply felt.

Crossing Lines v. the International Criminal Court

At the court, someone else told me:

> Generally it's the judges who have your attention, they're the ones you're watching. In *Bemba*, even from a purely aesthetic point of view, you've got three women [as judges] representing three different continents. There's something quite international and powerful about that image. . . . It's a trial primarily about sex crimes, and it's the first ever all-women panel in international criminal law—that means something. And you've got Asia, Africa, and Europe represented there. It's quite a powerful image I think, not only as a woman, but just as someone who's interested in the way that cultures clash at the ICC. . . . To see three judges from completely different backgrounds and legal systems, it's powerful.

The image of the court is another spectacular interface that invites emotional investment and proves prone to contestation. The image of three women judges, the image of an African woman serving as prosecutor, and the image of broad international cooperation each advances the court's normative goals. This interface is not limited to the images the court itself produces; others also produce images of the court over which it has little or no control.

As the *Bemba* trial proceeded, the ICC appeared on television, anchoring the plot of the series *Crossing Lines* (2013–2015). *Crossing Lines* was a German-French coproduction performed in English and created by a former Chicago police officer (Edward Allen Bernero) that had its world premiere in Italy. The show invented a "Special Investigations Unit" at the ICC, solving crimes that crossed international borders. It was a conventional police procedural show, featuring a team of beautiful cops transplanted to The Hague from the United States, the United Kingdom, Germany, France, and Italy; former belligerents of World War II united under a cosmopolitan banner of transnational policing. Intended to have broad appeal, the show also caught the eye of academics like me, who are devoted spectators of the court. One such spectator, Kevin Jon Heller, a legal scholar and contributing blogger on the website Opinio Juris, was not optimistic in his predictions for "what will no doubt be an absolute train-wreck of a TV show."[42]

Heller had some experience with Hollywood: in addition to his academic work, he had been employed as a staff writer on a courtroom drama, *The Court*, that aired on ABC in 2002. As Heller watched *Crossing Lines*, his initial pessimism was partly tempered. In his blog posts, he struggled to balance his appreciation for the show as an above-average genre exercise ("William Fichtner is fantastic as always")[43] with his distaste for the show's lack of fidelity to legal realities. He dutifully tabulated the ways that Bernero's fantasy violated the Rome Statute. Heller combined a blogger's snarkiness with an academic's precision to point out that "the ICC doesn't have a police force, international or otherwise,"[44] that the ICC "lacks jurisdiction over long-haul truckers who force families to hunt each other for sport,"[45] and that "it will be a very chilly day in the bad place when the ICC investigates a crime committed in Europe."[46] Heller continued blogging about the show through the summer of 2013. Though his posts grew increasingly brief, they also hinted that his attraction to the show was expanding. When Heller finally gave up on his recapping project, he made clear that the show had not lost him as a viewer: "I will continue to watch the show. I actually think, ICC silliness aside, that it's quite good."[47]

The ICC is composed of both its real activities and the ways it is represented: two fields of production stitched together as much by intermediaries in Africa as by spectators like Heller. While he was watching and blogging about *Crossing Lines*, he was also watching and blogging about the *Bemba* case and other prosecutions at the ICC.[48] Watching both the legal performance in The Hague and the police drama on television, Heller's spectatorship alternately produced and frustrated his intellectual and emotional attachment to apparatuses of international law. Whether one watches the court's theater in the public galleries in The Hague, in the body of an intermediary in the DRC, or on a television screen in the United States, each encounter impacts the work of the ICC by modulating the affects that surround it.

Jurisdictional issues proved particularly galling to Heller while watching *Crossing Lines*, in large part because the show engaged few other questions relevant to the ICC. The pilot episode allotted only ninety seconds to the series' longest discussion of the legal permissibility of the show's premise. In the scene, Michel Dorn, an "Inspector" for the ICC played by Donald Sutherland (styled to resemble Luis Moreno Ocampo), meets with Louis Daniel (Marc Lavoine) and Eva Vittoria (Gabriella Pession), leaders of the new Special Investigations Unit. Dorn relates the bad news: authorities within the ICC have refused to sanction the unit. Daniel presses for details before Vittoria interjects to revitalize Dorn's advocacy by appealing to the affective field the court generates:

> DORN: They're concerned they would be, or would appear to be, usurping the power of sovereign states.

DANIEL: I'm not asking for power, I just want to do my job.
DORN: Well, you're going to have to find another way to do your job.
VITTORIA: I don't understand.
DORN: The workings of the Court are very complicated—
VITTORIA: Not that, you. I don't understand you.
DORN: I beg your pardon?
VITTORIA: I read something you wrote once in a report, on Kosovo: "The mothers and wives of missing Serbs are begging for their loved ones to be found but they never will be. This court is the only"—
DORN: ". . . court is the only place for them to turn. We weep for those no one else weeps for."[49]

In scenes like this I share Heller's mixed feelings about the show. I share Heller's disappointment with the show's egregious interpretation of the Rome Statute, but I am attracted to its spectacular excesses: to the resemblance between Donald Sutherland's and Luis Moreno Ocampo's eyebrows, to the police shoot-outs set in European capitals that structure each episode, and to the substitution of melodramatic yearning for legal argumentation. I am less enthused than Heller regarding the show's ability to transcend the conventions of its genre, but I adore the breathless, dramatic dialogue that one would never find in The Hague. From Louis Daniel's pitch-perfect performance of a twenty-first-century global paladin to Vittoria and Dorn's mournful duet on genocide, the show harnesses television's penchant for sentimentality to an international legal mechanism that is suspicious of excessive theatricality. *Crossing Lines* reopens affective spaces that the work of the court implies but often mutes. These spaces are anxious and seductive to spectators like Heller as the reality of the court's work becomes distorted in representation, producing perceptions that feed back into the court itself, limiting or expanding its capacities.

In his discussion of the show's premiere, Heller worried over *Crossing Lines'* power to shift the world-historical trajectory of the court. He decried the show for spreading misinformation about the ICC, making the court's acceptance in places like the United States that much more difficult. But other elements of the show offered him the image of a court he might prefer. He wrote, "I could almost accept a show that gave the ICC its own police force; after all, who among us doesn't wish it had one?"[50] *Crossing Lines* responded to the criticism that the court is hobbled by its lack of an enforcement mechanism by providing a wish-fulfilling dream of a court that can back up its ambitions with action. As a spectator, Heller kept watching and stopped blogging as the show left the law behind, veering in its first two seasons towards action-packed scenes of Donald Sutherland carrying out extralegal executions as part of an unauthorized investigation into organized crime.

I am less concerned about the likelihood that *Crossing Lines* will make U.S. ratification of the Rome Statute more difficult, and more fascinated by the dream of power beyond the law it activates. The show prompts viewers to yearn for the exercise of violence to achieve resolutely moral ends without the inefficiency of legal means. This desire responds to sensations of political impotence fostered by the court's limited mandate and accomplishments. The unambiguous moral rightness of a police force attached to the International Criminal Court, making and preserving the law in a single gesture, emerges as a desired horizon where the capacities of international criminal law find their limit.

Heller's transit from defending the court against the treachery of images to his brief seduction by the image of violence as efficient means evinces the affective circuitry that emerges between the law, its representation, and the spectators who are attentive to each. Where the court's material capacities end, its representation on television extends a virtual field that calls for action in the face of atrocity. Where concerns over accuracy hold the real and representation in opposition, spectators who can keep each in view and articulate desires predicated on their relationship indicate that the law's power lies as much in the work of the court as that of its representation. Though neither *Crossing Lines* nor the ICC maintains a material power of enforcement, each mobilizes a cultural effort to remake the world.

As Heller and I orbit *Crossing Lines*, we each articulate our wish that we and others could act in the world in immediate and impactful ways. Heller wants a police force to enact the court's will, to make justice without any mess. I want art to intervene in the spectacles of global governmentality that are staged in international institutions. Though not equivalent, these desires travel similar vectors and are prompted by our shared engagements with international institutions and popular culture. We both entertain visions of action in spaces that are verbal and theatrical.

The *Bemba* case demonstrates that the court's power is a function of its theatricality. One informant told me the story of Bemba's arrest in 2008. She presented the tale secondhand, as something she had heard from colleagues, a bit of institutional folklore. The appeal of the story to those committed to the ICC's success is quite clear, insofar as it provides an image of a warmonger tripped up by the written and spoken word:

> Bemba was arrested when he was in Belgium. The Belgian police went to his apartment and he welcomed them inside. They were very surprised. They explained they were here, from the ICC, to arrest him. They didn't expect a very positive reception. So they don't know what to expect, but he pulls out his domestic papers from the DRC, to show that he has diplomatic immunity. Then one of the police officers pulls out the Rome Statute and opens to Article 27 and starts to read out loud the Article about irrelevance of official capacity. And then Bemba realized, "Oh, I'm in trouble. They're not just going to go away, they're going to try and arrest me."

The ICC exercises power theatrically, via those who take on its roles and enact its scripts. Bemba did not encounter William Fichtner or Donald Sutherland breaking down doors with their guns drawn, but local police who carried the Rome Statute and read aloud from it. Bemba's arrest, at least in this telling, affirms the power of verbal performance on the world stage. What is the power that theater wields, and what are the consequences of wielding power theatrically? If the ICC's theatricality risks impeding its efficacy (by exposing participants to danger, by tainting the reliability of evidence, or by outsourcing its mechanisms of enforcement), that same theatricality claims a world-making power beyond the brute force of armies or police. This is a power the court wields well, but over which it has no monopoly.

When the show reached its third and final season, Heller returned to watching *Crossing Lines*. On October 5, 2015, he blogged: "*Crossing Lines* Is Back! (And Actually Better Than Ever)."[51] At long last, the show had set scenes in a trial at the ICC; a trial that, to Heller's surprise and my own, could reasonably have fallen within the court's jurisdiction. Heller praised season three's new cast and improved plotting, "a sophisticated storyline—and one that is very realistic."[52] In the courtroom at last, Michel Dorn (still Donald Sutherland) was prosecuting the tyrant Fabrice Wombosi (played by Chukwudi Iwuji) for war crimes following the massacre of a village in the eastern DRC. The story incorporated elements of *Bemba*: the accused was a political leader, with plans to return to public life, who was charged with ordering a massacre by foreign mercenaries. Even the name of the fictional village of Banui, in which the crimes were alleged, seemed to be a creative transformation of the name of the capital of the CAR, Bangui, where the MLC had been active.

Posing questions to Wombosi, Dorn paced the open space between prosecution, defense, and judges. I recognized much of the courtroom I had seen at The Hague in the set design: blond wooden desks and paneled walls, lawyers wearing black robes with white jabots, evidence presented digitally on computer monitors set at each desk, and so on. The episodes even depicted the use of intermediaries: I was charmed to see the new investigator, Carine Strand (played by Elizabeth Mitchell), working through Médecins Sans Frontières to locate a key witness in a refugee camp; this witness was a child victim of Wombosi, Cedric Bofeko (played by Malachi Hallett). As gratifying as this increased fidelity to the realities of international criminal proceedings was, Heller also pointed out that "the show still has its fair share of minor annoyances."[53] Instead of the usual three judges, *Crossing Lines* sat a bench of at least eight. In the show, the public galleries occupied a corner of the courtroom itself, and the accused, public, and witnesses each had clear lines of sight connecting them, with no soundproofing or distortion. When Cedric Bofeko testified, he made direct eye contact with Wombosi. When Dorn introduced new evidence, the spectators' hubbub filled the courtroom without garnering a rebuke from court security.[54]

These changes are not surprising: they amplify the courtroom's theatricality and intensify its drama. They fill the court's spaces with feelings and sentiments it cannot usually abide. Heller noted that "the South African judge is a little too gleeful when he pronounces the defendant guilty,"[55] and I rolled my eyes when, upon hearing the verdict, Bofeko leaned his head on Strand's shoulder and began to cry. These creative decisions and others like them bring to the surface forces considered excessive by those who perform the law. Emotion is not absent from the ICC's courtrooms, but it is not spectacular there either. It emerges, displaced, at various removes from the courtroom: in the court's corridors and lobby, in the streets that surround it, on television and online, and so on.

On March 21, 2016, Trial Chamber III declared Jean-Pierre Bemba Gombo guilty of two counts of crimes against humanity and three counts of war crimes. The verdict was delivered in a hearing that was webcast live and later uploaded to YouTube. I watched the hearing some days after it took place, from my office in College Station, Texas. In December 2015, the ICC had moved into its permanent premises, a campus that had been custom-built for the court. The new courtroom was quite different from the temporary space I had explored in 2011, and also contrasted sharply with the courtroom in *Crossing Lines*. The new courtroom was cold and vast. Instead of blond wood, the walls and desks were shades of gray. Parties were arranged as they had been previously, but they occupied more space. An abyss separated the prosecution, defense, and judges. Throughout the verdict hearing, no one entered this void.

While the judges had been slightly raised in the KPN building, now they appeared to sit even higher above their clerks. The added height amplified the power of the image they projected. Presiding Judge Sylvia Steiner was flanked by Judge Joyce Aluoch and Judge Kuniko Ozaki; three women from Brazil, Kenya, and Japan, sitting in judgment. When the webcast cut to a medium close-up of Steiner wearing headphones, examining her monitor, and speaking into her microphone, I was also reminded of the distance dividing me from the court and of the ways I could collapse that distance. As she rendered judgment, so too was I invited (and even required), by virtue of my spectatorship and the court's mandate, to deliver my own.

The verdict hearing lasted 73 minutes; only Steiner spoke. She provided an oral summary of the 364-page judgment, methodically reciting the court's findings. Her speech lacked the gaps I had found in the public galleries and the transcripts; she provided a smooth and comprehensive story. Other elements of the dramaturgy had also shifted since the presentation of evidence and testimony had concluded. Unlike my experience in 2011, the camera now seemed to be looking for drama. It cut from Judge Steiner to Bemba, looking for reactions. From Bemba, it cut to Fatou Bensouda, who succeeded Moreno Ocampo as the chief prosecutor of the ICC in 2012. But this was not *Crossing Lines*: Steiner, Bemba, and Bensouda remained stoic throughout.

There was no hubbub as Steiner read out Bemba's verdict, nor did the webcast give any indication of the public galleries. "The Chamber has reached its decision unanimously," Steiner declared. "The Chamber finds Mr. Jean-Pierre Bemba Gombo guilty, under article 28A of the Statute, as a person effectively acting as a military commander for the following crimes: murder as a crime against humanity under article 7(1)(a) of the Statute . . ."[56] The webcast cut to a close-up of Bemba; he glanced to his left but was otherwise unmoved. Steiner continued to enumerate his further convictions: murder as a war crime, rape as a crime against humanity, rape as a war crime, and pillaging as a war crime.

In an interview with the website Justice Hub, Bemba's lead counsel, Peter Haynes, described his client's state following the trial: "I think he's alright. He has been in custody for eight years . . . He's disappointed, even angry about what happened. But it's round one. . . . That's the way he looks at it."[57] The French newspaper *Le Monde* offered more drama: "In the public gallery, Liliane Bemba, [the accused's] wife, collapsed in tears while in the street facing the Court, fifty or so of [Bemba's] supporters were demonstrating, surrounded by fifty or so Dutch police officers."[58]

In the days preceding the verdict, Justice Hub had reported that much of the Congolese press was predicting Bemba's acquittal, release, and return to the DRC.[59] After the verdict, and at a subsequent sentencing hearing, a reporter from the website spoke to supporters of Bemba in The Hague who expressed shock, and to other spectators who had more nuanced reactions:

> Yannick-Jenny Fernhout-Kottaud, who is originally from the CAR . . . said she had been following the trial from the beginning. "I was the only one in the courtroom regularly . . ." She watched the proceedings with interest. She noticed the women judges, the women in the defence team and a female chief prosecutor. . . . She was relieved by the sentence. "Reasonable" was the word she used. . . . Nonetheless, Kottaud said she is of the opinion "Africans should be judged in Africa."[60]

Perhaps *Crossing Lines* is right to spend so little time outside of Europe, when even those who find the court's work reasonable would prefer it stay there.

Diplomatic theater modulates our attachments to internationalism, attachments with material consequences for international institutions. The International Criminal Court is constituted by each of its interfaces, each a theatrical border where its work is experienced and a world system is imagined.

Where people interface with institutions, theater emerges. Often, this theater features a dramaturgy determined by the forms of vulnerability that are endemic to edges, borders, and exposed surfaces. The vulnerable dramaturgy so evident at the ICC is an amplification of the ways all international institutions prove susceptible to the impressions of those they encounter. The UN is also pliable at its interfaces: where it appears onstage, where it interposes bodies, where it attends a play, where it streams its webcast, and so on. Diplomatic theater invites destabilizing gazes, it inhabits uncontainable bodies, and it projects images over which the authorities have only so much control. Power is exercised and contested at these interfaces, and affects that are regulated in institutional centers emerge at these margins. With these affects, spectators push back, unsettling the theater through which they experience geopolitics.

Postscript

On June 8, 2018, Bemba was acquitted of the charges of war crimes and crimes against humanity of which he had been convicted in 2016. The reversal "came as a shock to many,"[61] myself included. Watching the webcast of the judgment hearing in the Appeals Chamber, gray institutional spaces greeted me on screen once more. I noted smaller contingents of lawyers for the Office of the Prosecutor and the defense. Bemba remained impassive behind his legal team. For a moment, the cameras caught a corner of the public galleries behind thick glass, packed with spectators looking down into the courtroom from the floor above.

Five judges entered and took their seats: Presiding Judge Christine Van den Wyngaert (Belgium), Judge Chile Eboe-Osuji (Nigeria), Judge Sanji Monageng (Botswana), Judge Howard Morrison (United Kingdom), and Judge Piotr Hofmański (Poland). After some introductions, Judge Wyngaert began reading the summary judgment. Later, Peter Haynes reported, "I knew pretty early on in the summary which way it was going."[62] After presenting the case background and the Appeals Chamber's initial findings, Judge Wyngaert arrived at the heart of the judgment: "The Appeals Chamber thus finds, by majority, Judge Monageng and Judge Hofmański dissenting, that the Trial Chamber's conclusion that Mr. Bemba failed to take all necessary and reasonable measures in response to MLC crimes in the CAR was materially affected by errors, and Mr. Bemba cannot be held criminally responsible under Article 28 for crimes committed by MLC troops during the CAR operation." She paused, dramatically, and looked up to the public galleries above her. "In these circumstances, the Appeals Chamber, by majority, reverses the conviction of Mr. Bemba." She paused again and then distant, muffled cheering could be heard on the webcast, jubilant sounds rumbling under her pronouncements. In the delay, the court's occlusions materialized once more: the muffled sounds I heard revealed at once the hard division the court erects between itself and its audience and the permeability of that same barrier.

Judge Wyngaert continued, "In relation to the remaining criminal acts, it enters an acquittal . . ." The cheer rose once more, louder and sharper, and

Judge Wyngaert paused again at the end of her sentence, not to embellish her own performance but in reaction to the acts of her spectators. The cameras refused to turn to the galleries, but could not hide the audience's presence or effects. The cheering continued, sounding distant on the webcast, as Judge Wyngaert glanced up to her left and right again. The webcast cut to a wider shot; most in the courtroom were looking up at the galleries.

Nearly thirty seconds of cheering passed before Wyngaert appealed for calm, her delivery halting as she seemed unable to look away from the galleries: "May I ask the registry to restore calm in the courtroom, in the public gallery? May I ask the registry to restore the order in the public gallery? Failing which, we will have to adjourn." The cheering continued as the court officer rose to respond, leaning into her own microphone: "Your honor, we are working on it." Wyngaert replied sharply, "I am not finished with reading the judgment," then spoke directly to the galleries, "Can you please sit down? Can you please sit down? May I ask you to sit down?" Calm returned a moment later, and Wyngaert began her summary of the minority's dissenting opinion.[63] In these two minutes in the courtroom, the delays and blockages that characterize the court's interface with its public revealed again the proximities at which the institution and its audience each lay claim to their unique authority—the authority of the law and of the audience that ratifies it—in a theater of states.

As the scene's effects reverberated among other audiences—Bemba's supporters cheering in Kinshasa,[64] victims of sex and gender-based violence lamenting in Bangui,[65] legal scholars worrying in the blogosphere[66]—the events in the courtroom revealed themselves to be an explicit materialization of the court's theatrical effects. In the reactions the court provokes, its theater continues; at the interface those reactions take their most concrete form. The scene of Bemba's acquittal makes clear that performances lauding or decrying the court follow a similar theatrical logic: they are operations of spectatorship in which the forces the court sets in motion are taken up or deflected by those the court addresses. Together, those who cheer the court and those who curse it establish a material space where the institution and its spectators may act and press on one another. When scholars and policy-makers fret over the court's future, they misrecognize relatively healthy theatrical operations. The old saw goes that justice must be seen to be done; this truism prompted the court to provide as much transparency as it feels it can to its audiences, which is an essentially theatrical gesture. But perhaps it is not just theater's visibility that proves essential to the law, but also theater's messiness, precarity, and incompleteness. Justice must also be seen to be a rehearsal, to be vulnerable, to be ongoing and forever opening onto its next performance, to be done but not finished.

Figure 7. Secretary-General Ban Ki-moon discusses the draft text of the Paris Agreement with his advisors at the UN Framework Convention on Climate Change's Twenty-First Conference of the Parties, December 12, 2015. UN Photo by Mark Garten.

6

✦

"No More Than a Piece of Paper"
The Written Word in a Theater of States

Fifteen men and women sit at a horseshoe table. They look officious. They are older, in their sixties or seventies. They all wear gray, black, or blue suits, with starched shirts and muted accessories. Younger colleagues sit behind them. A bronze globe dominates the rear wall of the room, flanked by the flags of ten nations; some superpowers (the United States) and some with less global clout (Finland). Placards set in front of each person at the table indicate the state he or she represents. The delegates of the United States and the United Kingdom, both graying white men, are in the midst of an argument. They heap vulgar abuse on each other. The U.S. delegate begins:

> Picture this
> I'm a bag of dicks
> Put me to your lips
> I am sick
> I will punch a baby bear in his shit
> Give me lip
> Imma send you to the yard, get a stick
> Make a switch
> I can end a conversation real quick

And the U.K. delegate gives as good as he gets:

> I am crack
> I ain't lyin', kick a lion in his crack
> I'm the shit, I will fall off in your crib, take a shit
> Pinch your momma on the booty
> Kick your dog, fuck your bitch.[1]

The U.S. delegate stands and begins to circle the table; the U.K. delegate rises to meet him. Their confrontation grows as their handlers and secretaries join them. The technocrats begin shoving one another and soon a brawl erupts, a melee that expands to all in the room. A pig darts across the floor, and a chicken flaps its wings to avoid rowdy politicians. Sheaves of paper are tossed into the air, floating briefly with feathers above the fracas. Books, clipboards, and files become bludgeons. The representative of the United Kingdom spies an opportunity to gain the upper hand: he lifts the U.S. flag from its stand and rushes toward his adversary. Brandishing the flag like a spear, he menaces his U.S. counterpart, who has fallen. Silence descends on the room and the belligerent representative lowers his weapon, embarrassed. A uniformed woman, a janitorial staffer, glares at him, dismayed by the mess she will have to clean up.

This is not the UN Security Council, but it is an interface with the Security Council—a theatrical image of the council that impacts its work. In late August 2016, DJ Shadow released a music video for his song "Nobody Speak," a collaboration with the hip-hop duo Run the Jewels. Though the U.S. and U.K. delegates in the video were played by actors Igor Tsyshkevich and Ian Bailey, respectively, their vulgar abuse was overdubbed by the rappers El-P and Killer Mike.[2] The music video for "Nobody Speaks" occupies an affective space opened between the international institution and contemporary hip-hop.

A press release from DJ Shadow's publicist makes the satirical content explicit:

> The video depicts a meeting of leaders that quickly descends into chaos, a scene not unlike what is unfolding in governments around the globe . . . Says DJ Shadow: "We wanted to make a positive, life-affirming video that captures politicians at their election-year best. We got this instead."[3]

The video attaches to and accelerates the feelings of political frustration that configure both international and domestic politics. This may not be the Security Council we have, but it remains a scene that many desire: a horizon that names an ideal political capacity of decisive action and energetic release. Killer Mike, who had spent much of the previous year campaigning for Bernie Sanders as he sought the Democratic Party's nomination for U.S. president, added to DJ Shadow's sentiments: "It's what I really wish Trump and Hillary would just do and get it over with . . ."[4]

In degrading the verbal art of diplomats with the spoken theatrics of hip-hop, the artists involved in the video elicit laughter that catches in my throat once I recognize the confluence of speech and violence in the song's repeated chorus: "Hey, you wanna hear a good joke? / Nobody speak, nobody get choked." Rapping is an intensely verbal art, and hip-hop music has often played on the relationship between words and violence, a relationship that also characterizes performative speech, the law, and international affairs. The chorus intertextually references Eazy-E's 1988 paean to crime, "Nobody Move," which sampled lines from the Reggae singer Yellowman: "Nobody move, nobody get hurt."[5]

"No More Than a Piece of Paper"

Transposing the bank robber's injunction, "nobody move," into a diplomat's threat, "nobody speak," the song and music video return the violence that runs rampant in our international system to the words and speech acts that would contain it. "Nobody Speak" proves an astute critique of our international institutions insofar as it plays on the same relationship between words, speech, and violence that is at the heart of the UN's dramaturgy.

In this book, I have elaborated a dramaturgy of international institutions composed of the affects and energies mobilized in culture or politics that circulate on a unified field of theatrical activity. This dramaturgy manages several relationships that are crucial to diplomacy, including relationships between past and present, between spectator and spectacle, and between power and performance. In the song's chorus, Run the Jewels reduces this dramaturgy to a simple, emblematic maxim. The line "Nobody speak, nobody get choked" presents the central concern of diplomatic theater (the negotiation over who has a right to speech, the right to impact policy) as a stark ultimatum. It is a threat that interpellates its targets to govern their behavior and that promises violence to a body that would perform.

Though Killer Mike and El-P rap these words, performing them aloud, the paper detritus that fills the space between the brawlers in the video reminds me that just as often this battle is contained to texts. "Nobody speak, nobody get choked" epitomizes the substantive content and affective quality of negotiations in which might is exercised as a right to speak and to determine the conditions for what speech will be allowed; a conflict that makes its final mark on the reams of paper the UN produces.

A remarkable relationship between text and performance underwrites the cases in each chapter of this book. This relationship is as constitutive of theater as it is of diplomacy, and suggests techniques that artists can use to infiltrate spaces of global administration. The work of the UN appears most explicitly in written documents that have a performative force, a historical life, and a spectacular impact, such as the Security Council resolutions that establish a peacekeeping mission or a sanctions regime. Just as significant, however, are the quotidian texts inscribed by the administrative life of international institutions, such as the transcripts of a Security Council meeting or the courtroom records of the International Criminal Court. These texts have been the raw material for my own dramaturgy, enacted in this book. This chapter takes on texts in three scenes of diplomatic theater: in the ICC's trial transcripts, in the negotiating practices of the UN General Assembly, and in postdramatic theaters that model global summitry.

Transcript

Counterintuitively, transcripts best represent the theatricality of international institutions even as they lie flat on the page. A transcript captures live performance and invites theatrical interpretation of the spoken dialogues it transcribes. Transcripts are a medium through which theater infiltrates disciplines like political science and history, disciplines that rely on such records as their raw materials. A transcript delivers the theater scholar's concern with the relationship between page and stage to arenas in which the distinction is often overlooked. The transcripts of UN meetings perform textual stability in order to recuperate the instability of live performance, which is more often than not an infelicitous effort. They collect comprehensive verbal details but omit excesses of tone, timbre, posture, and gesture.

Transcripts at the UN are often built of texts submitted by individual delegations, and these texts may not precisely match the words spoken live: the small errors that can accrue to one reading aloud from written notes are corrected for the historical record. The transcript is a battleground between the dynamism of the performed and the rigidity of the textual. Theater intervenes in history as a discipline and practice by drawing attention to the profundity of the fact that historical archives and artifacts index live, embodied events and highlight the ways in which historical meaning is constructed from the material traces left behind by performance. In these ways, verbatim transcripts are significant to the dramaturgy of diplomacy not as a record of the past, but as a central component of an ongoing performance event.

In its etymology and in contemporary practice, the word "diplomacy" signals the diplomat's embodied relationship to texts. Alexander Ostrower asserts the origin of the word in the Latin noun *diploma*, which originally referred to the folded document carried by early envoys as evidence that they acted on behalf of a state or imperial authority.[6] As diplomacy evolved into an art of statecraft, the word *diploma* transferred from the paper to its use, diplomacy, and the person who used it, the diplomat.[7] This history follows the same theatrical trajectory as the diplomatic practices described in this book: in diplomacy, the force of utterance and action transfers from textual instruments to live performance. Bodies replace papers. Yet the etymology of the word "diplomacy" leaves out an important subsequent movement in diplomatic practice. Though texts script diplomats, with their bodies replacing their papers, those diplomatic bodies work in turn to produce new texts (treaties, resolutions, transcripts, etc.). Neither the written nor the spoken word predominates in international institutions—as an event, diplomacy oscillates between text and performance, and neither pole can do without the other.

The question of the relationship between text and performance is also quite consequential in the study of theater.[8] As an object of study, theater often poses an immediate dilemma to the scholar, who must decide whether to privilege a written script that ostensibly endures or an instance of live performance that ostensibly disappears. Theater appears to the scholar as a tension between the written words that permit a play to be repeated and the performing bodies whose acts appear and disappear in an instant. In addition to these theoretical problems, the role of the text in performance also appears as a practical problem for all those who make theater. Even when Richard Schechner decenters the text in his *Environmental Theater*, writing that text "need be neither the starting point nor the goal of a production,"[9] he indicates the presence of the text in theater even in its absence. In theater (far more than in the adjacent field of ritual or the expanded field of performance), text is always a determinative component.

The devised and postdramatic works that are heirs to the innovations of environmental theater and similar twentieth-century performance practices provide fascinating analogues to the mise-en-scène of international institutions. When describing the disorientations, occlusions, and mediations of the ICC's courtrooms to other theater scholars, I have more than once been told that I sound like I'm describing something from New York City's downtown avant-garde theaters. In sleek public galleries, spectators, each with his or her own headphones, watch the performance through a glass wall. The performers may be entirely visible, may appear as pixelated images on TV screens, may be walled in by hanging curtains, or may break the fourth wall to acknowledge the audience. Photographs, documents, and video appear on screens that may or may not be wholly visible to the audience, and the performers can often be found reading from their own transcripts, reiterating scenes already played. This could be Rimini Protokoll, the Wooster Group, Temporary Distortion, or Gob Squad, but it is a war crimes trial at the International Criminal Court.

Thinking about the International Criminal Court as a site of devised performance offers new avenues to consider how power flows through diplomatic theater. In both the theater and the court, devising places pressure on hierarchical structures and the relations of power that attend them.[10] Though judges preside, they are not the only authors at the court. From words spoken to intermediaries in the Democratic Republic of the Congo, to a written statement prepared by defense or prosecution investigators, into the oral realm of the courtroom, through the voices of many interpreters, and onto the written page of the transcript, the official records of the court track disputed narratives as they travel between mouths, voices, and idioms; nations, states, and institutions. While the primary authorship of a witness, lawyer, or other participant is never lost, interpretation and transcription both serve to bring many hands and minds to bear on the final utterance that the court produces. In the courtroom, individual speech encounters a collective process of writing with historical consequences.

The minute negotiations in the courtroom indicate the degree to which a philosophy of collective creation pervades the court's work. As I heard Judge Bruno Cotte (France) tell the court on May 24, 2011, "the concern of the Chamber is that all the parties and participants should assist us to establish the truth." A day earlier, proceedings in the trial of Germain Katanga and Mathieu Ngudjolo Chui (former leaders of armed groups in Ituri during the transition following the Second Congo War, charged with three crimes against humanity and seven war crimes)[11] had come to a halt as a dynamic polyglot performance was stabilized and standardized for a written record.

On May 23, 2011, nearly two years into the trial, the court intended to receive testimony from defense witnesses. As a witness, identified as Mr. Akurotho Obia, was brought into the room, Judge Cotte assured Jean-Pierre Fofé, the co-counsel for Mathieu Ngudjolo Chui, that requested changes to the previous day's transcript had been made. Fofé began his line of questioning by summarizing the corrected transcript, which prompted an objection from Lucio Garcia, of the prosecution, "to remind Mr. Fofé that this is an examination of the witness" and not a time to make statements. While the lawyers on each side spoke either English or French when posing their questions, the witness responded in Swahili, with the help of unseen interpreters. Nearby, court clerks transcribed all that was said to create English and French texts. Some minutes later Garcia began his cross-examination, and Fofé provided his own intervention. "I beg your pardon, your Honour," Fofé began, "I was just rising to inform the Prosecutor that he should—he should pause for a while and give the interpreters time to completely translate the answers provided by the witness." Checking the real-time transcript scrolling across the monitor on his desk, he added, "And I would like to seek your leave that the answer which has been given on page 11, lines 19 to 21, be verified."[12]

Judge Cotte acceded to the request and began reading the transcript aloud to the witness, repeating the prosecutor's recent questions and the witness's answers. Before the witness could confirm the transcript, David Hooper, lead counsel for the defense, offered his own intervention. I have reproduced the scene that followed by editing seven pages of the transcript, reducing it to its most theatrical moments (see below). Here I am acting as a dramaturge to indicate the theatrical opportunity presented by the performed work of international institutions and the texts they leave behind. In this excerpt, the court's primary work is to negotiate between oral performance and the textual record that guarantees its historical significance. These negotiations both maintain their own theatricality and resemble the collaborative methodologies of many postdramatic theater-makers. These collaborators work through a space where meaning may be infinite to establish and revise a historical record in a common language. Focused on a glossary, the transcript, and overlapping speakers, my excerpt catalogs the textual difficulties that the court routinely encounters. In effect, the dramaturgy of international institutions becomes explicit in the thing they do most often: collectively inscribing a text built from live and embodied verbal performance. In this context, the problem of collective action—the central problem in international institutions for securing peace and stability by harmonizing competing interests and individuals—becomes an expressly theatrical dilemma.

English Transcript Excerpts from Trial Chamber II—Courtroom I, 23 May 2011

MR. HOOPER: Can I, before the question's answered, just say one thing. I understand that the words that are being used are the French words, "*combattant*," "*soldat*," "*milice*." . . . It might be a useful exercise . . . to establish the nomenclature that we're going to use if [Mr. Garcia is] using shades of meaning like that . . .

PRESIDING JUDGE COTTE: (Interpretation) That is indeed the difficulty we have been facing right from the start of this trial . . . I think, Mr. Garcia, that you should make the appropriate distinction . . .

MR. FOFÉ: (Interpretation) I beg your pardon, your honor . . . shouldn't we rather ask for the interpreters to tell us how they translate into Swahili the term "combatant," "militia member," "soldier"? Maybe we could establish a glossary . . .

PRESIDING JUDGE COTTE: (Interpretation) Fine. Interpreters, you can see that we depend fully on you. Can you please tell us . . . how you translate into Swahili the word "militia member"? Do you have different words for "militia member," "combatant," and "soldier"? . . .

THE INTERPRETER: (Interpretation) Thank you, your Honour, for the question. In Swahili we translate "combatant" by "*wanamgambo*" . . . However, when . . . the witness understands French, we borrow the word from French and would use "*combattant*" . . .

MR. FOFÉ: (Interpretation) Your Honour, can the interpreter repeat what he said, because I have the impression that word "*wanamgambo*" is used to designate both combatants and the militia members . . .

PRESIDING JUDGE COTTE: (Interpretation) Interpreter, give us the Swahili word for interpreter—sorry, for "combatant" and the Swahili word for "militia member."

THE INTERPRETER: (Interpretation) Thank you, your Honour. For "*combattant*" we say "*wapiganji*." And for "*militaire*" we say "*jeshi*" or "*askari*." And for the last word, "*milicien*," we say "*wanamgambo*."

PRESIDING JUDGE COTTE: (Interpretation) At least phonetically speaking, I heard three different words. I think it will be appropriate that the transcript should reflect the three Swahili terms . . .

MR. HOOPER: . . . My understanding is those Swahili words have not been employed before . . . I think from what I've heard relayed to me is these are—these words, Swahili words, themselves aren't used in Ituri . . .

MR. GARCIA: (Interpretation) Your Honour, maybe we should simply ask the witness . . . and let him tell us what he understands . . .

PRESIDING JUDGE COTTE: (Interpretation) . . . For once it would be interesting to have one of the accused persons participate actively in our proceedings . . . Mr. Katanga, we're listening to you . . .

MR. KATANGA: (Interpretation) I beg your pardon, your Honour. I would like to establish a relationship between the word "combatant" and the word "soldier." Yes, I do confirm that these two words have been used here in your Chamber. However, with regard to the term "militia member," they used the French word "*milice.*" They do not use another term. It is today that I have heard that the term "militia member" is translated as "*wanamgambo*" into Swahili, but ever since I have been here I have never heard that equivalent being used . . .

MR. MACDONALD: (Interpretation) The accused person just made a statement to the Chamber. We have been holding proceedings in Lingala for the accused person for the past three years, and today he is raising objections about the Swahili interpretation, and therefore I would like to—I would like to—

THE INTERPRETER: Overlapping speakers, your Honour. We cannot interpret everybody.

PRESIDING JUDGE COTTE: (Interpretation) Mr. MacDonald, please complete what you're saying calmly.[13]

As this excerpt gains momentum, it expands to include more and more of the speech situation: from individual words, to intersecting languages, to the authority of the bodies who speak them. The disputation over spoken and written words forms a repeated structure organizing the court's work. Contrasting with the desire for immediate justice, the dramaturgy of the courtroom is characterized by delay; it plods along and doubles back on itself. An informant who had worked in chambers described the courtroom participation: "You're following all the transcripts as you're looking at your computer. You do get the impression that people are focusing heavily on making sure that it's accurate; it is kind of a moving-along process, it requires editing, it isn't perfect right away." The attentions of those in the courtroom shift back and forth between the live event and its record in a daily practice that combines the gestures of performance and documentation. Prompting questions and receiving answers, the transcript establishes a virtual historical space filled by the testimony of those who come to the court, but it also anchors legal conflicts that expand in the courtroom. The dramaturgical space opened by the transcript runs perpendicular to the teleological time implied by the law's imperative to pass judgment, expanding time laterally, a bubble in history.

The heteroglossia of the court fills these spaces, as is evident from the mutating dispute over the languages used by the witnesses, the interpreters, and the accused in my excerpt. The hierarchy that privileges the court's working languages (French and English) over its other official languages (Arabic,

Chinese, Russian, and Spanish) receives consistent challenge from each new language deemed necessary by the Registry or by judges for the court's operations: Swahili, Lingala, and so on. These languages enter the court on an ad hoc basis, circulating around, below, and beyond the texts in English and French that capture the court's work. Language deterritorializes geographic difference: languages come from specific places, but they travel with people, over airways, and across wires and networks. At the ICC, languages mark geographic origins and localities in the context of a global project. Distinct languages assert local particularities in a space dedicated to normalizing global behaviors, tentatively destabilizing the colonial heritage that the court cannot escape as it addresses formerly colonized peoples from its home in the Netherlands. The polyglot courtroom provides a counter-image to the monolithic historical record that the court promises.

Taking collective action as a theatrical dilemma offers ways to understand how dramatic conflict becomes an instrument of power. Katanga's intervention exasperated a senior trial lawyer with the prosecution, Eric MacDonald, who was livid that Katanga should be following the proceedings in French or Swahili when the court had gone to great expense to provide Lingala interpretation—an additional regional dialect from central Africa—exclusively for his use. Perhaps MacDonald was also irked that the judge chose to ignore his colleague Garcia's suggestion to pose the question of translation to the witness, and instead made space for the accused himself to speak.

International institutions foreground authority, and so invite challenges to the duly authorized. This moment, which is captured at the end of my excerpt, is significantly de-dramatized in the pages of the transcript. Heightened emotions are tamped down, and the reader cannot hear the cacophony of voices filling the courtroom; the exceptional character of Macdonald's outburst is only captured indirectly by the interpreter's complaint and Judge Cotte's admonishment. Though this would not be the last quibble over language and lexicon in the *Katanga* case, by the afternoon the trial seemed to be back on track and Mr. Obia was able to continue his testimony.

International institutional spaces rely on consensual performances to maintain the hierarchy of powers that provide their sanction. These are spaces of decorous performance, where text and performance work in tandem to regulate speakers and their speech. Transcripts contain speech, resisting scenes of dissensus by relegating all performance to a past record in the moment it is performed. Official history is not devoid of conflict, but it does curate that conflict. It is decorous speech that mutes violence by admitting no rejoinder.

[Brackets]

Though I have previously characterized the UN Charter as the promise that founded the institution, I need only shift my dramaturgical gaze slightly to suggest that the UN was also founded under threat. Between the signing of the Charter of the United Nations on June 26, 1945, and its coming into force on October 24, 1945, the world entered the nuclear age. The work of the UN has always played in the shadow of the atomic bomb. The General Assembly's first resolution, in January 1946, took up the question of nuclear disarmament, and the question continues to be of primary importance on the UN's agenda.[14] In disarmament debates, states respond to the generalized threat of nuclear weapons. Nuclear weapons, which are so destructive that their only conscionable employment is as a deterrent, operate performatively as an implicit threat designed to keep hostile others at bay. In this they intensify the relationship between speech and action that is inherent in any interstate threat, materializing the matrix of threats and promises organizing world affairs in specific weapons.

The UN responds with its textual instruments. Article 2, Paragraph 4 of the United Nations Charter sets out the basic tenets of the organization's approach to managing international peace and security: "All Members shall refrain in their international relations from the *threat or use* of force against the territorial integrity or political independence of any state."[15] Throughout its nineteen chapters, the charter equates the use of force with the threat of force. This is a textual effort and performative promise that wavers infelicitously in the face of the Bomb.

Nuclear weapons predetermined the work imputed to the UN in the twentieth century by providing a generalized existential threat that was irreducible to a conflict between two states. Charging the arms race and foreclosing on creative solutions to global conflicts, nuclear weapons hemmed in the repertoire available to actors on the world stage. Jose Ayala-Lasso, the minister for foreign relations of Ecuador, said as much at the General Assembly's First Special Session on Disarmament in 1978, where he noted that the specter of nuclear annihilation "emerges from the shadows when major world leaders maintain that total war is inevitable, though it may be postponed; when high officers of other Powers in public statements do not reject the possibility; and when the main actors of this great military drama increase their nuclear arsenals."[16] Nuclear weapons point despairingly to the limits of a diplomacy that is measured only by the success and failure of its acts, rather than by accounting broadly for the forces that embodied performance unleashes.

Nuclear weapons curtail the capacity of international institutions to stage collective action, and here theater must intervene. Though theater's scripts contain the fates of those they depict, suggesting that theater is an art of the inevitable, in the transit from page to stage that art reveals its investment in the notion that its repetitions may bring unexpected ends. The play that is played again and again traffics in difference and newness as much as it does in similarity and oldness. Live performance holds an audience's attention in part by suggesting that something unanticipated might emerge from that liveness.[17] Unanticipated performance is rare at the UN, but in this book

I have invested in its possibility as a disruptive event that can shift the trajectory of world affairs. I have found it in plays that replay history, movie stars that intrude on institutional spaces, concerts that disconcert their auditors, and speechmakers who go off script. I have also sought unanticipated meanings where reiteration passes the cordon dividing political spectacles from the publics they require; where political performances are represented on theatrical stages, and aesthetic performances invade the diplomats' conference rooms.

These cases are each examples in which certain speech appeared where it was not supposed to, a figure I first found at the UN by poring over the transcripts of the General Assembly's First Special Session on Disarmament. In its time, that session was "the largest conference on disarmament in human history,"[18] and though its impact on the progress of interstate affairs may be debated, the changes it made to the machinery for negotiating and debating nuclear disarmament remain operative in the twenty-first century. Like the arguments in Judge Cotte's courtroom, the First Special Session on Disarmament staged a battle over speech: over who can speak when and on what. This battle had documentary precursors and became enshrined in further documents. Disarmament debates make urgent the question of who has a right to perform on the world stage in order to distribute what the world holds in common. The debate over who can participate in negotiations on nuclear disarmament reduces the politics of diplomatic theater to its most essential terms and to what the philosopher Jacques Rancière describes as the essence of politics: "a quarrel over the issue of speech itself."[19]

At the Special Session, states from the Non-Aligned Movement (NAM)—states that publicly disavowed submission to either the U.S. or Soviet spheres of influence[20]—staged a scene of dissensus.[21] Nuclear disarmament negotiations in the first decades of the Cold War had bypassed the UN, and especially the General Assembly, excluding a majority of states from participation. According to the nuclear power brokers, these exclusions were founded on sound, unassailable logic: nuclear disarmament "talks were to be held between those who had 'scientific claims' for participation."[22] In 1978, the NAM challenged this status quo by staging diplomatic theater to rearrange global hierarchies.[23] This theater was written down, after weeks of live speech-making, in the session's outcome, the Final Document of the Tenth Special Session of the General Assembly, which was adopted as General Assembly Resolution S-10/2.[24]

The Final Document was a text intended to counter nuclear war, to capture and contain its potential violence, and so to provide its power to particular state actors in varying intensities. Many texts at the UN suggest a similar trajectory as violence loses its materiality, becomes speech, and is transcribed as text. During the General Debate of the session, states performed for the text—both for the Final Document and for the verbatim transcript recording each day of the month-long session. Belligerents took aim at one another across the

General Assembly hall. As Iraq prepared a resolution (ultimately unsuccessful) organizing a military boycott of Israel, Afghanistan pressed the same case in the General Debate, declaring: "The covert proliferation of nuclear weapons to Israel and South Africa is a disturbing violation of the international Treaty on the Non-Proliferation of Nuclear Weapons."[25] This spectacular performed accusation became only a brief allusion in the Final Document.[26]

In his own speech, the head of the Israeli delegation, Permanent Representative Chaim Herzog, responded to the accusations that had piled up. He remediated the language of official reports, composed of the precise alphanumeric signifiers of modern warfare, to represent the balance of power in the Middle East. He maintained Israel's official policy of nuclear opacity, but painted an image of his region that would underscore his state's need for a deterrent. He reported that arms expenditures in the Middle East had exceeded all previous records, "$35 thousand million so far, of which $24 thousand million have been expended by Saudi Arabia alone," and that Syria, Libya, and Iraq were buying Soviet weapons, "including thousands of T-62 and T-72 tanks, hundreds of Mig-23 fighter aircraft, as well as Suchoy fighters, 'Scud' surface-to-surface missile launchers, and Komar and Osa missile boats."[27] Crammed with details, Herzog's speech was designed with its continuing textual life in mind. His performance anticipated the page it would be printed on, a page where the numbers would read starkly.

Herzog had experience with diplomacy's oscillation between performance and text. In 1975, his first year as Israel's permanent representative, the General Assembly debated Resolution 3379, which was notorious for equating Zionism with racism. Speaking to the Assembly before the vote, Herzog recognized that a history recorded in texts and transcripts was the ultimate medium for which he and his colleagues played:

> The vote of each delegation will record its country's stand on anti-Semitic racism and anti-Judaism. You yourselves bear the responsibility for your stand before history, for as such will you be viewed in history . . . For us, the Jewish people, this is no more than a piece of paper and we will treat it as such.[28]

Herzog concluded his speech by raising the resolution above the podium, and tearing it in half to emphasize his disdain. His performance admitted and denied the power of diplomatic writing in adjacent gestures: he claimed both the power of a vote inscribed in a historical record, and the impotence of a text that is not consummated in action. Texts provide performance with historical traction (writing attaches the unfolding present to the record of history), and performance decides the potency of texts (documents can only deliver their forces in contingent moments of performance in the present).

Texts also contain and tamp down the theatrical excesses to which live performance can give rise. At the Special Session on Disarmament, one finds these dramas in the margins: in Nigeria sniping with the United States over South Africa in meetings of the Credentials Committee, or Somalia and Ethiopia trading barbs over the Ogaden War, or Chile and Bolivia airing territorial disputes at the end of each debate, during time reserved for the Right of Reply. U.S. news reports on the Special Session gave little, if any, ink to these conflicts, even where U.S. interests were involved. To the event's official spectators, these unanticipated moments were outliers that were beyond the thrust of the session as a whole, and outside the scope of an ascendant NAM, superpower politics, or the Final Document.

The regular appearance of these moments under the Right of Reply affirms their marginal status. The Right of Reply allows for unscheduled speakers to make off-the-cuff statements following the speeches from the official list. Here the session's scripted material gives way to ungoverned speech. Replying to Herzog's statements, Jamil Baroody of Saudi Arabia found a timbre to match Run the Jewels's rough speech:

> Do not fool yourself, Mr. Herzog: there is no future for you and the people who believe that they are the chosen people of God . . . And you throw mud at Saudi Arabia because it is buying some defensive arms? Why do you not curse from this podium the country that is selling it the arms? Do you not dare, or is it Khazar duplicity? Tell us. You go and connive there in Washington and everywhere else . . .[29]

Living up to George H. W. Bush's description of him as an "unguided missile,"[30] Baroody avoided polite argument in favor of expressive vitriol that was unconcerned with advancing an agenda or achieving diplomatic agreement. Baroody's massed invective overwhelmed his speech. His words bristled with anger. Baroody was infamous for past performances in the General Assembly. In 1971 he threw a punch at the undersecretary for General Assembly affairs, Constantin Stavropolous (who deftly blocked the right cross), when Baroody was denied the opportunity to exercise (out of turn) his Right of Reply to a speech by the Israeli foreign minister, Abba Eban.

Baroody's outburst erupted in the hall, but the transcripts stripped away the nonverbal cues that could capture his anger more fully in the historical record. Returning to text, the UN's dramaturgy encourages purely instrumental speech and performance to keep at bay the bad feelings prompted by global injustice. "Simply put," Raymond Cohen asserts in his treatise on body language in diplomacy, *Theatre of Power*, "diplomacy rests on orderly dialogue."[31] An ideal of orderly dialogue, in which anger and other emotions evaporate, dominates UN performance, an ideal embodied in the institution's many textual lives. Texts contain and conserve the force of action on the world stage, drawing that force from live performance, and saving it to be redeployed at a later date.

The least spectacular work of diplomats consists in collectively negotiating the most potent of these texts. At the First Special Session on Disarmament, an Ad Hoc Committee was convened to finalize the Final Document, and to reconcile the competing verbal contributions of more than 100 delegations. In the drafts of the Final Document, disputed paragraphs, phrases, and words were enclosed by square brackets, a standard working method in UN negotiations. In her ethnography of negotiators at UN-sponsored conferences in the mid-1990s, Annelise Riles notes that

> the bracket was more than a representational marker of the lack of consensus among states. It was also a self-representational graphic entity, and the project of removing brackets engendered a commitment that was independent of [negotiators'] commitment to the conference's substantive political goals. For negotiators brackets were not asides, pauses, or explanatory devices but focal points to which attention was immediately drawn . . . The argument happened within the brackets.[32]

Brackets inhere drama in policy documents. They are a textual site of disagreement; an ephemeral space in which disputes are staged. They maintain an unstable performativity as "a point of potentially infinite internal expansion,"[33] a textual corollary to the infinite possibilities of the theatrical stage. They are theatrical in the affects they generate and in the energies that attend to them: the excited and embodied work of negotiators to eliminate them.

Within brackets, individual diplomats assert themselves and the states they represent. Within brackets, speech acts are staged as text acts. As the imperative to find consensus increases disagreements, no quibble proves too trivial for inclusion within brackets. Shades of meaning reveal their fine gradations where alternative words, phrases, sentences, paragraphs, and pages jostle alongside one another. Replete with brackets, draft documents at the UN reveal dialogic tendencies. Though diplomats' speeches brook no interruption, brackets break into the spaces between written words, allowing states to establish occupied territories on pages penned by others. On the page, brackets allow the United States to invade Russia or the Non-Aligned Movement to retaliate against the P-5. In brackets, a global bureaucracy stages its most dramatic conflicts.

I have reproduced a sample comparison of bracketed and final text from the Final Document in the extract below. These brackets represent interventions by Western and Eastern regional alliances, the Non-Aligned Movement, and individual efforts by France, Mexico, Pakistan, the United States, and the Soviet Union. The brackets are the hurdles to be overcome in a performance of policy-making, when the administrative engines of technocrats are pushed to peak efficiency. Henryk Jaroszek, the permanent representative of Poland to the UN, and chair of one of two Working Groups subsidiary to the Ad Hoc Committee, described the "debracketing venture" as "indispensable spade work" and "a vivisectional operation."[34] The draft Final Document featured not just brackets side by side, but brackets within brackets, and still more brackets within those. These brackets reiterate the dissensual character of the Special Session, staging disagreement and providing action with a textual locus at a site of potentially infinite expansion.

Comparison between the Final Document and draft text:

Paragraph 33 of the Final Document of the Tenth Special Session of the General Assembly:

> The establishment of nuclear-weapon-free zones on the basis of agreements or arrangements freely arrived at among the States of the zone concerned and the full compliance with those agreements or arrangements, thus ensuring that the zones are genuinely free from nuclear weapons, and respect for such zones by nuclear-weapon States constitute an important disarmament measure.

Corollary draft text on nuclear-weapon-free zones:

> [[Taking into account the distinction to be made between zones where nuclear weapons are an element of the general equilibrium and zones where its introduction would constitute a dramatic factor of imbalance] [The creation [where appropriate] of nuclear-weapon free zones constitutes one of the most effective disarmament measures that can [and should] be initiated by the non-nuclear-weapon states.] The nuclear-weapon states should undertake [wherever possible] [legally binding] obligations to respect the statutes of nuclear-weapon-free zones, [to refrain from contributing in any way to the performance in the territories forming part of the zone of acts which involve a violation of such statutes and to refrain from using or threatening to use nuclear weapons against the States included in the zone [provided that such zones are genuinely free of nuclear weapons, that relevant agreements contain no loopholes and fully correspond to the generally recognized norms of international law.]] [The establishment of zones of peace in various regions of the world can also contribute to the strengthening of security and promotion of friendly relations among states within such zones and international peace and security as a whole.]][35]

The expansive movement of the bracket chafes at the diplomat's desire for stability. At the 15th meeting of the Ad Hoc Committee, which was exhausted by the seemingly endless process of de-bracketing drafts, Hazem Nuseibeh, the permanent representative of Jordan to the United Nations, suggested that "the General Assembly might adopt the final draft document with the remaining brackets intact."[36] This idea did not find support. When the Ad Hoc Committee met again the next day, a bracketless draft had appeared. This was forwarded to the Plenary Meeting, which adopted it on June 30. At the adoption, nearly one-third of the states present exercised their right to give statements. Even before the ink was dry, the Final Document had prompted further live performance.

Among those forty-four speakers, some applauded the "miracle" (USA)[37] that consensus had been reached in spite of negotiations that often seemed "like the ritual death dance of dying elephants" (UK).[38] But others undercut the surface calm of "general satisfaction" (Nigeria)[39] with the session by noting "general reservations" (Brazil)[40] with the Final Document, especially the fact that "unexpectedly, the brackets disappeared last night as though someone had waved a magic wand" (El Salvador).[41] "In the marathon process of removing the square brackets . . . we must honestly admit that the content of the Final Document . . . has been deprived of much of its substance, clarity and determination" (Malta).[42] These speakers indicate the affective excesses generated by the elimination of brackets, by foreclosing on the potentially infinite expressivity of an incomplete policy document, the fact that it *could be* so substantive, so clear, so determined.

The Final Document intervened at the level of debate, establishing new disarmament machinery and new stages for new diplomatic theater. The Final Document established two venues: the Disarmament Commission and the Committee on Disarmament. Under the auspices of the General Assembly, the Disarmament Commission was to be a *deliberative* body in which all UN member states would participate to make recommendations on disarmament. Meanwhile, the Committee on Disarmament would be the primary *negotiating* forum on disarmament, where states would hash out their binding commitments. Here participation would be limited to the declared nuclear-weapon-states and between 32 and 35 other nations chosen by the General Assembly president, subject to review at regular intervals. Power demonstrated its intractability in the Final Document, in which meaningful work on disarmament remained the purview of the few.

The policies scripted in diplomatic theater are at once an invitation to and a constraint on future theatricality—they compose a metadrama to regulate diplomacy's stages. Sri Lanka's permanent representative to the United Nations, B. J. Fernando, summed up the views of the Non-Aligned Movement:

> It is not my wish on a day like this, after having joined in this consensus, to introduce a note of disharmony or a voice of dissent. But silence or a passive acquiescence in all that is contained in this document would amount to a departure from the principles to which the non-aligned movement has long adhered . . . that all states have

the right to participate in disarmament negotiations and the United Nations is the only body in which all States are represented.[43]

Diplomacy prefers consensus for the same reasons that it prefers orderly dialogue. In consensus, states coalesce around a particular image of the world. Consensus is also an event structured by theater: a live enactment presented for public consumption. Theater realizes consensus, but it also undermines the certainty that that consensus will have lasting effects. Consensus is only a moment in an ongoing and dynamic global drama, and is preceded and succeeded by the more common disagreements that divide states. Diplomacy turns to theater to negotiate between agreement and disagreement. This hunger for consensus is the final evidence that diplomacy cannot do without theater, and the fissures that are revealed when consensus is performed are the final evidence that diplomacy should not do without theater.

Paul Newman, a famous actor and a disarmament activist, attended the Special Session as part of a U.S. delegation headed by Vice President Walter Mondale (President Jimmy Carter stayed in Washington). Newman recognized that his presence likely had more to do with the capacity of his renown to attract media attention than it did with his extensive antinuclear campaigning. In an interview for *NBC News* given during the session, Leonard Probst asked him, "Paul, do you feel used? Do you feel the government is getting a story out by appointing you as delegate?" Newman responded, "I'm realistic about that. People listen to me for the wrong reasons, but if I can get their concentration on the issue, then I certainly don't care. My ego isn't hurt. I think the big job now is to make people aware of what's going on and get them hopping mad."[44] Newman's response limits his role at the conference to one of amplification, ignoring other radical effects that may attend to a film actor recast in diplomatic theater. The Carter administration used Newman's star power to broadcast its nonproliferation agenda, and Newman used that same power to propel his more radical disarmament goals. In either case, the effort fails to account for the fact that political and aesthetic performance can do more than get a spectator hopping mad.

What both efforts overlook is that Newman, as an artist and citizen, shares the potential for the unexpected and unanticipated found in the Assembly hall or the diplomats' brackets. Though he had established that Newman's relevance to the Special Session lay in his powers of star attraction, Probst also asked Newman about the source of his expertise on disarmament. Newman replied, "There are no disarmament or nuclear experts. There are only theorists. And no experts on nuclear war. . . . There is no expert who can confidently say, 'Well this is what the society is going to be like.' "[45] Newman invokes a citizen's dissensus against the performative constrictions of the nuclear disarmament debate. He is not applauding ignorance—he had extensive experience with the disarmament issue—only the markers of office and authority (performative conditions in their own right) that permit certain speech to be valued over the noise of the disenfranchised. As diplomacy oscillates between text and speech, it offers reminders that not only politicians and movie stars can take advantage of their nonexpert status to shift the trajectory of power. What is unexpected and unanticipated more often accompanies those who are unauthorized and displaced, the spectators and actors that institutions admit unwittingly.

Model

"I like to start with something that is not really jumping in your face, saying, 'Hey, I'm the most exciting person or thing,'" Imanuel Schipper related to me when I asked what had compelled him and his collaborators, the German theater-makers Rimini Protokoll, to stage their own version of the UN Framework Convention on Climate Change's 21st Conference of the Parties, a play they titled *World Climate Conference*.[46] He continued, suggesting that his own penchant for subjects that are not exciting at first glance might be shared by his collaborators, "Maybe that's one of the reasons why [our company is] called Rimini Protokoll and not Manhattan Transfer. Boring people go to Rimini [a resort town in Italy] to just lay down in the sun and have their holidays, but they do it every summer the same, those are the people that go to Rimini."[47]

Schipper has worked with Rimini Protokoll as a dramaturge for more than a decade. Rimini Protokoll is the collective label for the work of three self-described author-directors, Helgard Haug, Stefan Kaegi, and Daniel Wetzel, who have collaborated together since 2000. Rimini Protokoll's work spans spaces, genres, and media. Their best-known pieces, shows like *Call Cutta in a Box*, *Cargo Sofia-x*, *Remote X*, and *Situation Rooms* (to name a small representative sample), place audiences singly or in groups into more or less theatricalized encounters with the people, technology, and places that compose our everyday worlds. Audience members at a Rimini show may find themselves in conversation with a call center worker half a world away, rumbling down the streets of a European capital in a cargo truck, walking the avenues of a global metropolis directed by a synthetic voice received via headphones, or wandering a building-sized film set following a trail indicated by a small tablet computer. If this survey indicates that the group's dramaturgy is centrally interested in technology, it is no less interested in text.

In conducting research for *World Climate Conference*, Schipper was initially attracted by the volume of documents produced for and by the UN. Finding his way to the website of the UN Framework Convention on Climate Change (UNFCCC), "a huge web presence with a huge documentation of all the conferences and meetings and agendas and every transcript and everything," he marveled, "I had never seen such a thing, a thing so well documented like that." At the heart of Rimini Protokoll's working method lies the search for "protocols"—units of behavior, sentence structures, ways of thinking, or, as Schipper defines them, "the nodes of something that has happened"—that will form the basis for the production and its dramaturgy. Schipper and Rimini Protokoll dug through the UNFCCC's archives "to see if there was some kind of protocol that we could restage . . . and it was so unbelievably boring and so unbelievably hard to read . . . And then we found in the text, in the resolutions, these brackets."

To Schipper, the brackets were an artifact of a massive human drama, the evidence and by-product of a theater of states appearing in conferences and summits. "We were starting to think that this could be something for the play, because it was really interesting: the whole [conference] with 13,000 persons is in fact just to make a text." To build their play, Rimini Protokoll seized on the theatricality of collective action as a textual and performative problem— "it was a question of the text, how to produce a text in common"—and identified that problem with their own working methods: "As Rimini we do that often, we work on Google [Documents] at the same time or different times, but on the same thing, and sometimes you don't know who changed what . . . Collectively writing one text is an interesting thing." The spectators at *World Climate Conference* may not be asked to write or debate language at the show, but their experience is configured at each moment by a peculiar relationship to text.

Upon arriving at the Deutsches Schauspielhaus in Hamburg (where *World Climate Conference* played periodically between November 2014 and December 2015), each audience member was given a red lanyard from which hung a small booklet printed with the flag and name of one of the 196 nations that were parties to the UNFCCC.[48] Assigned to delegations (diplomas in hand), the spectators were asked to inhabit that nation as a role, and spent much of the evening learning the predicted consequences of climate change for their nation. The nineteen-page booklet was rife with data: maps to locate the nation in its region, and figures on land use, current climatological conditions, population, industry, gross domestic product, energy use, and greenhouse gas emissions. During an introductory session set in the main hall of the Schauspielhaus, the delegations became acquainted with their members, were oriented toward the data in their booklets, and were given their charge for the day: to commit their nation to explicit carbon emissions reductions by 2020 and 2050.

Following the initial forty-minute plenary session, the delegations and groups of delegations split apart to engage with different experts. Some stayed in the main hall for a session titled "Two Degree Limit," a reference to a target that is often debated in climate negotiations, whether to keep global temperatures from rising more or less than 2 degrees Celsius (3.6 degrees Fahrenheit) above pre-industrial levels. In the session, the meteorologist and climate negotiator Rosemarie Benndorf introduced delegates to the brackets that had captivated me, Schipper, and the scholars before us. She spoke at a lectern near the edge of the stage, with curtains drawn behind her. Above her a one-story-tall projection of a bracketed sentence indicated international disagreement over emissions targets and mitigation efforts. "The negotiation papers are the product of a lengthy and arduous collaboration between representatives from all countries—that's all of you," she told the assembled delegates.

Other groups found their way to scenes set in and around the Schauspielhaus: in its café, on board a bus zooming around the neighborhood, and elsewhere. Backstage, the delegations from Scandinavian countries sat in a few rows of raked seating while the physicist Dr. Bernd Hezel paced in front of them, presenting from a few notecards. Benndorf and Hezel, like most of the performers in *World Climate Conference*, are not professional actors who have taken on roles, but are scientists and diplomats performing their real expertise filtered through the theatrical designs and dramaturgical efforts of Rimini Protokoll. Where Paul Newman's interview with *NBC News* had been prefaced in print by the warning that he spoke not "as an 'expert' but . . . express[ed] compelling common sense about the nuclear predicament,"[49] Rimini Protokoll takes an alternate tack, mobilizing experts defined by their expertise into encounters with audiences who are "Experts of the Everyday,"[50] calling on all for speech and action by virtue of their expert status.

"The climate problem is a hard nut to crack," Hezel told his group. "The whole world needs to be involved. Here, for example, is Africa." He gestured to the remainder of the space, where a section of the stage slowly rotated. More spectators, cast as delegates from African nations, lay on cots arranged in concentric circles on the revolving stage. At their center, another expert loomed over them, standing atop a raised, telescoping, hydraulic lift. "And we had just gotten used to being the heroes of the Anthropocene," Hezel continued, extending his arms in a grand gesture to emphasize his point. Bright, warm lights came up on the rotating cots, illuminating the prone, spinning delegates, who wore headphones to listen to the man perched above them. Kenneth Gbandi, the president of the Germany Chapter of the Nigerians in Diaspora Organization Europe, explained what was in store for the continent in the coming years: "Africa will get hotter and hotter." Alongside steam and rain effects, he implored his charges not to sell their nations short: "For you as an African politician, there can be no question, because you are vital for the global community." Rimini Protokoll's artistry lies in dynamizing the encounter between an audience and an individual marked by policy experience, putting the transmissions that drive interstate political machinery under a theatrical microscope.

In these scenes, stage theatricality and the theatricality of conferencing take over from the theatricality of transcripts. In our conversation, Schipper enumerated the details that caught his eye:

> As the dramaturge of the work, I was interested in the question, "What is a conference?" And what is the outcome of a conference, and what does it bring, and how does it work? How is the conference? What is the plan of the structure of a conference? They are so huge and there are so many things going on at the same time. And what is in the places that we can see and what is outside of those places—in the ways, in the doorways, in the places where you get food? Where is the coffee machine?

Rimini Protokoll's *World Climate Conference* paid attention to the details of the UNFCCC's Conference of Parties. Rimini Protokoll used every part of the Deutsches Schauspielhaus to capture the multi-sited and diffuse mise-en-scène of international summitry. As the play entered its second hour, each delegation was allotted time for bilateral discussions with one other delegation, and the small groups filled the halls, loges, and galleries of the Schauspielhaus, Germany's largest capacity theater. Filling these spaces, and implying their corollaries in the auditoriums, hallways, and foyers of international institutions, points to the conceptual figure that guided Rimini Protokoll: that their production would be a "model."

Schipper described the discussions that led the collaborators to settle on the figure of the model: "With this show especially [we asked], are we going to do a reenactment? That is not possible. Are we going to do a simulation, like we do like it was? Are we actually going to do a better climate conference? We decided that we did not want to do a better one, we did not want to do a reenactment." In their model, Rimini Protokoll sought a relationship between performance and the real that was not prefigured by extant conceptions of where and how theater could impact political and institutional structures. Rimini Protokoll eschewed the figure of reenactment that drives so much documentary theater, the figure of simulation that informs varieties of immersive and interactive theater, and the utopian motivations of those who make theater for social justice—this was no rehearsal for the revolution.

Rimini Protokoll was also uninterested in making audiences empathize with the plight of our planet and its people, or with amplifying a specific environmental policy message. Schipper elaborated:

> So what does it mean, a model? A model is something like the original, but in a different size. It is somehow like the original, but with slightly different rules. It has in some parts the same rules and in some parts other rules. It can be done without the original people, it can be done without the original time frame. And this model, modeling an event of that size, gives some feelings, or in some parts there will be some emotions, some sensations transported that could also be at the [real Climate Conference].

Rimini Protokoll's model Climate Conference, a scene of diplomatic theater, provides the mechanisms that transmit energies between the UNFCCC Conference of the Parties and the audiences in Hamburg. This affective transmission is not an empathetic transmission, it is the circulation of political will as a material force manifested by art or by politics. Schipper estimates that more than 10,000 audience members participated in the *World Climate Conference* model over the course of its run, a reasonable approximation given the Deutsches Schauspielhaus's 1,200-seat capacity. Thus, if the model condensed the human magnitude of the UNFCCC Conference of the Parties on any given night, it approximated its contours when taken as a whole: more than 10,000 people at work on a single text, seeking a collective response to a global existential crisis. As these audiences navigated between the aesthetic rules of the model and the structures of diplomatic negotiation, they inhabited previously ignored spaces where art and politics meet.

Jacques Rancière asserts that "politics plays itself out in the theatrical paradigm as the relationship between the stage and the audience, as meaning produced by the actor's body, as games of proximity or distance."[51] *World Climate Conference* integrates the spirit of this observation into its structures in a manner that disavows the expressly political content of the show. Pressed on the politics of his model, Schipper said: "We do not intend to have an effect on politics. Normally, Rimini does not intend to have an effect on politics in or through their plays or their shows." The model is neither agitprop nor *Lehrstücke* (i.e., "teaching-plays"); though Schipper admitted that audiences could learn much through the program, the purpose was not to raise consciousness or reform political subjectivities. In video documentation of the performance, the spectators appear serious and engaged during their brief bilateral meetings near the evening's end. The audience members pore over the data in their booklets, share suggestions, and laugh at the horse-trading they are occasionally reduced to.

Though spectators were brought into close proximity with Rimini's stage, this was also not a democratic exercise:

> I think that we as Rimini are not so much interested . . . in the personal opinions of the audience. We are interested in how they would act if they were Zimbabwe, but we are not interested in the opinion of Peter . . . we are not there to debate, . . . we want to see what would you do if you were Zimbabwe.

If politics evaporates (as a conceptual category) in *World Climate Conference*, it does so by virtue of Rimini Protokoll's efforts to collapse together the aesthetic and political valences of representation. Insofar as Rancière's observation quoted earlier hinges on the actor's body that creates meaning, the audience member who is asked to represent Zimbabwe in both a political and an aesthetic sense becomes a new source of meaning on the world stage, an infinitely expressive nonexpert (or at least one whose everyday expertise is not perfectly matched to the task of being Zimbabwe) whose unanticipated signification may shift policy.

Thinking about how to do things with art involves a broader field of art and politics than even Rancière admits when he speaks of games of proximity and distance. If politics and art attach to one another in the distance between stage and spectator, efforts to impact policy must begin from a detailed understanding of how art and politics work together to emplace a spectator in the world. Dramaturgical analysis of a theater of states can reveal the spectatorial and theatrical terms that construct subjects on the world stage, and provide those subjects with the conceptual tools to renegotiate their place in global spectacle. In some ways, *World Climate Conference* returns my discussion to the first performance discussed in this book, Bennett Miller's *Dachshund UN*. Though either production could easily be explicated as a reflection (parodic or otherwise) of the institution it represents, both become more meaningful when viewed in light of their capacity to expand or condense the affective and energetic fields that international institutions, states, and regimes require to realize their goals.

World Climate Conference was integrated with its subject in key ways—if it reproduced some of the energies of the UNFCCC Conference of the Parties, it also spoke to and heard from its analogue when possible. During performances held in the first two weeks of December 2014, the audiences in Hamburg received live updates via Skype from two experts on the ground in Lima, Peru (where the 20th Conference of the Parties was in session): the head of an NGO working to influence negotiations, and a journalist reporting on them. In these scenes, the energies generated in Hamburg interfaced with those circulating in the institutional space in Lima. In video documentation of the show, a member of Rimini Protokoll in Germany asked the journalist in Lima what had been accomplished so far. "Well," the journalist responded, "nothing has happened here at all besides a lot of talk."

Similar complaints were leveled at the Special Session on Disarmament. An intolerance of verbosity inhabits certain critiques of the ICC. And Muammar Qaddafi was lambasted for being long-winded. Opposing speech with action in order to denigrate internationalism is quite common, but to do so refuses the central role that artists play in global governance. The UN's texts attest that action on the world stage must also be speech—like theater, it often proceeds from performance to written word, and must resolve into new performances in turn.

As the delegates filed back into the main hall for a closing plenary session at the end of *World Climate Conference*, scenes of protests at previous Conferences of the Parties played on the screen behind the podium. "Less talk! More action!" men and women chanted in Doha (Qatar) in 2012. The urgency of activism contrasted with the pragmatic playing that audiences had experienced throughout the evening. The scenes coincided with a final call to action, as delegations were asked to submit their commitments to be compiled together. Schipper points out that "the time is too short for everything. It is too short, you're always too late, the information is too much, so this whole flow of information and the necessity of time . . . the time is not enough to solve it, which is actually also the problem of climate change anyway." In the video documentation of the show, Schipper appeared onstage at the show's end to announce the results of the conference, an aggregation of the Declarations of Intent submitted by each audience delegation. Present on stage, the dramaturge eliminated brackets to finalize a document that had been collectively written, transcribing the conference's efforts to script the future actions of states and individuals. Schipper's turn on stage underscored the significance of dramaturgy to politics.

Unique dramaturgical challenges confront a theater company that is dedicated to staging experts and not actors, challenges that revisit the occasional aversion between theater and politics. According to Schipper, "because the Schauspielhaus has this big and very famous ensemble of very good actors, [they asked], Could you not use our actors?" Only one professional actor appeared in the play, Ute Hannig, who told the audience: "I stand before you not as an expert but as a concerned citizen. I am one of the billions of people around the world who want to solve our climate crisis. As an actress, I pretend for a living. I play fictitious characters often solving fictitious problems." Audience members representing Saudi Arabia nodded in agreement with her call to action, as behind her a video projection of her speech slowly faded into footage of Leonardo DiCaprio at the General Assembly dais. Hannig revealed her dissembling: "I was just pretending that the speech was mine; it was actually delivered by my colleague Leonardo DiCaprio at a UN Summit." To the problem of an actor among their experts, Schipper found a solution in the UN webcast, as he watched "hours and hours" of the webcast from the UN's 2014 Climate Summit before landing on DiCaprio's speech. I feel a particular kinship for Schipper, having watched the UN's broadcasts in a similar mode for years: looking for their unique theatricality, for performances that disrupt, displace, and disconcert.

World Climate Conference investigates the UN's reliance on DiCaprio as a tool to amplify its message. Though DiCaprio excoriated the delegates assembled in 2014 for their lack of action on climate change, he remained deeply imbricated in their spectacle, and was part and parcel of a political dispute that plays out in theatrical modes. DiCaprio's appearance at the UN and his reappearance in Hamburg establishes and then estranges the emotional dimensions of international responses to climate change. In Schipper's words, DiCaprio appeared at the UN to exert "emotional pressure"—a limited and limiting way to conceive of the theatricality of international relations. *World Climate Conference* interrogates this political and theatrical mechanism, which is a mainstay of conventional thought on the relationship between art and policy. Schipper continued:

> This is something that I think is always a theme of the shows for Rimini Protokoll. Why do we not talk about actors? Actors are mainly professionals for emotions. But do we really want to present emotions on stage? No . . . But when is it good to have professionals for emotions? . . . How can they be used? Maybe they can be used in politics.

Schipper's response does not suggest either that politicians should become more practiced at performing emotions, or that performance can produce a more empathetic politics. Rather, he acknowledges the degree to which aesthetics and politics have each prefigured the other, in a finely woven coupling that can be mined by artists, activists, and spectators.

Hannig doubles DiCaprio, who in function reiterates Newman. Political performance is doubled in its transcript and becomes reiterated in new performances. Rimini Protokoll models the UNFCCC's 21st Conference of the Parties, and Bennett Miller models the Human Rights Council. Run the Jewels, Edward Allen Bernero, and David Hare each reconstruct the architecture of international institutions. Psy, Pharrell, Karen Sunde, *Battlestar Galactica*, the Viva Vox Choir, and Shakespeare's Globe invade institutional spaces. *Fun Home* and *Ruined* invite the diplomats to Broadway. In each case, the encounter between arts and politics proves as material and tangible as it is affective. There is action here, the sort of action concretized by policy documents that provide malleable and theatrical points of entry into global political discourses. Heads of state, diplomats, artists, activists, and citizens all stitch together culture and policy as spectators, receiving and transmitting the energies that generate constituent power and drive political action. We feel and act at the theatrical interface between international institutions and our lived experiences. These experiences vary widely—we may be a witness from the Democratic Republic of Congo, a Dutch legal clerk, the permanent representative of Saudi Arabia to the United Nations, an American movie star, a German dramaturge, or a spectator named Peter asked to play Zimbabwe—but the structures that assign us each differential powers of speech and action become suspended in a theater of states.

In a theater of states, policy reveals its malleability as it travels between performance and text. For the international institutions that respond to global crises, collective action is often born of collective writing, a collaborative process that holds consensus and disagreement in tension with one another. With a dramaturgical eye, one can reopen the spaces foreclosed by consensus to see the disagreements performed in bodies or brackets. In the transit from page to stage (and on from there), authorship and authority are challenged by a theatrical process which asserts that the work of making meaning from global events rests as much with the world's spectators as with any others.

Figure 8. Nikki R. Haley, the permanent representative of the U.S. to the UN, speaks to journalists before presenting her credentials to Secretary-General António Guterres, on January 27, 2017. UN Photo by Mark Garten.

Epilogue

◆

"On Notice" and "Taking Names"

On March 7, 2016, the U.S. mission to the United Nations (US-UN) hosted a dinner for the Foundation for Art and Preservation in Embassies: "An Evening Celebrating Alexander Hamilton." Ambassador Samantha Power gave introductory remarks:

> It is rare that I get to speak to Grammy and Tony award winners—not too many of those across the street [at UN headquarters]. So let me just start by noting that I too am a musician. I sing in a band of other UN Ambassadors called "UN Rocks." The Korean Ambassador plays the drums—this is not a joke, it's real life; the Thai Ambassador plays the bass; the Serbian and Danish ambassadors play the electric guitars; and the ambassador from Tonga plays the keyboard. And I wanted to take this opportunity to announce that I have some availability for gigs starting around January 20th, 2017. In case anybody is interested.[1]

Here, some months before the end of her tenure at the UN, Power looked ahead to her transition back into the role of a citizen spectator. She highlighted the collaborative musicking that had gone hand in hand with her statecraft, a practice that may have been fun, but was not a joke at all. The bulk of this study was undertaken during Barack Obama's two terms as president of the United States, a period of nominal internationalism and engagement with international institutions that was bookended by George W. Bush's efforts to spread democracy with war and Donald Trump's efforts to put America first.

On January 27, 2017, Ambassador Nikki Haley, Power's successor, arrived at Turtle Bay. She spoke to the press in the lobby of the Secretariat building, on her way to deliver her credentials to Secretary-General António Guterres, who had succeeded Ban Ki-moon in the position just a month earlier (figure 8). Turning left and right, smiling cheerfully as the cameras flashed, she announced:

> There is a new US-UN . . . You are going to see a change in the way we do business. . . . Our goal with the administration is to show value

159

at the UN, and the way that we'll show value is to show our strength, show our voice, have the backs of our allies, and make sure that our allies have our back, as well. For those who don't have our back, we're taking names.[2]

Haley emphasized what her performance would show and what her audience would see, and then made a promise to the United States' allies and a threat to the United States' enemies. Though there was a new US-UN, its dramaturgy was not so different from that of its predecessors.

When North Korea tested an intercontinental ballistic missile in July 2017, she told the council: "Time is short. Action is required. The world is on notice." Her succinct declarative statements built urgency from live performance.[3]

In December 2017, with the General Assembly set to adopt a resolution opposing President Donald Trump's order to move the U.S. embassy in Israel to Jerusalem, Haley told her colleagues: "America will put our embassy in Jerusalem . . . No vote in the United Nations will make any difference on that. But this vote will make a difference on how Americans look at the UN and on how we look at countries who disrespect us in the UN. And this vote will be remembered."[4] While both denying and affirming the resolution's significance in adjacent gestures, she harnessed it to a collective memory that would be maintained only in performance.

As Iran violently repressed protests in Tehran in January 2018, the United States requested an emergency meeting of the Security Council. There Haley appealed to fundamental human rights, to the UN's ideals, and to our collective responsibility to heed the cry of the oppressed:

> Once again, the people of Iran are rising up. They are asking for something that no government can legitimately deny them: their human rights and fundamental freedoms. They are calling out, "Think of us." If the founding principles of this institution mean anything, we will not only hear their cry, we will finally answer it. The Iranian regime is now on notice. The world will be watching what you do.[5]

Haley restaged and re-voiced real and imagined individuals at hemispheric distances to hail a set of spectators into alignment around Iran in an effort to undo a diplomatic promise: the Joint Comprehensive Plan of Action agreed to by Iran, the permanent members of the Security Council, and Germany in 2015, an agreement which effectively halted Iran's efforts to develop fissionable materials for use in atom bombs.

There are, of course, differences between Haley's US-UN and Power's US-UN, but to overinvest in them would risk losing sight of the fact that the work of diplomats at an international institution still rests in the dramaturgy they conduct. We risk dismissing Haley's threats as bluster, her promises as empty, and her grandstanding as a distraction; as so much sound and fury to stand in for the real work of politics happening elsewhere, behind closed doors, in the halls of power, in global capitals. Politics is not usefully understood as such a sleight of hand. Rather, those places where a diplomat makes a verbal attack, tears up a written document, or redeploys a platitude on the world stage are as much the location of politics as is the negotiating table.

In these scenes of diplomatic theater, Haley deploys and manages the eyes and ears of others, placing her spectators, and placing us. She tells stories and modifies them as necessary to keep her audience in place. She exercises power in speech that is performed live to stratify the world, in an effort to maintain a global hierarchy that keeps the United States at its pinnacle. She puts her rivals on notice, conflating threat, surveillance, and attention, and sets to work taking names, an embodied, textual practice aimed at a historical record. I am not treating her idioms too literally. In these repeated metaphors, Haley reveals that she knows the dramaturgy of international institutions well.

Haley is a twofold spectator: she is not just a diplomat who notices and takes names, but is also an engaged cultural consumer. On Twitter she has expressed both her love for FX's thriller about Russian spies in the United States, *The Americans*,[6] and her disdain for the appearance of the anti-Trump exposé, *Fire and Fury*, at the Grammy Awards ceremony.[7] Where she watches, we should be reminded that theater is also an interface where artists, activists, and citizens act on politics. Though we may not be capable of perceiving in an instant the universe of forces that bear on the experience of politics in the present, political action must begin from our sensitive acknowledgment that art and politics share the field on which we watch and perform. On such a shared field, the political uses of art will extend beyond intersubjective empathy, mass protest, and dystopian visions to encompass theatrical models, historical revisions, and spectators displaced. Theater is more than a tool, it is an interface with the shared field of political and aesthetic action that reveals the machinations of power to subjects who watch and act on the world stage.

Diplomatic theater is our point of entry, where we press back using the images, sounds, and texts produced by diplomats. In identifying scenes of diplomatic theater we may be displaced, we may refuse to be interpellated by hegemons, we may rewrite their scripts. The dramaturgy of international institutions invites the insurrections of its spectators.

We are also on notice; we are also taking names.

NOTES

Introduction

1. Beverley Knowles, "Fierce Festival, Bennett Miller, Dachshund U.N.," This Is Tomorrow, April 2, 2012, http://www.thisistomorrow.info/viewArticle.aspx?artId=1223.
2. Katie McMillan, "Out of the Doghouse: Katie McMillan on Dachshund UN," *Harbourfront Centre Blog*, March 4, 2013, http://www.harbourfrontcentre.com/blog/2013/03/katie-mcmillan-discusses-dachshund-un/.
3. Pat Donnelly, "FTA Calls Off the Dogs Today but Nella Tempesta Storms On," MontrealGazette.com, May 25, 2013, http://blogs.montrealgazette.com/2013/05/25/fta-calls-off-the-dogs-today-but-nella-tempesta-storms-on/.
4. Now Magazine (@nowtoronto), "Hey turns out the #DaschundUN is totally ineffective and has no consequent bearing on international law . . . just like the real UN! #rimshot," Twitter, March 3, 2013, 3:31 p.m., https://twitter.com/nowtoronto/status/308313724433862656.
5. Kelly Stone, "News—Dachshunds for World Peace," Museum of Contemporary Art Australia, May 30, 2012, http://www.mca.com.au/news/2012/05/30/dachshunds-world-peace/.
6. J. Kelly Nestruck, "Why Man's Best Friend Is the Ultimate Performance Artist," *The Globe and Mail*, February 26, 2013, http://www.theglobeandmail.com/arts/theatre-and-performance/why-mans-best-friend-is-the-ultimate-performance-artist/article9094230/.
7. Vitaly Churkin, "SC President, Vitaly I. Churkin (Russian Federation) on Central African Republic (CAR), Syria—Security Council Media Stakeout (20 March 2013)," United Nations Webcast streaming video, 17:58, March 20, 2013, http://webtv.un.org/search/sc-president-vitaly-i.-churkin-russian-federation-on-central-african-republic-car-syria-security-council-media-stakeout-20-march-2013/2240819371001.
8. Gérard Araud, "Gérard Araud (France) and Philip Parham (United Kingdom) on Syria—Security Council Media Stakeout (20 March 2013)," United Nations Webcast streaming video, 10:10, March 20, 2013, http://webtv.un.org/search/g%C3%A9rard-araud-france-and-philip-parham-united-kingdom-on-syria-security-council-media-stakeout-20-march-2013/2240792345001.
9. For an analysis of the role that chemical weapons played in diplomatic responses to the Syrian Civil War, see Michelle Bentley, *Syria and the Chemical Weapons Taboo* (Manchester, Eng.: Manchester University Press, 2016).
10. For a concise history of the UN's founding, see Jean E. Krasno, "Founding the United Nations: An Evolutionary Process," in *The United Nations: Confronting the Challenges of a Global Society*, ed. Jean E. Krasno (Boulder, Colo.: Lynne Rienner, 2004), 19–45.

11. United Nations, Charter of the United Nations, June 26, 1945, Article 4, http://www.un.org/en/documents/charter/.

12. United Nations, "Growth in United Nations Membership, 1945–Present," 2018, http://www.un.org/en/sections/member-states/growth-united-nations-membership-1945-present/.

13. United Nations, Charter, "Preamble."

14. Krasno, "Founding the United Nations," 26.

15. The authors of *The United Nations and Changing World Politics* argue that "the veto saved the organization from wrecking itself in operations against its most powerful members." Thomas George Weiss, David P. Forsythe, Roger A. Coate, and Kelly-Kate Pease, *The United Nations and Changing World Politics*, 5th ed. (Boulder, Colo.: Westview, 2007), 8.

16. Mark Mazower writes, "One can view the Charter and especially its preamble, along with the Universal Declaration on Human Rights and the Genocide Convention, as testifying to the foundational imperatives of the new world order established in the fight against Nazism. Or one can read them as promissory notes that the UN's founders never intended to be cashed." Mark Mazower, *No Enchanted Palace: The End of Empire and the Ideological Origins of the United Nations* (Princeton, N.J.: Princeton University Press, 2009), 8.

17. Inis L. Claude, Jr., *The Changing United Nations* (New York: Random House, 1967), 3.

18. United Nations, Charter.

19. Alex J. Bellamy and Paul D. Williams with Stuart Griffin, *Understanding Peacekeeping*, 2nd ed. (Cambridge: Polity, 2010), 82–83.

20. See Weiss et al., *Changing World Politics*, 27–36; and Bellamy et al., *Understanding Peacekeeping*, 81–88.

21. Krasno, "Founding the United Nations," 38.

22. Benjamin Rivlin, "The UN Secretary-Generalship at Fifty," in *The United Nations in the New World Order: The World Organization at Fifty*, ed. Dimitris Bourantonis and Jarrod Weiner (New York: St. Martin's Press, 1995), 87.

23. I take these numbers from figures 2.1 and 3.1 of Weiss et al., *Changing World Politics*, 35, 47.

24. Thomas G. Weiss, Tatiana Carayannis, Louis Emmerij, and Richard Jolly, *UN Voices: The Struggle for Development and Social Justice* (Bloomington: Indiana University Press, 2005), 281.

25. Weiss et al., *Changing World Politics*, 100.

26. This structure is implicit in a question occasionally posed of the UN: whether it is an actor in its own right, or a framework that facilitates the acts of the independent states that engage it. "The UN is most fundamentally an intergovernmental organization in which key decisions are made by governments representing states. . . . However, the UN is also a broad and complex system of policymaking and administration in which some decisions are made by individuals who are not instructed by states." Weiss et al., *Changing World Politics*, lii.

27. United Nations, Charter, Article 24.

28. See Cathy Turner and Synne Behrndt, *Dramaturgy and Performance*, rev. ed. (New York: Palgrave Macmillan, 2016), for a comprehensive overview of the history and practice of dramaturgy in the performing arts.

29. Jacques Rancière, *The Politics of Aesthetics: The Distribution of the Sensible*, trans. Gabriel Rockhill (London: Continuum, 2004), 13.

30. See Richard Schechner, *Performance Theory* (New York: Routledge, 1988); Victor Turner, *From Ritual to Theatre: The Human Seriousness of Play* (New York: PAJ Publications, 1982); and Victor Turner, *On the Edge of the Bush: Anthropology as Experience* (Tucson: University of Arizona Press, 1985).

31. Schechner, *Performance Theory*, 214–15.

32. As Turner recognized, the figure of the infinity loop is overly "equilibrist" (Turner, *From Ritual to Theatre*, 74) and suggests that the processes it maps are "endless" and non-responsive to external stimuli (Turner, *On the Edge of the Bush*, 301). Turner sought to revise the loop with a spiraling figure that would interpellate bystanders: "philosophers feed their work into the spiraling process; poets feed their poems into it; politicians feed their acts into it; and so on" (ibid., 301).

33. See Tracy C. Davis, "Theatricality and Civil Society," in *Theatricality*, ed. Tracy C. Davis and Thomas Postlewait (New York: Cambridge University Press, 2003), 127–55.

34. Ibid., 149.

35. Ibid., 147.

36. Ibid., 153, emphasis added.

37. Samuel Weber, *Theatricality as Medium* (New York: Fordham University Press, 2004), 68.

38. Jenny Edkins and Adrian Kear, introduction to *International Politics and Performance: Critical Aesthetics and Creative Practice*, ed. Jenny Edkins and Adrian Kear (London: Routledge, 2013), 8.

39. See, for example, Charlotte M. Canning's study of the U.S. State Department's cultural programming in the twentieth century: *On the Performance Front: U.S. Theatre and Internationalism* (London: Palgrave Macmillan, 2015); or Wendy S. Hesford's study of the aesthetics deployed by humanitarian nongovernmental organizations: *Spectacular Rhetorics: Human Rights Visions, Recognitions, Feminisms* (Durham, N.C.: Duke University Press, 2011).

40. See James C. Scott, *Seeing like a State: How Certain Schemes to Improve the Human Condition Have Failed* (New Haven, Conn.: Yale University Press, 1998); and Jeffrey Edward Green, *The Eyes of the People: Democracy in an Age of Spectatorship* (Oxford: Oxford University Press, 2010). See also James Der Derian, *Virtuous War: Mapping the Military-Industrial-Media-Entertainment Network*, 2nd ed. (New York: Routledge, 2009), for another map of the interconnections between politics and culture, and the spectators inhabiting there.

41. Green, *The Eyes of the People*, 8.

42. Green outlines a theory of citizen spectatorship and a plebiscitarian ethics that "supplies an ethical perspective to the passive spectator, supplements the ethical perspective of the active partisan and supplants the ethical perspective of the democrat committed to popular sovereignty" (ibid., 31).

43. I elaborate this point in James R. Ball III, "The Live Archive of the World Stage: Engagement and Spectatorship in the United Nations Webcast," *e-Misférica* 9, nos. 1 and 2, http://hemisphericinstitute.org/hemi/en/e-misferica-91/ball.

44. For one similar method, see Canning, *On the Performance Front*, 7. Canning describes her method as dramaturgical to capture the ways she stages the past using varied archival materials and transmits it to an audience.

45. See, for example, Jacques Rancière, *The Emancipated Spectator*, trans. Gregory Elliott (London: Verso, 2009).

Chapter 1

1. Dominic Dromgoole, Ladi Emeruwa, Miranda Foster, Rawiri Paratene, and Iona Thomas, "The Globe Theatre—Press Conference," United Nations Webcast, streaming video, 30:09, August 4, 2014, http://webtv.un.org/search/the-globe-theatre-press-conference/3712745997001.

2. Quoted in Colum Lynch, "Exclusive: Russia Vetoes House of Cards," *Foreign Policy*, July 2, 2014, http://foreignpolicy.com/2014/07/02/exclusive-russia-vetoes-house-of-cards/.

3. Quoted ibid.

4. Dromgoole et. al., "The Globe Theatre—Press Conference."

5. Ibid.

6. Graham Holderness and Bryan Loughrey, "Arabesque: Shakespeare and Globalization," *Essays and Studies* 59 (2006): 24.

7. To be entirely fair to Dromgoole and his collaborators, the international conversation to which he referred included Shakespeare's Globe's original Globe to Globe festival, in 2012, where each of Shakespeare's thirty-six plays was performed in London by ensembles drawn from around the world, including areas of conflict like Palestine and Afghanistan. Dromgoole's unwillingness to recognize the soft power project in which he participated may stem from his sense that the force he and his artists projected into the world was reciprocal to the gesture of receiving global players at home.

8. William Shakespeare, *Hamlet*, ed. Harold Jenkins (London: Arden Shakespeare, 1982), 3.2.181–82. References are to act, scene, and line.

9. Mary Douglas, *How Institutions Think* (Syracuse, N.Y.: Syracuse University Press, 1986), 69.

10. Security Council Report, "Security Council Working Methods: A Tale of Two Councils?" Special Research Report, March 25, 2014, 12, http://www.securitycouncilreport.org/special-research-report/security-council-working-methods-a-tale-of-two-councils.php.

11. Ibid.

12. James Hammersmith, "Hamlet and the Myth of Memory," *ELH* 45, no. 4 (1978): 603–4, emphasis in original.

13. Dromgoole et al., "The Globe Theatre—Press Conference."

14. Colin Powell, "Iraqi Weapons Compliance Debate," *C-Span*, February 5, 2003, streaming video, 3:35:44, https://www.c-span.org/video/?174942-1/iraqi-weapons-compliance-debate. Quoting UN Security Council, "The Situation between Iraq and Kuwait," S/PV.4692 (January 27, 2003), 3, 10, http://www.un.org/Docs/journal/asp/ws.asp?m=S/PV.4692.

15. Hans Blix, *Disarming Iraq* (New York: Pantheon Books, 2004), 153.

16. Powell, "Iraqi Weapons Compliance Debate."

17. Ibid.

18. Carol Martin notes that "inherent in the very idea of documentary is an anxiety about truth and authenticity." Carol Martin, "Introduction: Dramaturgy of the Real," in *Dramaturgy of the Real on the World Stage*, ed. Carol Martin (London: Palgrave Macmillan, 2010), 1. The essays collected by Martin elaborate

the variety of ways in which documentary theater-makers investigate truth and its construction.

19. Powell, "Iraqi Weapons Compliance Debate." Here, Powell's live performance diverged significantly from the transcript of the session published by the UN, which made no mention of Powell's prop or his references to the 2001 anthrax attacks on the U.S. Senate. The UN's published transcripts are often based on texts provided by the speaker and his or her embassy. See UN Security Council, "The Situation between Iraq and Kuwait," S/PV.4701 (February 5, 2003), http://www.un.org/Depts/dhl/resguide/scact2003.htm.

20. The Daily Show, "Dude Is Crazy," *The Daily Show with John Stewart*, February 5, 2003, streaming video, 1:58, http://www.cc.com/video-clips/04ik13/the-daily-show-with-jon-stewart-dude-is-crazy.

21. See Iraq Body Count, http://www.iraqbodycount.org.

22. Ngũgĩ Wa Thiong'o, *Penpoints, Gunpoints, and Dreams: Towards a Critical Theory of the Arts and the State in Africa* (Oxford: Clarendon, 1998), 37.

23. David Hare, *Stuff Happens* (London: Faber and Faber, 2004), [vi].

24. June Thomas, "Bad Theatre Happens: The Problem with David Hare's Iraq Play," Slate, April 14, 2006, http://www.slate.com/articles/news_and_politics/theater/2006/04/bad_theater_happens.html.

25. Hare, *Stuff Happens*, 15.

26. Ibid., 59.

27. Ibid., 92.

28. Ibid., 120.

29. UN Security Council, S/PV.4701, 20.

30. Hare, *Stuff Happens*, [vi].

31. Ibid., 105–6.

32. Ibid., 107.

33. Ibid., 106.

34. See Blix, *Disarming Iraq*, 152–56.

35. ABC News, "Colin Powell on Iraq, Race, and Hurricane Relief," *ABC 20/20*, September 8, 2005, http://abcnews.go.com/2020/Politics/story?id=1105979&page=1#.T0J-q3JWrPs.

36. Hare, *Stuff Happens*, 52.

37. Ibid., 84–85.

38. Ibid., 97.

39. Janelle Reinelt, "Review: *Stuff Happens* by David Hare, Nick Hytner," *Theatre Journal* 57, no. 2 (2005): 303–6.

40. David Hare, *Obedience, Struggle, and Revolt* (London: Faber and Faber, 2005), 118.

41. Ibid., 4.

42. Hare, *Stuff Happens*, 118–19.

Chapter 2

1. My descriptions and citations of the event in this chapter are my own transcriptions of video documentation of the event available via the UN Webcast. See Kiyotaka Akasaka, Radhika Coomaraswamy, David Eick, Whoopi Goldberg, David Howe, Mary McDonnell, Craig Mokhiber, Ronald D. Moore, Edward James Olmos, Robert Orr, and Famatta Rose Osode, "Special Event: UN Public

Information Department, Sci Fi Channel to Co-Host a Panel with Battlestar Galactica Creators to Raise Profile of Humanitarian Concern," United Nations Webcast RealVideo, 2:04:00, March 17, 2009, http://www.un.org/webcast/2009a.html.

2. The event was sponsored by the UN's Creative Community Outreach Initiative and moderated by Whoopi Goldberg. Representing the UN were Craig Mokhiber of the Office of the High Commissioner for Human Rights; Radhika Coomaraswamy, the special representative of the secretary-general on children and armed conflict; Robert Orr, assistant secretary-general for policy planning; and Famatta Rose Osode, the deputy permanent representative of Liberia to the UN.

3. See Diana Taylor, *The Archive and The Repertoire: Performing Cultural Memory in the Americas* (Durham, N.C.: Duke University Press, 2003), 4: "performance also functions as an epistemology. Embodied practice, along with and bound up with other cultural practices, offers a way of knowing."

4. *Battlestar Galactica*, "Miniseries," directed by Michael Rymer, written by David Eick and Ronald D. Moore, aired December 8 and 9, 2003, on the Sci Fi Channel.

5. See chapter 1.

6. Ian Williams, "An Un-Green Noggin Heads Earth Summit," *New York Observer*, May 11, 1992.

7. Karen Sunde, interview with author, New York, February 2011.

8. United Nations, "'Ruined': Ban Attends Theatre Play," YouTube video, 2:57, June 19, 2009, http://www.youtube.com/watch?v=Ftd0G67-ZUk.

9. I have built each of the case studies in this chapter primarily using the UN's own documents—a methodological effort to see as the UN sees and to stage conflicts using the media with which they were staged for institutional eyes. To stage UNIFIL, I begin with letters to the Security Council, Security Council resolutions, and reports of the secretary-general, and I conduct an extended close reading of the memoirs of the mission's first commander, Emmanuel Erskine. To stage MONUC, I emphasize the secretary-general's regular reporting to the Security Council on the mission. These reports are the primary conduit by which information collected in a mission's area of operation makes its way to the council. However, as Séverine Autesserre points out, such reporting can often indicate institutional blind spots; see *The Trouble with the Congo: Local Violence and the Failure of International Peacebuilding* (Cambridge: Cambridge University Press, 2010), 228. Thus, I supplement the secretary-general's reports with others by nongovernmental organizations and other UN agencies. In this way, my cases are intended as examinations not just of what the UN sees or does not see in peacekeeping, but how the UN sees through peacekeeping.

10. Pinhas Eliav, "Letter dated 13 March 1978 from the Charge d'affaires a.i. of the Permanent Mission of Israel to the United Nations addressed to the Secretary-General" (S/12598), March 13, 1978, 1–2, http://www.un.org/en/ga/search/view_doc.asp?symbol=s/12598.

11. Ghassan Tuéni, "Letter dated 15 March 1978 from the Permanent Representative of Lebanon to the United Nations Addressed to the President of the Security Council" (S/12600), March 15, 1978, 1, http://www.un.org/en/ga/search/view_doc.asp?symbol=s/12600.

12. For more on Palestinian refugees in Lebanon, see Rebecca Roberts, *Palestinians in Lebanon: Refugees Living with Long-Term Displacement* (London: I.B. Tauris, 2010).

13. William Harris, *Lebanon: A History 600–2011* (Oxford: Oxford University Press, 2012), 240.

14. Ahron Bregman, *Israel's Wars: A History since 1947*, 4th ed. (London: Routledge, 2016), 157.

15. For analyses of UNIFIL's evolving mandate, successes, and failures, see Vanessa F. Newby, *Peacekeeping in South Lebanon: Credibility and Local Cooperation* (Syracuse, N.Y.: Syracuse University Press, 2018); and Ray Murphy, *UN Peacekeeping in Lebanon, Somalia and Kosovo: Operational and Legal Issues in Practice* (Cambridge: Cambridge University Press, 2007).

16. In *Understanding Peacekeeping*, Alex J. Bellamy and Paul D. Williams complicate a simple chronological division between traditional and next-generation peacekeeping. Nonetheless, they recognize that such a view remains salient for many scholars and policy-makers. See Bellamy et al., *Understanding Peacekeeping*, 17.

17. In this chapter I examine one traditional peacekeeping operation, UNIFIL, and one next-generation operation, MONUC.

18. United Nations Secretary-General, "Report of the Secretary-General on the Implementation of Security Council Resolution 425 (1978)," (S/12611), March 19, 1978, http://unispal.un.org/UNISPAL.NSF/0/00ECA24D7952AD83852568 BA0070C4B9.

19. François Debrix, *Re-Envisioning Peacekeeping: The United Nations and the Mobilization of Ideology* (Minneapolis: University of Minnesota Press, 1999), 12–15, 109.

20. Paul Higate and Marsha Henry, *Insecure Spaces: Peacekeeping, Power and Performance in Haiti, Kosovo and Liberia* (London: Zed Books, 2009), 58–73.

21. Emmanuel A. Erskine, *Mission with UNIFIL: An African Soldier's Reflections* (New York: St. Martin's Press, 1989), 98.

22. Vanessa F. Newby writes, "The UNIFIL mission is a case that causes us to reevaluate what the terms *success* and *failure* mean in the context of peacekeeping and peacebuilding." Newby, *Peacekeeping in South Lebanon*, 4. Newby's reevaluation of success and failure points to the intrinsic performativity of peacekeeping.

23. United Nations Secretary-General, "Report of the Secretary-General on the Implementation of Security Council Resolution 1701 (2009)," (S/2017/591), July 11, 2017, https://www.un.org/en/ga/search/view_doc.asp?symbol=S/2017/591/.

24. Erskine, *Mission*, 22.

25. Analyzing UN Observer missions like the UN Truce Supervision Organization (UNTSO, which often works with UNIFIL), John Hillen notes, "It was hoped that [observers'] moral authority and responsibility would give all the belligerents the confidence that the other side was not flagrantly violating the accords of the peace settlement. This would strengthen the trust needed to implement a cease-fire or peace settlement." Hillen also indicates those places where these activities may develop into "quasi-juridical functions," as peacekeepers are called on to adjudicate small disputes in their areas of operation. John Hillen, *Blue Helmets: The Strategy of UN Military Operations*, 2nd ed. (Washington, D.C.: Brassey's, 2000), 51, 54.

26. Erskine, *Mission*, 50.
27. Ibid., 52.
28. Ibid., 53.
29. Ibid., 109.
30. Ibid., 110.
31. My MONUC case study, below, examines these reports in greater detail.
32. Karen Sunde, *Plays by Karen Sunde* (New York: Broadway Play, 2001), 109.
33. Ibid.
34. Ibid., 117.
35. Sunde, interview.
36. Sunde, *Plays*, 106.
37. Ibid., 128. The incident remains close to its source material. On the same day that the *New York Times* published Hezbollah's statement that "we have grabbed the criminal American serpent by the throat . . . an agent of the Central Intelligence Agency and one of the biggest spies," it also noted that "the Defense Department told reporters today that Colonel Higgins was formerly an aide to Secretary of Defense Caspar W. Weinberger." Ihsan A. Hijazi, "Pro-Iranian Group Claims Abduction," *New York Times*, February 20, 1988, A1.
38. Sunde, *Plays*, 128.
39. In *Mission*, Erskine offered another image of the gray area between observing and spying. Turning to UNTSO, he notes, "it is the only organization in the world where US and Soviet military—not even civilians—live, eat, sleep and work together . . . I queried one Soviet observer . . . about his compatriots' obvious wish to share observation post duties with Americans. 'Yes, General,' he replied, 'we Soviets always want to be with our US colleagues because we know they are CIAs and they know we are KGBs." Erskine, *Mission*, 149.
40. Rey Chow, for one, shows the contours of this connection at a macrocosmic level: "War and knowledge enable and foster each other." Chow, *The Age of the World Target: Self-Referentiality in War, Theory, and Comparative Work* (Durham, N.C.: Duke University Press, 2006), 36. Chow's argument centers on the implicit and explicit collusion between area studies departments in American universities and the institutions that carry out the United States' interventionist foreign policy.
41. Sunde, *Plays*, 128.
42. See Harris, *Lebanon*, 247, for more on this history.
43. Sunde, *Plays*, 119.
44. Sunde, interview with author.
45. Sunde went on to tell me, "so much of what motivates us arises from obstacles we felt in high school," an insight that led her to superimpose several scenes from Hogan's high school days—playing football, lingering by the hall lockers, reciting poetry to prepare for English class, and so on—over UNIFIL's efforts to know their own situation and territory.
46. Sunde, *Plays*, 118.
47. Ibid.
48. Ibid., 143.
49. Ibid., 165.
50. Ibid., 162.

51. Ibid., 166.
52. Sunde, interview with author.
53. Lynn Nottage, *Ruined* (New York: Theatre Communication Group, 2009), 92–94.
54. Ibid., 95.
55. Séverine Autesserre details the horrific violence of Belgium's colonial authorities, and notes the ill effects not only of the physical violence committed, but also of the perception and stereotype it contributed to: that the violence in the Congo in the late twentieth and twenty-first centuries was a normal state of affairs, an "atavistic or primordial" situation that was not worth addressing. See Autesserre, *The Trouble with the Congo*, 76–78.
56. Gérard Prunier, *Africa's World War: Congo, the Rwandan Genocide, and the Making of a Continental Catastrophe* (Oxford: Oxford University Press, 2009), xxix.
57. Autesserre, *The Trouble with the Congo*, 133–34.
58. Ibid., 135–40.
59. Prunier, *Africa's World War*, 24–25. Others put the number of refugees at 1.5 million: see Philip Roessler and Harry Verhoeven, *Why Comrades Go to War: Liberation Politics and the Outbreak of Africa's Deadliest Conflict* (Oxford: Oxford University Press, 2016), 133. Autesserre reports 2 million: see Autesserre, *The Trouble with the Congo*, 47.
60. Prunier, *Africa's World War*, 73–112; Autesserre, *The Trouble with the Congo*, 47; Roessler and Verhoeven, *Why Comrades Go to War*, 151–57.
61. See Roessler and Verhoeven, *Why Comrades Go to War*, for a detailed study of the shifting alliances of the First Congo War.
62. Alan Doss, "United Nations Organization Mission in the Democratic Republic of the Congo (MONUC)," in *The Oxford Handbook of United Nations Peacekeeping Operations*, ed. Joachim A. Koops, Norrie Macqueen, Thierry Tardy, and Paul D. Williams (Oxford: Oxford University Press, 2015), 657.
63. Séverine Autesserre reminds her readers that though the transitional period was described by many in the UN and elsewhere as "postconflict," the local situation, especially in the eastern DRC, "saw large-scale fighting between 'former' war enemies, led to the deaths of hundreds of combatants and civilians, the displacement of hundreds of thousands, and very nearly caused the collapse of the regional and national peace processes." Autesserre, *The Trouble with the Congo*, 67.
64. United Nations Secretary-General, "Thirteenth Report of the Secretary-General on the United Nations Organization Mission in the Democratic Republic of the Congo" (S/2003/211), February 21, 2003, 3–4, http://www.un.org/en/ga/search/view_doc.asp?symbol=S/2003/211.
65. United Nations Secretary-General, "Second Special Report of the Secretary-General on the United Nations Organization Mission in the Democratic Republic of the Congo" (S/2003/566), May 17, 2003, 4, http://www.un.org/en/ga/search/view_doc.asp?symbol=S/2003/566.
66. United Nations Secretary-General, "Third Special Report of the Secretary-General on the United Nations Organization Mission in the Democratic Republic of the Congo" (S/2004/650), August 16, 2004, 22, http://www.un.org/en/ga/search/view_doc.asp?symbol=S/2004/650.

67. Médecins Sans Frontières, "Nothing New in Ituri: The Violence Continues," MSF Report, August 2005, http://www.msf.org/sites/msf.org/files/old-cms/source/countries/africa/drc/2005/ituri_violence_2005report.pdf. In some ways, Ituri proved more visible than comparable Congolese provinces. Autesserre notes that "Ituri enjoyed significantly more international attention and resources than did any other eastern province," even though the violence there was on a par with that seen in other parts of the country during the transition (Autesserre, *The Trouble with the Congo*, 207). Ituri proved an exception to the "vicious circle" by which "the view of violence as an insignificant matter led many intermediaries to filter out data on local conflicts when they transmitted information from UN field offices to the UN Headquarters" (ibid., 228). Autesserre diagnoses a problem of UN spectatorship, and attributes the Ituri region's visibility to the occurrence of events that "proved so shocking that they grabbed international attention and inspired increased intervention" (ibid., 213). Among the mechanisms giving visibility to the violence, she includes the reports of nongovernmental organizations, like the 2005 MSF report. This increased scrutiny led to the arrest and prosecution of Thomas Lubanga, Germain Katanga, and Mathieu Ngudjolo Chui by the International Criminal Court. I discuss the Lubanga case in chapter 5, and the cases against Katanga and Ngudjolo Chui in chapter 6.

68. Secretary-General, "Third Special Report," 8.

69. See Bonnie Kovatch, "Sexual Exploitation and Abuse in UN Peacekeeping Missions: A Case Study of MONUC and MONUSCO," *Journal of the Middle East and Africa* 7, no. 2 (2016): 157–74.

70. Elisabeth Rehn and Ellen Johnson Sirleaf, *Women, War and Peace: The Independent Experts' Assessment on the Impact of Armed Conflict on Women and Women's Role in Peace-Building* (New York: United Nations Development Fund for Women, 2002), 11–12.

71. The gaze of peacekeepers calls to mind the male gaze investigated by film theorists. The crime of patriarchal cinema rests on the inevitable association of the film's structure with the eye and agency of a male subject, simultaneously reducing the female subjects depicted to the status of objects without agency who exist for the satisfaction and pleasure of that male subject. See Laura Mulvey, "Visual Pleasure and Narrative Cinema," in *Film Theory and Criticism: Introductory Readings*, ed. Leo Braudy and Marshall Cohen, 5th ed. (New York: Oxford University Press, 1999), 833–44.

72. Quoted in Paul Higate, "Peacekeepers, Masculinities, and Sexual Exploitation," *Men and Masculinities* 10, no. 1 (2007): 107.

73. Ibid., 105.

74. Nottage, *Ruined*, 20.

75. Ibid., 21.

76. Ibid., 29–30.

77. See David Krasner, "Empathy and Theater," in *Staging Philosophy*, ed. David Krasner and David Z. Saltz (Ann Arbor: University of Michigan Press, 2006), 258–59.

78. Ben Brantley, "War's Terrors, through a Brothel Window," *New York Times*, February 11, 2009, C1.

79. Robert Skloot, "Review Essay: Old Concerns and New Plays in the Theater of Genocide," *Genocide Studies and Prevention* 5, no. 1 (2010): 115.

80. Sharon Friedman, "The Gendered Terrain in Contemporary Theatre of War by Women," *Theatre Journal* 62 (2010): 609, quoting Wendy Hesford, "Rhetorical Memory, Political Theater, and the Traumatic Present," *Transformations* 16, no. 2 (2005): 105–6.

81. David Krasner uses language that makes the transgressive quality of empathy quite clear: "Empathy . . . *allows us to transcend the limits of our own world* . . . it allows us to cross the boundaries between us, boundaries that are especially evident in this moment of world history." Krasner, "Empathy and Theatre," 256.

82. Nottage, *Ruined*, 38.

83. Ibid., 94. Each of the three essays in the "Special Section on *Ruined*" in a recent volume on Nottage's work highlights this moment. See Jocelyn L. Buckner, ed., *A Critical Companion to Lynn Nottage* (London: Routledge, 2016), 139, 153, 171.

84. For a discussion of how the play's melodramatic structure encloses the disruptive forces it otherwise unleashes, see Jennifer-Scott Mobley, "Melodrama, Sensation, and Activism in *Ruined*," in *A Critical Companion to Lynn Nottage*, ed. Jocelyn L. Buckner (London: Routledge, 2016), 130–31. See the same essay, and Jeff Paden, "Renegotiating Realism: Hybridity of Form and Political Potentiality in *Ruined*," in *A Critical Companion to Lynn Nottage*, ed. Jocelyn L. Buckner (London: Routledge, 2016), 144–60, for a discussion of how the play impacted U.S. foreign policy.

85. Sunde, interview.

86. Ibid.

87. Ibid.

88. Ibid.

89. Kate Whoriskey, introduction to *Ruined* by Lynn Nottage, ix–x.

90. Ibid.

91. Michel Foucault, *Security, Territory, Population: Lectures at the Collège de France, 1977–78*, ed. Michel Senellart, trans. Graham Burchell (New York: Palgrave Macmillan, 2007), 122.

92. See ibid., 190–98; and Michel Foucault, *Dits et écrits II, 1976–1988* (Paris: Gallimard, 2001), 1056.

93. Foucault, *Security*, 310–60.

94. Lieutenant-General Erskine begins his memoir by noting, "the only international combat exposure to which Ghanaian soldiers, both officers and men, who were on active service in the early 1960s could lay claim was their participation in the United Nations Operation in the Congo, ONUC." *Mission*, 1. Erskine paints the colonial contours of this pedagogy by noting that the only other training available to Ghana's armed forces at the time of independence had come from its former colonial master, Britain. Where the UN takes the place of the colonial power, it continues colonialism's civilizing mission. Erskine confirms Roland Paris's hypothesis that a continuum exists between the work of peace support operations today and the "mission civilisatrice, or the colonial-era belief that the European imperial powers had a duty to 'civilise' dependent populations and territories." Roland Paris, "International Peacebuilding and the 'Mission Civilisatrice,'" *Review of International Studies* 28, no. 4 (2002): 637. Peacekeepers bring home what they learn by performing in the theater of peacekeeping. For

Erskine, the mission in Lebanon provided a pretext to keep the battalion under his command from becoming embroiled in a coup d'etat in Ghana. This event, and the financial gain to individual Ghanaian soldiers paid by the United Nations (enabling them to purchase appliances to bring home), led Erskine to quip, "the benefits of [involvement with UNIFIL] to [the Ghanaian] personnel extended to the government and consequently the entire people of Ghana." Erskine, *Mission*, 156–57. Erskine draws a line that connects the effects of peacekeeping on the bodies of his troops to the constitution of the Ghanaian state and the population inhabiting there. His troops appear more civil both because they are kept from participating in an undemocratic attempt at regime change at home, and by virtue of their entry into a middle-class consumer society and their engagement with a global marketplace.

95. MONUC's intimate involvement with the process of disarmament, demobilization, and reintegration of paramilitary groups into the national armed forces demonstrates its function as a node through which forces flowed. In these processes, MONUC directly addressed the bodies and subjectivities of soldiers, conducting their conduct. Disarmament, demobilization, and reintegration began with public spectacle: armed forces in the DRC "present[ed] themselves to MONUC," making themselves visible to the UN and international community in a public performance designed to recuperate them into national and international systems. At the Security Council's request, MONUC also "contributed to army integration through basic training for units undergoing brassage," and provided them training "on human rights and international humanitarian law." United Nations Secretary-General "Thirty-First Report of the Secretary-General on the United Nations Organization Mission in the Democratic Republic of the Congo" (S/2010/164), March 30, 2010, 2, 8, http://www.un.org/en/ga/search/view_doc.asp?symbol=S/2010/164.

96. Implicit in the logic of governmentality is also its capacity to overlook—to exclude from view the individuals who disrupt the statistical thrust of the whole. Responding to sexual exploitation and abuse by MONUC personnel, the UN works on bodies in two ways: first by addressing the conduct of its peacekeepers with new reports, guidelines, codes, and training; and second by investigating perpetrators and returning them to their home countries. Since the United Nations lacks legal authority over peacekeeping troops provided by member states, the greatest punishment it can mete out is to expel perpetrators from its ranks, hoping they are punished at home. In these cases of repatriation, the logic of governmentality allows individual cases of deviance to be set aside so that the statistical thrust of the population remains favorable. The soul of one is abandoned in order to best shepherd the rest. As Foucault puts it in his discussion of the Christian pastorate that preceded contemporary forms of governmentality, "the sheep that is a cause of scandal . . . must be abandoned, possibly executed, chased away." Foucault, *Security*, 169.

97. Ibid., 196.

98. Quoted in Anneke Van Woudenberg, "MONUC: A Case for Peacekeeping Reform," Human Rights Watch, February 28, 2005, https://www.hrw.org/news/2005/02/28/monuc-case-peacekeeping-reform.

99. Autesserre highlights these as "shocking events." *The Trouble with the Congo*, 213.

Chapter 3

1. Unless otherwise noted, direct quotations of speakers at the event are my own transcriptions from audio recordings of the event.

2. Guy Debord, *The Society of the Spectacle*, trans. Donald Nicholson Smith, (New York: Zone Books, 1994), 115.

3. LGBTI is the initialism used by the U.S. Mission to the UN, and by Ambassador Power in public speeches. I have followed suit with its use, though I also occasionally use "queer" as a synonym, one that recognizes there are forms of experience worth protecting that are not included in the categories of lesbian, gay, bisexual, transgender, and intersex.

4. See Kalle Oskari Mattila, "Selling Queerness: The Curious Case of *Fun Home*," *The Atlantic*, April 25, 2016, http://www.theatlantic.com/entertainment/archive/2016/04/branding-queerness-the-curious-case-of-fun-home/479532/; and Advocate Contributors, "That Time the U.N. Ambassador Came to See *Fun Home*," The Advocate, March 14, 2016, http://www.advocate.com/commentary/2016/3/14/time-un-ambassador-came-see-fun-home, for reporting on the show.

5. Power made this frame explicit in the talkback when she revealed to the cast the U.S. Mission's "desire to take advantage of American soft power: which is our culture and everything you offer."

6. Fun Home on Broadway, "Welcome to FUN HOME at Circle in the Square Theatre," April 15, 2016, YouTube video, 1:24, https://www.youtube.com/watch?v=510IdY6xPr4.

7. Quoted in Advocate Contributors, "That Time the U.N."

8. Samantha Power, "Remarks on 'I Know You: Making LGBTI Rights Human Rights at the UN and Abroad' at the Human Rights Campaign's Equality Convention," March 12, 2016, http://usun.state.gov/remarks/7185.

9. Diplomacy is structured by these speech acts that compose it, its diplomatic performatives. These are the basic units of diplomacy: the individual written, spoken, or performed speech acts of states and their representatives. Much like J. L. Austin's performative utterance, each diplomatic performative is uttered to enact rather than describe a particular configuration of world affairs; each has intended consequences and unintended effects; and each brooks little concern for truth and falsity, only a stark reckoning of success and failure. See J. L. Austin, *How to Do Things with Words*, ed. J. O. Urmson and Marina Sbisà (Cambridge, Mass.: Harvard University Press, 1955). The most common diplomatic performatives are threats (the threat of war, sanctions, etc.) and promises (the promise of peace, aid, etc.). Threats and promises reduce the field of international relations to manageable terms that interpellate states as subjects on the world stage. Threats and promises organize the performances of states and their agents; they arrange individual and state subjects to enable or foreclose on the repertoire of action available to each. Threats and promises leverage an imagined future to configure the present and past, in an unstable operation that may be interrupted.

10. Barack Obama, "United States of America, General Debate, 66th Session," September 21, 2011, United Nations Webcast streaming video, 36:31, http://www.unmultimedia.org/tv/webcast/2011/09/united-states-of-america-general-debate-66th-session.html.

11. Barack Obama, "Presidential Memorandum—International Initiatives to Advance the Human Rights of Lesbian, Gay, Bisexual, and Transgender Persons,"

December 6, 2011, https://obamawhitehouse.archives.gov/the-press-office/2011/12/06/presidential-memorandum-international-initiatives-advance-human-rights-l.

12. Power, "Remarks on 'I Know You.'"

13. Ibid.

14. Ibid.

15. According to Security Council Report, only Angola and Chad were absent from the meeting. See Security Council Report, "September 2015 Monthly Forecast—Status Update," August 31, 2015, http://www.securitycouncilreport.org/monthly-forecast/2015-09/status_update_33.php.

16. Samantha Power and Subhi Nahas, "Samantha Power (USA) and Subhi Nahas on LGBT in the Middle East—Security Council Media Stakeout, Arria formula (24 August 2015)," United Nations Webcast streaming video, 14:44, August 24, 2015, http://webtv.un.org/search/samantha-power-usa-and-subhi-nahas-on-lgbt-in-the-middle-east-security-council-media-stakeout-arria-formula-24-august-2015/4441763676001/.

17. Guy Debord, *Critique de la separation*, streaming video hosted by UbuWeb Film, 17:23, 1961, http://ubu.com/film/debord_critique.html.

18. Debord, *Society of the Spectacle*, 15.

19. Lisa Kron, foreword to *Fun Home*, music by Jeanine Tesori, book and lyrics by Lisa Kron, Acting Edition ([New York]: Samuel French, 2015), 7.

20. Ibid., 8.

21. Ibid., 7.

22. Alison Bechdel, *Fun Home: A Family Tragicomic* (Boston: Houghton Mifflin Harcourt, 2007), 220–21.

23. Judith Butler, *Excitable Speech: A Politics of the Performative* (New York: Routledge, 1997), 14.

24. Ibid., 163.

25. Debord, *The Society of The Spectacle*, 96.

26. Barack Obama, "'Responsibility for Our Common Future' Address to the United Nations General Assembly," September 23, 2009, [1], https://gadebate.un.org/sites/default/files/gastatements/64/64_US_en.pdf.

27. Muammar Qaddafi, "General Debate of the 64th Session (2009)," United Nations Webcast RealVideo, English translation, 1:36:00, September 23, 2009, http://www.un.org/en/ga/64/generaldebate/LY.shtml.

28. Yoweri Museveni, "Statement by H.E. Yoweri Kaguta Museveni, President of the Republic of Uganda, at the United Nations General Assembly,'" September 23, 2009, 9, https://gadebate.un.org/sites/default/files/gastatements/64/64_UG_en.pdf.

29. Leonard Doyle, "Has Colonel Gaddafi Lost His Chance to Meet Barack Obama?" *The Telegraph*, September 6, 2009, http://www.telegraph.co.uk/news/worldnews/northamerica/usa/6143761/Has-Colonel-Gaddafi-lost-his-chance-to-meet-Barack-Obama.html.

30. Patrick Worsnip, "Obama Debut, Gaddhafi, Ahmedinejad a Potent U.N. Brew," *Reuters*, September 6, 2009, http://www.reuters.com/article/2009/09/06/us-un-assembly-idUSTRE5850DX20090906.

31. By 2011, though, the revolutions of the Arab Spring had reversed Qaddafi's fortunes once more: he was killed by rebel forces (supported by a NATO mission authorized in Security Council Resolution 1973) that October. Dirk Vandewalle's *A History of Modern Libya*, 2nd ed. (Cambridge: Cambridge University Press),

places Qaddafi's reign, Libya's nuclear program, and the civil war that toppled Qaddafi in historical context.

32. Quoted in Alexander Mooney, "Obama Says Time to Rid World of Nuclear Weapons," CNN.com, July 16, 2008, http://www.cnn.com/2008/POLITICS/07/16/obama.speech/.

33. Barack Obama, "Remarks by President Barack Obama," speech given in Prague, Czech Republic, April 5, 2009.

34. Quentin Peel, "Gaddafi Offers Mere Sideshow to Main Event," *Financial Times*, September 25, 2009, 6, https://www.ft.com/content/2560cb3a-a94f-11de-9b7f-00144feabdc0.

35. Qaddafi, "General Debate."

36. Contradictions of this sort may be engrained in the charter. Mark Mazower asks, "what to make of the fact that Jan Smuts, the South African statesman, helped draft the UN's stirring preamble? How could the new world body's commitment to universal rights owe more than a little to the participation of a man whose segregationist policies back home paved the way for the apartheid state? Smuts, an exponent of racial superiority, and a believer in white rule over the African continent, casts an enigmatic shadow over the founding of the new United Nations Organization at the end of the Second World War." Mazower, *No Enchanted Palace*, 19.

37. Qaddafi, "General Debate."

38. Davis, "Theatricality and Civil Society," 148–49.

39. United Nations, Charter.

40. My argument in this chapter and elsewhere in this book has some affinities with Jeffrey Edward Green's ocular model of popular power, which "recognizes the leaders who are watched as the ultimate medium wherein popular empowerment makes its impact felt." Green, *The Eyes of the People*, 128. Green's model emphasizes the gaze of a citizen spectator; my own efforts in this chapter seek to elaborate the theatricality of the situation that a citizen spectator experiences, and additional avenues by which she may act.

41. Walter Benjamin, "Theses on the Philosophy of History," in *Illuminations*, trans. Harry Zohn, ed. Hannah Arendt (New York: Schocken Books, 1968), 257–58.

42. I also remember David Hare's Colin Powell, in *Stuff Happens*, for whom history had become a river of shit flowing around him.

43. UN Security Council, "Security Council [Meeting]: Maintenance of International Peace and Security—Nuclear Non-Proliferation and Nuclear Disarmament," United Nations Webcast RealVideo, English translation, 1:44:00, September 24, 2009, http://www.un.org/webcast/2009.html.

44. UN Security Council, Resolution 1887, "Maintenance of International Peace and Security: Nuclear Non-Proliferation and Nuclear Disarmament," S/RES/1887, September 24, 2009, 3, http://www.un.org/Docs/sc/unsc_resolutions09.htm.

45. United Nations, Treaty on the Non-Proliferation of Nuclear Weapons, July 1, 1968, http://www.un.org/en/conf/npt/2005/npttreaty.html.

46. UN Security Council, "Security Council [Meeting]: Maintenance of International Peace and Security—Nuclear Non-Proliferation and Nuclear Disarmament."

47. Ibid.

48. Aili Mari Tripp describes the political system headed by Museveni in Uganda as "semi-authoritarian," in her study of his rule. Tripp, *Museveni's Uganda: Paradoxes of Power in a Hybrid Regime* (Boulder, Colo.: Lynne Rienner, 2010), 20. For a discussion of Museveni's presidency in a broader historical context, see Richard J. Reid, *A History of Modern Uganda* (Cambridge: Cambridge University Press, 2017). Both authors discuss the "draconian Anti-Homosexuality Bill that proposed life imprisonment [and in some cases the death penalty] for acts of homosexuality." Tripp, *Museveni's Uganda*, 96.

49. Adam Taylor, "Worldviews: MAP: The U.S. Military Currently Has Troops in These African Countries," *Washington Post*, May 21, 2014, https://www.washingtonpost.com/news/worldviews/wp/2014/05/21/map-the-u-s-currently-has-troops-in-these-african-countries/.

50. Ty McCormick, "Is the U.S. Military Propping up Uganda's 'Elected' Autocrat?" *Foreign Policy*, February 18, 2016, http://foreignpolicy.com/2016/02/18/is-the-us-military-propping-up-ugandas-elected-autocrat-museveni-elections/. See also Reid, *A History of Modern Uganda*, 95, for further discussion of what he describes as the "quid pro quo" between the United States and Uganda.

51. I am borrowing this phrase from Homi Bhabha, who takes it from an 1818 sermon by Archdeacon Potts. After quoting the sermon, Bhabha elaborates its significance: "the native refusal to satisfy the colonizer's narrative demand . . . represents a frustration of that nineteenth-century strategy of surveillance, the confession, which seeks to dominate the 'calculable' individual by positing the truth that the subject has but does not know. The incalculable native produces a problem for civil representation in the discourses of literature and legality." Bhabha, *The Location of Culture* (New York: Routledge, 1994), 141.

52. Gordon Brown, Barack Obama, and Nicolas Sarkozy, "Iranian Nuclear Program," *C-Span*, streaming video, 8:04, September 25, 2009, https://www.c-span.org/video/?289138-1/iranian-nuclear-program.

53. Debord, *The Society of The Spectacle*, 19.

Chapter 4

1. Ban Ki-moon and Park-Jae Sang, "Secretary-General Ban Ki-moon and PSY, Korean Singer," United Nations Webcast streaming video, 8:50, October 23, 2012, http://webtv.un.org/%E2%80%A6/we%E2%80%A6/watch/secretary-general-ban-ki-moon-and-psy-korean-singer/1920431996001.

2. United Nations, Charter.

3. Ban Ki-moon and Park-Jae Sang, "Ban Ki-moon and PSY."

4. Marcus Tan, "K-Contagion: Sound, Speed, and Space in 'Gangnam Style,'" *TDR: The Drama Review* 59, no. 1 (spring 2015): 86.

5. The image, which is in the public domain, is hosted online by Wikimedia Commons at https://commons.wikimedia.org/wiki/File:Strauss_I_-_Wiener_Scene_-_Der_gro%C3%9Fe_Galop.jpg.

6. For an example, see GNRSlashLover, "Chubby Checker—Pony Time," YouTube video, 2:07, September 18, 2010, https://www.youtube.com/watch?v=JyaxcvHSyZY. Though the video does not include its source or the original air date of the material, in the video Chubby Checker teaches the dance to a small group of young people, who demonstrate for viewers.

Notes to Pages 93–100

7. See MosesTKrikey, "TEEN TIME—The Horse," YouTube video, 4:44, February 11, 2008, https://www.youtube.com/watch?v=l4XFk2VCgVc. The uploader's annotations indicate that this clip came from an episode of the television program *Teen Time* that aired in the late 1960s in Steubenville, Ohio.

8. Christopher Small, *Musicking: The Meanings of Performing and Listening* (Middletown, Conn.: Wesleyan University Press, 1998), 135–36.

9. Conor Cruise O'Brien, *United Nations: Sacred Drama* (New York: Simon and Schuster, 1968), 19.

10. See Kent Schroeder, *Politics of Gross National Happiness: Governance and Development in Bhutan* (New York: Palgrave Macmillan, 2017), for an analysis of how Gross National Happiness programs have been implemented in Bhutan.

11. Karma Ura, Sabina Alkire, Tshoki Zangmo, and Karma Wangdi, *A Short Guide to Gross National Happiness Index* (Thimphu: Centre for Bhutan Studies, 2012), 15.

12. Ibid., 1.

13. UN General Assembly, Resolution 66/281, "International Day of Happiness," A/RES/66/281, June 28, 2012, 1, https://undocs.org/A/RES/66/281, emphasis in original.

14. Sara Ahmed, *The Promise of Happiness* (Durham, N.C.: Duke University Press, 2010), 29.

15. United Nations Foundation, "What We Do: Campaigns and Initiatives," 2013, http://www.unfoundation.org/what-we-do/campaigns-and-initiatives/.

16. Katherine Yester, "Happy Math," *Foreign Policy*, October 14, 2009, http://foreignpolicy.com/2009/10/14/happy-math/.

17. Foucault, *Security*, 190–98.

18. Here, again, I am following Sara Ahmed's lead. In *The Promise of Happiness* Ahmed argues that "happiness is a form of world making" (2) and that it "becomes a duty" (7); I concur with her deep suspicion of the "instrumentalization of happiness as a technique" (10).

19. As of December 2017, the website was still available at https://www.globalhappyparty.com.

20. Pharrell Williams, "Happy," track 5 on *GIRL*, Columbia, 2013.

21. United Nations, "International Day of Happiness Event," UN Webcast streaming video, 55:05, March 20, 2015, http://webtv.un.org/search/international-day-of-happiness-event/4129206146001?term=pharrell.

22. Ibid.

23. Ibid.

24. Small asserts that this is true of music venues: "In the concert hall, as at any other kind of musical event there is an underlying kinship between the members of the audience . . . There are certain kinds of behavior they can expect of one another and other kinds that they need not." Small, *Musicking*, 41.

25. I discuss the performances of Baroody and Herzog in chapter 6.

26. UN General Assembly, "Viva Vox Choir (Belgrade)—New Year's Concert of the 67th Session of the General Assembly," UN Webcast streaming video, 1:03:31, January 14, 2013, http://webtv.un.org/search/viva-vox-choir-belgrade-new-years-concert-of-the-67th-session-of-the-general-assembly/2094291812001?term=viva%20vox.

27. In the introduction to their collection *Music and Diplomacy*, Damien Mahiet, Mark Ferraguto, and Rebekah Ahrendt outline the history of the metaphor, and the ways that scholars have taken it apart. They write: "The symbolic relationship between terrestrial and celestial harmony as manifested in musical objects has itself been a powerful tool in diplomatic endeavors. . . . If the harmony of the spheres could control the motions of the soul, it was then but a short road to concluding that music, as a universal human practice, also had universal effects. . . . From the perspective of societies organized around a sovereign . . . ensemble playing could suggest a submersion of the individual's identity within the production of unified (albeit polyphonic) sound." Rebekah Ahrendt, Mark Ferraguto, and Damien Mahiet, eds., *Music and Diplomacy: From the Early Modern Era to the Present* (New York: Palgrave Macmillan, 2014), 3–6.

28. UN General Assembly, "Viva Vox Choir (Belgrade)."

29. Viva Vox Choir, "Choir History," 2015, http://www.vivavoxchoir.com/eng/choir-history.

30. UN General Assembly, "Viva Vox Choir (Belgrade)."

31. John Lennon, "Imagine," track 1 on *Imagine*, Abbey Road Studios, 1971.

32. Haris Alibasic, Ajila Delkic, Emir Ramic, and Sanja Segerovic-Drnovsek, "Protest Letter to Ban Ki-moon, UN Secretary-General," Bosniak.org, Congress of North American Bosniaks, January 15, 2013, http://www.bosniak.org/protest-letter-to-ban-ki-moon-un-general-secretary/.

33. Martin Nesirky, "Daily Press Briefing: SG in California, Syria, Syria—UNRWA, Secretary-General's Appointments, Security Council, Darfur, DRC, Mali," UN Webcast streaming video, 15:32, January 17, 2013, http://webtv.un.org/search/daily-press-briefing-sg-in-california-syria-syria-%E2%80%93-unrwa-secretary-general%E2%80%99s-appointments-security-council-darfur-drc-mali/2101083964001/?term=2013-01-17&sort=date.

34. U.S. Department of State, "Seventh Report on War Crimes in the Former Yugoslavia," in *U.S. Department of State Dispatch* 4 (April 19, 1993).

35. Quoted in Michelle Nichols, "Serbian Military Song at U.N. Concert Sparks Bosnian Outcry," *Reuters*, January 17, 2013, http://www.reuters.com/article/us-serbia-bosnia-un-song-idUSBRE90G1D520130117.

36. Steven Connor, "The Help of Your Good Hands: Reports on Clapping," in *The Auditory Culture Reader*, ed. Michael Bull and Les Back (Oxford: Berg, 2003), 72.

37. Ibid., 68.

38. Baz Kershaw puts this another way: "Applause is the moment in which the collective aims to assert itself over the individual, in which an imagined community is forged. So the pitch of applause—whether it is a standing ovation or a desultory clap—indicates different types of consensual abandon, a giving up of individual judgement: we lose something of ourselves in putting our hands together with others in public." Kershaw, "Oh for Unruly Audiences! or, Patterns of Participation in Twentieth-Century Theatre," *Modern Drama* 44, no. 2 (summer 2001): 135.

39. Abjection is a psychological and a sociocultural function. It is a process that stabilizes an individual's sense of self and that polices the borders of a given community. According to Julia Kristeva, "the abject and abjection are my safeguards. The primers of my culture." Kristeva, *Powers of Horror: An Essay on Abjection*,

trans. Leon S. Roudiez (New York: Columbia University Press, 1982), 2. Abjection is the process of casting off what might otherwise be considered constitutive of the subject, "I." Multiple affects index the scene of abjection: fear, disgust, shame, hate, and others. Where these erupt, the subject may be said to be in a process of self-stabilization, erecting and maintaining his or her psychological boundaries. As Kristeva puts it, "I experience abjection only if an Other has settled in place and stead of what will be 'me'" (ibid., 10). In abjection, subjectivity emerges from self-alienation, where this Other is cast off and cast out. In invoking Kristeva's theory of abjection, I am also following Karen Shimakawa's assertion of "the paradigm of abjection as a national/cultural identity forming process." Shimakawa engages abjection not as an exclusive psychoanalytic explanation for the formation of specific identities, but "as a descriptive paradigm in order to posit a way of understanding the relationship linking the psychic, symbolic, legal, and aesthetic dimensions of national identity." Shimakawa, *National Abjection: The Asian American Body Onstage* (Durham, N.C.: Duke University Press, 2002), 3–4.

40. Connor, "Reports on Clapping," 72.

41. Kristeva acknowledges this same horror: "The border has become an object. How can I be without a border?" *Powers of Horror*, 4.

42. Weiss et al., *Changing World Politics*, 11.

43. O'Brien, *Sacred Drama*, 121.

44. Aurel Kolnai, *On Disgust*, ed. Barry Smith and Carolyn Korsmeyer (Chicago: Open Court, 2004), 103.

45. Here I am following Sara Ahmed's lead once more: "Harmony would be a demand for accordance. This is why I would argue that the powers-that-be might want their subjects happy rather than sad . . . The good encounter could be read as being how bodies stay in place or acquire a place in which they can stay, by agreeing with what they receive. The bad encounter can be read as how bodies refuse to be placed by disagreeing with what they receive." Ahmed, *Happiness*, 213.

46. Kolnai, *Disgust*, 99.

47. Ahmed, *Happiness*, 40.

Chapter 5

1. Abdalmahmood Mohamad, "Media Stakeout: Informal Comments to the Media by the Permanent Representative of Sudan, H. E. Mr. Abdalmahmood Abdalhaleem Mohamad on the Situation in Sudan," United Nations Webcast RealVideo, 10:00, June 5, 2009, http://www.un.org/webcast/2009.html.

2. UN Security Council, "Reports of the Secretary-General on the Sudan," S/PV.5125 (February 16, 2005), 3, http://www.un.org/en/sc/meetings/records/2005.shtml.

3. For a detailed history of recent conflicts in Darfur, see Julie Flint and Alex de Waal, *Darfur: A New History of a Long War* (London: Zed Books, 2008).

4. Mohamad, "Media Stakeout."

5. The International Criminal Court began work in 2002, following the entry into force of the Rome Statute of the International Criminal Court (1998), an international treaty detailing the court's organization, functions, and jurisdiction. Though it is independent of the UN, the ICC reports to the Security Council on its work, performing in the same geopolitical spectacles as the UN where the

institutions meet. Cases at the ICC develop from "situations," scenes of insecurity, war, or oppression that are actively investigated by the court's prosecutors, a performative process that focuses global spectatorship on particular regions. Not every situation worth investigating comes to the attention of the court, and not every situation under investigation requires regular reports to the Security Council (only those originally referred to the court in a Security Council resolution). Investigations by the International Criminal Court begin in one of three ways: through referral by a State Party to the Rome Statute, referral by the Security Council, or through acts of the prosecutor *proprio motu* (on his or her own initiative) based on information received through third parties.

6. The literature on performance and the law is rapidly expanding. Lara D. Nielsen's article "Institutionalizing Ensembles: Thinking Theatre, Performance, and 'the Law,'" *Law, Culture and the Humanities* 4, no. 2 (2008): 156–78, nicely synthesizes academic studies of the affinities between the three realms from the perspective of performance studies. The essays that make up Austin Sarat, Lawrence Douglas, and Martha Merrill Umphrey, eds., *Law and Performance*, (Amherst and Boston, Mass.: University of Massachusetts Press, 2018) provide examples of recent scholarship in the field of performance and the law. Approaches that look at trials themselves as forms of theater form a subset of this literature and include Milner S. Ball, "The Play's the Thing: An Unscientific Reflection on Courts under the Rubric of Theater," *Stanford Law Review* 28, no. 1 (1975): 81–116; Bernard J. Hibbitts, "'Coming to Our Senses': Communication and Legal Expression in Performance Cultures," *Emory Law Journal* 41, no. 4 (1992): 873–960; Shoshana Felman, *The Juridical Unconscious: Trials and Traumas in the Twentieth Century* (Cambridge, Mass.: Harvard University Press, 2002); and Pnina Lahav, "Theater in the Courtroom: The Chicago Conspiracy Trial," *Law and Literature* 16, no. 3 (2004): 381–474.

Branislav Jakovljevic's "From Mastermind to Body Artist: Political Performances of Slobodan Milošević," *TDR: The Drama Review* 52, no. 1 (2008): 51–74, considers international criminal tribunals from the perspective of performance studies, and so comes closest to my own approach. Eric Stover, *The Witnesses: War Crimes and the Promise of Justice in The Hague* (Philadelphia: University of Pennsylvania Press, 2005), synthesizes approaches that apply a theatrical metaphor to tribunals following mass atrocity. These approaches include Lawrence Douglas, *The Memory of Judgment: Making Law and History in the Trials of the Holocaust* (New Haven, Conn.: Yale University Press, 2001); and Mark Osiel, *Mass Atrocity, Collective Memory, and the Law* (New Brunswick, N.J.: Transaction, 1997). Stover also notes those who see limits to the utility of finding theater in an international courtroom, such as Ian Buruma, *The Wages of Guilt: Memories of War in Germany and Japan* (New York: Farrar, Straus and Giroux, 1994). Approaches to performance and international criminal law largely consider the experiences of persons engaged by international courts (as in Stover), and the circulation and reception of global juridical spectacles. See Kamari M. Clarke, *Fictions of Justice: The International Criminal Court and the Challenge of Legal Pluralism in Sub-Saharan Africa* (New York: Cambridge University Press, 2009). The *relationship* between individual experiences of international law and the global spectacles to which those experiences contribute has received less attention. This relationship is the focus of this chapter.

7. See Tatiana Carayannis, "CAR's Southern Identity: Congo, CAR, and International Justice," in *Making Sense of the Central African Republic*, ed. Tatiana Carayannis and Louisa Lombard (London: Zed Books, 2015), 244–66, for detailed accounts of the CAR's relationship with the DRC and the MLC's interventions in the CAR.

8. *The Prosecutor v. Jean-Pierre Bemba Gombo*, ICC-01/05–01/08, Trial Transcript, May 17, 2011, 3–4, https://www.icc-cpi.int/Transcripts/CR2015_02625.PDF. I have supplemented the notes I took while in the public galleries with official court transcripts. In some cases, I would have heard things spoken in open court that would be redacted in the transcripts, while in other cases, the transcripts revealed moments of the proceedings that were held in private or closed session but were reclassified for release at a later date. I will discuss the place of transcripts and transcription in the court's work in greater depth in the next chapter.

9. For a discussion of the precedents set by *Bemba*, see Janine Natalya Clark, "The First Rape Conviction at the ICC: An Analysis of the *Bemba* Judgment," *Journal of International Criminal Justice* 14 (2016): 667–87. See Chantal Meloni, *Command Responsibility in International Criminal Law* (The Hague: T.M.C. Asser, 2010), for a detailed history of how international tribunals have dealt with the question of command responsibility. Analyses of these precedents in light of Bemba's acquittal in 2018 were not available at the time of writing.

10. *Bemba*, Trial Transcript, May 17, 2011, 6.

11. Throughout the *Bemba* proceedings, this term was used to refer to MLC troops in the CAR, as it was widely used by the witnesses called by the prosecution. However, as Felix Mukwiza Ndahinda argues, such a use of the ethnonym "Banyamulengue" risks criminalizing a wider community that was not involved in the MLC's crimes, and absolves the crimes of those members of the MLC who did not belong to the Banyamulengue community. See Felix Mukwiza Ndahinda, "The Bemba-Banyamulenge Case before the ICC: From Individual to Collective Criminal Responsibility," *International Journal of Transitional Justice* 7 (2013): 476–96.

12. *Bemba*, Trial Transcript, May 17, 2011, 6–7.

13. That the Rome Statute provides opportunities for victims to participate throughout the court's proceedings is another historic innovation of the ICC. Several offices at the court deal with victims: the Victims and Witnesses Unit provides protection and psychological support to those who appear at the court, the Victims Participation and Reparations Section handles applications to become participating victims in the proceedings (and thus be eligible for reparations), and the Office of Public Counsel for the Victims provides legal assistance to those victims who take part in trials. Lawyers for the victims sit in the courtroom alongside the prosecution, and are given an opportunity to pose questions to witnesses throughout the trial, in addition to the usual direct and cross-examinations carried out by the prosecution and defense teams.

14. This view is widespread. Tatiana Carayannis reports: "Bemba's arrest immediately and predictably prompted outrage in the DRC, glee among Bozizé's inner circle in Bangui, and accusations throughout Africa that the ICC is a political instrument of Western powers aimed against African leaders." Carayannis, "CAR's Southern Identity," 261.

15. See Channa Wickremesekera, *The Tamil Separatist War in Sri Lanka* (London: Routledge, 2016), for a military history of the war in Sri Lanka.

16. See chapter 2 for more background on the Ituri conflict.

17. *The Prosecutor v. Thomas Lubanga Dyilo*, ICC-01/04–01/06, Trial Transcript, January 28, 2009, 35–40, http://www.icc-cpi.int/iccdocs/doc/doc1385048.pdf, emphasis added.

18. Mike Corder, "Testimony of Former Congo Child Soldier Halted," *San Diego Tribune*, January 29, 2009, http://www.sandiegouniontribune.com/sdut-eu-international-court-congo-012909-2009jan29-story.html.

19. *Lubanga*, "Closing Submissions for Victims a/0001/06, a/0002/06, a/0003/06, a/0007/06 a/00049/06, a/0149/07, a/0155/07, a/0156/07, a/0162/07, a/0149/08, a/0404/08, a/0405/08, a/0406/08, a/0407/08, a/0409/08, a/0523/08, a/0610/08, a/0611/08, a/0053/09, a/0249/09, a/0292/09 and a/0398/09," June 1, 2011, https://www.icc-cpi.int/CourtRecords/CR2012_00959.PDF.

20. Registry of the International Criminal Court, "Guidelines Governing the Relations between the Court and Intermediaries," March 2014, 5, http://www.icc-cpi.int/en_menus/icc/legal%20texts%20and%20tools/strategies-and-guidelines/Documents/GRCI-Eng.pdf.

21. Ibid., 6.

22. *Lubanga*, Trial Transcript, January 28, 2009, 9.

23. During and in the wake of the *Lubanga* verdict, a small but growing legal literature on the use of intermediaries has developed, including Elena Baylis, "Outsourcing Investigations," *UCLA Journal of International Law and Foreign Affairs* 14, no. 121 (spring 2009): 121–47; Christian de Vos, "Case Note: Prosecutor v. Lubanga: 'Someone Who Comes between One Person and Another': *Lubanga*, Local Cooperation and the Right to a Fair Trial," *Melbourne Journal of International Law* 12 (2011): 217–36; Emily Haslam and Rod Edmunds, "Managing a New 'Partnership': 'Professionalization,' Intermediaries and the International Criminal Court," *Criminal Law Forum* 24, no. 1 (March 2013): 49–85; and Caroline Buisman, "Delegating Investigations: Lessons to Be Learned from the Lubanga Judgment," *Northwestern Journal of International Human Rights* 11, no. 3 (summer 2013): 30–82.

24. *Lubanga*, "Judgment Pursuant to Article 74 of the Statute," March 14, 2012, 91, http://www.icc-cpi.int/iccdocs/doc/doc1379838.pdf.

25. *Lubanga*, Rule 68 Deposition, Transcript, November 16, 2010, 37, http://www.icc-cpi.int/iccdocs/doc/doc1298128.pdf.

26. Ibid., 54.

27. Registry of the ICC, "Guidelines," 4.

28. Robert Cover, "Violence and the Word," in *Narrative, Violence, and the Law: The Essays of Robert Cover*, ed. Martha Minow, Michael Ryan, and Austin Sarat (Ann Arbor: University of Michigan Press, 1993), 238.

29. *Lubanga*, "Judgment Pursuant to Article 74 of the Statute," 219.

30. Buisman, "Delegating Investigations," 32.

31. Scholars who consider performance and the law often hit upon this apparent conflict between the live and the documentary at the heart of courtroom proceedings. Philip Auslander argues that the live performance of recollection is essential to the law; see *Liveness: Performance in a Mediatized Culture* (London: Routledge, 1999), 125. Diana Taylor takes a historical view

Notes to Pages 120–127

to establish the preference of colonizing powers for archival evidence over embodied knowledge; see *The Archive and the Repertoire*. And Shoshana Felman argues that the prosecution in the 1961 trial of Adolf Eichmann chose to add live witnesses to their documentary evidence in order to "transmit history as an experience"; see *The Juridical Unconscious,* 133. Caught in these same debates, the Lubanga trial wrangled with questions of memory, transmission, and power, attaching political questions (of justice) to aesthetic questions (of medium).

32. *Lubanga*, "Judgment Pursuant to Article 74 of the Statute," 128.
33. Ibid., 122–23.
34. Ibid., 123.
35. Diana Taylor usefully summarizes: "In some cases, the emphasis on the constructedness of performance reveals an antitheatrical prejudice; in more complex readings, the constructed is recognized as coterminous with the real." Taylor, *The Archive and the Repertoire,* 4.
36. *Lubanga*, "Judgment Pursuant to Article 74 of the Statute," 157.
37. *Lubanga*, "Separate and Dissenting Opinion of Judge Odio Benito," March 14, 2012, 12, http://www.icc-cpi.int/iccdocs/doc/doc1379838-O.pdf.
38. Registry of the ICC, "Guidelines," 2.
39. Haslam and Edmunds, "Managing a New 'Partnership,' " 57.
40. *Lubanga*, Trial Transcript, January 28, 2009, 49–50.
41. Quoted in Olivia Bueno, "14 Years: Too Much or Not Enough?" International Justice Monitor, July 16, 2012, http://www.ijmonitor.org/2012/07/14-years-too-much-or-not-enough/.
42. Kevin Jon Heller, " 'Crossing Lines' Is Going to Be a Disaster . . . ," Opinio Juris, May 12, 2013, http://opiniojuris.org/2013/05/12/crossing-lines-is-going-to-be-a-disaster/.
43. Kevin Jon Heller, "The Problem with 'Crossing Lines,' " Opinio Juris, June 24, 2013, http://opiniojuris.org/2013/06/24/the-problem-with-crossing-lines/.
44. Heller, " 'Crossing Lines' Is Going to Be a Disaster . . ."
45. Kevin Jon Heller, "Crossing Lines S01E04 ('Long-Haul Predators')," Opinio Juris, July 9, 2013, http://opiniojuris.org/2013/07/09/crossing-lines-s01e04-long-haul-predators/.
46. Heller, " 'Crossing Lines' Is Going to Be a Disaster . . ."
47. Kevin Jon Heller, "Crossing Lines S01E07 ('Animals')," Opinio Juris, August 1, 2013, http://opiniojuris.org/2013/08/01/crossing-lines-s01e07-animals/.
48. See, for example, Kevin Jon Heller, "The Curious Timing of the Bemba Arrests," Opinio Juris, November 27, 2013, http://opiniojuris.org/2013/11/27/curious-timing-bemba-arrests/.
49. *Crossing Lines*, season 1, episode 1, "Pilot," directed by Daniel Percival, written by Edward Allen Bernero, featuring Marc Lavoine, Gabriella Pression, and Donald Sutherland, aired June 23, 2013, on NBC.
50. Heller, "The Problem with 'Crossing Lines.' "
51. Kevin Jon Heller, "Crossing Lines Is Back! (And Actually Better Than Ever)," Opinio Juris, October 5, 2015, http://opiniojuris.org/2015/10/05/crossing-lines-is-back-and-actually-better-than-ever/.
52. Ibid.
53. Ibid.

54. *Crossing Lines*, season 3, episode 1, "Redux," directed by Niall McCormick, written by Frank Spotnitz, featuring Donald Sutherland, aired September 30, 2015, on Netflix; and *Crossing Lines*, season 3, episode 2, "Whistleblower," directed by Niall McCormick, written by Wendy Battles, featuring Donald Sutherland, aired September 30, 2015, on Netflix.

55. Heller, "Crossing Lines Is Back!"

56. IntlCriminalCourt, "Bemba Case: Verdict, 21 March 2016," YouTube video, 1:13:50, March 21, 2016, https://www.youtube.com/watch?v=Uy4y-pinGWY.

57. Sophie van Leeuwen, "This Is Round One, Says Bemba's Lawyer," Justice Hub, March 22, 2016, https://justicehub.org/article/round-one-says-bembas-lawyer.

58. Stéphanie Maupas, "Jean-Pierre Bemba jugé coupable de crimes contre l'humanité en Centrafrique," *Le Monde*, March 21, 2016, http://www.lemonde.fr/afrique/article/2016/03/21/l-ancien-vice-president-congolais-juge-coupable-de-crimes-contre-l-humanite-en-centrafrique_4887192_3212.html.

59. Elvis Katsana, "Jean-Pierre Bemba Is Eagerly Awaited by Many in the DRC," Justice Hub, March 18, 2016, https://justicehub.org/article/jean-pierre-bemba-eagerly-awaited-drc.

60. Brian Obara, "'He Will Appeal. He's Our President'—Reactions to Bemba's Sentencing," Justice Hub, June 23, 2016, https://justicehub.org/article/he-will-appeal-hes-our-president-reactions-bembas-sentencing.

61. Fritz Streiff, "The Bemba Acquittal: Checks and Balances at the International Criminal Court," International Justice Monitor, July 18, 2018, https://www.ijmonitor.org/2018/07/the-bemba-acquittal-checks-and-balances-at-the-international-criminal-court/.

62. Janet Anderson, "Bemba's Lawyer: The Fact That There Are Victims Doesn't Mean That the Man in the Dock Is Guilty," Justice Hub, June 13, 2018, https://justicehub.org/article/bembas-lawyer-fact-there-are-victims-doesnt-mean-man-dock-guilty.

63. IntlCriminalCourt, "Bemba Case: ICC Appeals Chamber Judgement, 8 June 2018," YouTube video, 48:00, June 8, 2018, https://www.youtube.com/watch?v=M_NK5nopbsM.

64. For reports of reactions to the Bemba acquittal in Africa, see Olivia Bueno, "Impact of the Bemba Acquittal Already Seen in the Democratic Republic of Congo," International Justice Monitor, August 2, 2018, https://www.ijmonitor.org/2018/08/impact-of-the-bemba-acquittal-already-seen-in-the-democratic-republic-of-congo/.

65. See Amnesty International, "CAR: Acquittal of Bemba a Blow to Victims," Amnesty International, June 8, 2018, https://www.amnesty.org/en/latest/news/2018/06/car-acquittal-of-bemba-a-blow-to-victims/.

66. While the conviction had been hailed as historic, the appeal raised new concerns about the court's future. To some, the majority's findings "turn[ed] the Court's procedures upside down," (Alex Whiting, "Appeals Judges Turn the ICC on Its Head with Bemba Decision," Just Security, June 14, 2018, https://www.justsecurity.org/57760/appeals-judges-turn-icc-head-bemba-decision/), indicating "an apparent drift away from the assignment of responsibility for international crimes" (Diane Amann, "In Bemba and Beyond, Crimes Adjudged

to Commit Themselves," EJIL: Talk! June 13, 2018, https://www.ejiltalk.org/in-bemba-and-beyond-crimes-adjudged-to-commit-themselves/). Others lauded the majority for not "reducing [the Appeals Chamber] to a sort of 'court of cassation'" (Jacques B. Mbokani, "The Bemba Appeals Judgment: The ICC Facing the Tower of Babel?" International Justice Monitor, June 26, 2018, https://www.ijmonitor.org/2018/06/the-bemba-appeals-judgment-the-icc-facing-the-tower-of-babel/) and soberly reminded readers that it would "be inappropriate to bemoan the decay of everything the ICC stands for" (Alexander Heinze, "Some Reflections on the Bemba Appeals Chamber Judgment," Opinio Juris, June 18, 2018, http://opiniojuris.org/2018/06/18/some-reflections-on-the-bemba-appeals-chamber-judgment/).

Chapter 6

1. DJ Shadow and Run the Jewels, "DJ Shadow ft. Run The Jewels—Nobody Speak," dir. Sam Pilling, Vimeo video, 3:46, 2016, https://vimeo.com/180016993.

2. Killer Mike and El-P are present in the video, though they are displaced from their own voices. The also sit at the table, positioned as spectators who watch with dismay as the situation deteriorates.

3. Shore Fire Media, "DJ Shadow Unveils 'Nobody Speak' Music Video Featuring Run the Jewels," press release, August 24, 2016, http://shorefire.com/releases/entry/dj-shadow-tour-dates-nobody-speak-music-video-featuring-run-the-jewels.

4. Quoted ibid.

5. "Nobody Speak Lyrics," Genius.com, accessed September 23, 2016, http://genius.com/9016845.

6. Alexander Ostrower, *Language, Law, and Diplomacy* (Philadelphia: University of Pennsylvania Press, 1965), 108.

7. Ostrower explains, "Toward the end of the eighteenth century the word 'diploma' had undergone a process of transformation . . . the meaning of the word shifted from the form of the document to its contents, from the paper itself to what it actually represented in international relations. The new word *diplomatie* (diplomacy) thus derived signified the art or business of the *diplomarius* of the French *diplomâte*, and the English *diplomatist*, or *diplomat* by contraction. Thus diplomacy had become the craft of a person entrusted with an official mission by a state in its intercourse with other countries." Ostrower, *Language*, 109. See also Costas M. Constantinou, *On the Way to Diplomacy* (Minneapolis: University of Minnesota Press, 1996), 69–95.

8. For example, Marvin Carlson has outlined the historical transformation of the question, debates ongoing since the romantic period over whether the stage illustrates, translates, fulfills, or supplements the page in his article "Theatrical Performance: Illustration, Translation, Fulfillment, or Supplement?" *Theatre Journal* 37, no. 1 (March 1985): 5–11; Marco De Marinis has argued for the expanded category of the "performance text" in the analysis of theatrical events in *The Semiotics of Performance* (Bloomington: Indiana University Press, 1993); and Jacques Derrida has investigated the place of the written word in theories of the speech act in his essay "Signature, Event, Context," in *Limited, Inc.*, trans. Samuel Weber and Jeffrey Mehlman (Evanston, Ill.: Northwestern University Press, 1988), 1–25.

9. Richard Schechner, *Environmental Theater* (New York: Applause, 1973), xli.

10. Both a 2005 special issue of *Theatre Topics* (vol. 15, no. 1) on devising and a 2010 special issue of *TDR* (T208) on new devising ensembles feature extended discussions of the relationship between individual artists, the collectives in which they operate, and the broader national and transnational communities in which their work appears.

11. At the time of my visit to the court, Katanga and Ngudjolo were codefendants accused as military commanders of two armed groups in Ituri in the eastern Democratic Republic of the Congo of recruiting and employing child soldiers and ordering an attack on the civilian village of Bogoro in February 2003. The trials were split in November 2012. Ngudjolo was acquitted and released in December 2012, while Katanga was convicted on five counts in March 2014 and sentenced to twelve years imprisonment. For an overview of the conflicts in the DRC, see chapter 2.

12. *The Prosecutor v. Germain Katanga and Mathieu Ngudjolo Chui*, ICC-01/04–01/07, Trial Transcript, May 23, 2011, 11, https://www.icc-cpi.int/Transcripts/CR2011_07222.PDF.

13. Ibid., 12–18.

14. See chapter 3.

15. United Nations, Charter.

16. UN General Assembly, Tenth Special Session, 9th Plenary Meeting, A/S-10/PV.9, May 30, 1978, 176, http://undocs.org/en/A/S-10/PV.9.

17. Janelle Reinelt writes, "Performance makes visible the micro-processes of iteration and the non-commensurability of repetition, in the context of historically sedimented and yet contingent practices, in order that we might stage theatricality, and render palpable possibilities for unanticipated signification." Reinelt, "The Politics of Discourse: Performativity Meets Theatricality," *SubStance* 31, no. 2/3 (2002): 213.

18. Homer A. Jack, *Disarmament Workbook: The U.N. Special Session and Beyond* (New York: World Conference on Religion and Peace, 1978), iii.

19. Jacques Rancière, *Disagreement: Politics and Philosophy*, trans. Julie Rose (Minneapolis: University of Minnesota Press, 1999), 23.

20. The Non-Aligned Movement emerged from the 1955 Bandung Conference of Asian and African Nations, and was formally constituted at the 1961 Conference of the Non-Aligned Nations in Belgrade, Yugoslavia, where initial calls were made for a global nuclear disarmament conference, calls fulfilled in the Special Sessions on Disarmament. See Naoko Shimazu, "'Diplomacy as Theatre': Recasting the Bandung Conference of 1955 as Cultural History," Working Paper Series No. 164 (Singapore: Asia Research Institute, 2011), for a discussion of the Bandung Conference's cultural effects and theatricality. See Richard L. Jackson, *The Non-Aligned, The UN, and the Superpowers* (New York: Praeger, 1983), for a history of the Non-Aligned Movement written in the wake of the two Special Sessions on Disarmament.

21. "Dissensus" is Rancière's term for disruptive speech that reveals the inequality in professedly egalitarian political formations; see Rancière, *Disagreement*, 23.

22. Dimitris Bourantonis, *The United Nations and the Quest for Nuclear Disarmament* (Cambridge, Mass.: Dartmouth, 1993), 53. Bourantonis's book

Notes to Pages 143–150

provides an excellent history of nuclear disarmament at the UN, including the role of the Non-Aligned Movement.

23. Ibid., 145–62.

24. Though this session was the First Special Session on Disarmament, it was the Tenth Special Session convened by the UN General Assembly.

25. UN General Assembly, Tenth Special Session, 19th Plenary Meeting, A/S-10/PV.19, June 6, 1978, 351, http://undocs.org/en/A/S-10/PV.19.

26. Jack, *Disarmament Workbook*, 57.

27. UN General Assembly, Tenth Special Session, 12th Plenary Meeting, A/S-10/PV.12, June 1, 1978, 234–35, http://undocs.org/en/A/S-10/PV.12.

28. UN General Assembly, 2400th Plenary Meeting, A/PV.2400, November 10, 1975, 776, http://undocs.org/en/A/PV.2400.

29. UN General Assembly, Tenth Special Session, 13th Plenary Meeting, A/S-10/PV.13, June 1, 1978, 260, http://undocs.org/en/A/S-10/PV.13.

30. Quoted in "Jamil the Irrepressible," *Time* 98, no. 24 (December 13, 1971): 46.

31. Raymond Cohen, *Theatre of Power: The Art of Diplomatic Signaling* (London: Longman, 1987), 1.

32. Annelise Riles, "Infinity within the Brackets," *American Ethnologist* 25, no. 3 (1998): 390.

33. Ibid.

34. UN General Assembly, Verbatim Record of the 13th Meeting of the Ad Hoc Committee of the Tenth Special Session, A/S-10/AC.1/PV.13, June 23, 1978, [33], http://undocs.org/en/A/S-10/AC.1/PV.13.

35. This comparison appeared in Jack, *Disarmament Yearbook*, 55. The relevant paragraph of the Final Document can also be found in UN General Assembly, Final Document of the Tenth Special Session of the General Assembly, A/S-10/2, adopted as a resolution, June 30, 1978, 6, http://undocs.org/en/A/S-10/2.

36. UN General Assembly, Verbatim Record of the 15th Meeting of the Ad Hoc Committee of the Tenth Special Session, A/S-10/AC.1/PV.15, June 28, 1978, [10], http://undocs.org/en/A/S-10/AC.1/PV.15.

37. UN General Assembly, Tenth Special Session, 27th Plenary Meeting, A/S-10/PV.27, June 30, 1978, 508, http://undocs.org/en/A/S-10/PV.27.

38. Ibid., 474.

39. Ibid., 511.

40. Ibid., 486.

41. Ibid., 480.

42. Ibid., 504.

43. Ibid., 481.

44. Center for Defense Information, "Paul Newman: U.S. Delegate," *Defense Monitor* 7, no. 7 (1978): 3.

45. Ibid.

46. The UN Framework Convention on Climate Change is an environmental treaty adopted in 1992 that provides for annual conferences among its parties on efforts to address climate change. It can be found online at http://www.unfccc.int/.

47. Imanuel Schipper, interview with author, August 2016. All subsequent direct quotations of Schipper are from this interview.

48. My descriptions of the performance's details are all based on video documentation of the performance of *World Climate Conference* on December 12, 2014, made available online by Rimini Protokoll. See Rimini Protokoll, "WELT-KLIMAKONFERENZ (World Climate Change Conference) | Helgard Haug, Stefan Kaegi, Daniel Wetzel (with English Subtitles)," Vimeo video, 54:34, 2015, https://vimeo.com/129199465.

49. Center for Defense Information, "Paul Newman," 1.

50. Miriam Dreysse and Florian Malzacher, eds., *Experts of the Everyday: The Theatre of Rimini Protokoll* (Berlin: Alexander Verlag, 2008).

51. Rancière, *The Politics of Aesthetics*, 17.

Epilogue

1. Samantha Power, "Remarks on 'From Turtle Bay to Broadway: The Power of Art in American Diplomacy' at the Foundation for Art and Preservation in Embassies (FAPE) Dinner," March 7, 2016, https://2009-2017-usun.state.gov/remarks/7178.

2. Nikki Haley, "Remarks to Press before the Presentation of Credentials to the UN Secretary-General," January 27, 2017, https://usun.state.gov/remarks/7659.

3. Nikki Haley, "Remarks at an Emergency UN Security Council Meeting on Nonproliferation in the Democratic Republic of Korea," July 5, 2017, https://usun.state.gov/remarks/7890.

4. Nikki Haley, "Remarks before a UN General Assembly Vote on Jerusalem," December 21, 2017, https://usun.state.gov/remarks/8232.

5. Nikki Haley, "Remarks at an Emergency UN Security Council Briefing on Iran," January 5, 2018, https://usun.state.gov/remarks/8248.

6. Nikki Haley (@nikkihaley), "Loving the Americans!" Twitter, February 19, 2017, 10:43 p.m., https://twitter.com/nikkihaley/status/833522357037854720.

7. Nikki Haley (@nikkihaley), "I have always loved the Grammys but to have artists read the Fire and Fury book killed it. Don't ruin great music with trash. Some of us love music without the politics thrown into it." Twitter, January 28, 2018, 10:12 p.m., https://twitter.com/nikkihaley/status/957813664207245313.

BIBLIOGRAPHY

ABC News. "Colin Powell on Iraq, Race, and Hurricane Relief." *ABC 20/20.* September 8, 2005. http://abcnews.go.com/2020/Politics/story?id=1105979&page=1#.T0J-q3JWrPs.
Advocate Contributors. "That Time the U.N. Ambassador Came to See *Fun Home*." The Advocate. March 14, 2016. http://www.advocate.com/commentary/2016/3/14/time-un-ambassador-came-see-fun-home, for reporting on the show.
Ahmed, Sara. *The Promise of Happiness.* Durham, N.C.: Duke University Press, 2010.
Ahrendt, Rebekah, Mark Ferraguto, and Damien Mahiet, eds. *Music and Diplomacy: From the Early Modern Era to the Present.* New York: Palgrave Macmillan, 2014.
Akasaka, Kiyotaka, Radhika Coomaraswamy, David Eick, Whoopi Goldberg, David Howe, Mary McDonnell, Craig Mokhiber, Ronald D. Moore, Edward James Olmos, Robert Orr, and Famatta Rose Osode. "Special Event: UN Public Information Department, Sci Fi Channel to Co-Host a Panel with Battlestar Galactica Creators to Raise Profile of Humanitarian Concern." United Nations Webcast RealVideo, 2:04:00. March 17, 2009. http://www.un.org/webcast/2009a.html.
Alibasic, Haris, Ajila Delkic, Emir Ramic, and Sanja Segerovic-Drnovsek. "Protest Letter to Ban Ki-moon, UN Secretary-General." Bosniak.org. Congress of North American Bosniaks. January 15, 2013. http://www.bosniak.org/protest-letter-to-ban-ki-moon-un-general-secretary/.
Amann, Diane. "In Bemba and Beyond, Crimes Adjudged to Commit Themselves." EJIL: Talk! June 13, 2018. https://www.ejiltalk.org/in-bemba-and-beyond-crimes-adjudged-to-commit-themselves/.
Amnesty International. "CAR: Acquittal of Bemba a Blow to Victims." Amnesty International. June 8, 2018. https://www.amnesty.org/en/latest/news/2018/06/car-acquittal-of-bemba-a-blow-to-victims//
Anderson, Janet. "Bemba's Lawyer: The Fact That There Are Victims Doesn't Mean That the Man in the Dock Is Guilty." Justice Hub. June 13, 2018. https://justicehub.org/article/bembas-lawyer-fact-there-are-victims-doesnt-mean-man-dock-guilty.
Araud, Gérard. "Gérard Araud (France) and Philip Parham (United Kingdom) on Syria—Security Council Media Stakeout (20 March 2013)." United Nations Webcast streaming video, 10:10. March 20, 2013. http://webtv.un.org/search/g%C3%A9rard-araud-france-and-philip-parham-united-kingdom-on-syria-security-council-media-stakeout-20-march-2013/2240792345001.

Auslander, Philip. *Liveness: Performance in a Mediatized Culture*. London: Routledge, 1999.
Austin, J. L. *How to Do Things with Words*. Edited by J. O. Urmson and Marina Sbisà. Cambridge, Mass.: Harvard University Press, 1955.
Autesserre, Séverine. *The Trouble with the Congo: Local Violence and the Failure of International Peacebuilding*. Cambridge: Cambridge University Press, 2010.
Ball III, James R. "The Live Archive of the World Stage: Engagement and Spectatorship in the United Nations Webcast." *e-Misférica* 9, nos. 1 and 2. http://hemisphericinstitute.org/hemi/en/e-misferica-91/ball.
Ball, Milner S. "The Play's the Thing: An Unscientific Reflection on Courts under the Rubric of Theater." *Stanford Law Review* 28, no. 1 (1975): 81–116.
Ban Ki-moon and Park-Jae Sang. "Secretary-General Ban Ki-moon and PSY, Korean Singer." United Nations Webcast streaming video, 8:50. October 23, 2012. http://webtv.un.org/%E2%80%A6/we%E2%80%A6/watch/secretary-general-ban-ki-moon-and-psy-korean-singer/1920431996001.
Baylis, Elena. "Outsourcing Investigations." *UCLA Journal of International Law and Foreign Affairs* 14, no. 121 (spring 2009): 121–47.
Bechdel, Alison. *Fun Home: A Family Tragicomic*. Boston: Houghton Mifflin Harcourt, 2007.
Bellamy, Alex J., and Paul D. Williams with Stuart Griffin. *Understanding Peacekeeping*. 2nd edition. Cambridge: Polity, 2010.
Benjamin, Walter. "Theses on the Philosophy of History." In *Illuminations*, translated by Harry Zohn, edited by Hannah Arendt, 253–64. New York: Schocken Books, 1968.
Bentley, Michelle. *Syria and the Chemical Weapons Taboo*. Manchester, Eng.: Manchester University Press, 2016.
Bhabha, Homi. *The Location of Culture*. New York: Routledge, 1994.
Blix, Hans. *Disarming Iraq*. New York: Pantheon Books, 2004.
Bourantonis, Dimitris. *The United Nations and the Quest for Nuclear Disarmament*. Cambridge: Dartmouth, 1993.
Brantley, Ben. "War's Terrors, through a Brothel Window." *New York Times*. February 11, 2009, C1.
Bregman, Ahron. *Israel's Wars: A History since 1947*. 4th edition. London: Routledge, 2016.
Brown, Gordon, Barack Obama, and Nicolas Sarkozy. "Iranian Nuclear Program." *C-Span*. Streaming video, 8:04. September 25, 2009. https://www.c-span.org/video/?289138-1/iranian-nuclear-program.
Buckner, Jocelyn L., ed. *A Critical Companion to Lynn Nottage*. London: Routledge, 2016.
Bueno, Olivia. "14 Years: Too Much or Not Enough?" International Justice Monitor. July 16, 2012. http://www.ijmonitor.org/2012/07/14-years-too-much-or-not-enough/.
———. "Impact of the Bemba Acquittal Already Seen in the Democratic Republic of Congo." International Justice Monitor. August 2, 2018. https://www.ijmonitor.org/2018/08/impact-of-the-bemba-acquittal-already-seen-in-the-democratic-republic-of-congo/.

Buisman, Caroline. "Delegating Investigations: Lessons to Be Learned from the Lubanga Judgment." *Northwestern Journal of International Human Rights* 11, no. 3 (summer 2013): 30–82.

Buruma, Ian. *The Wages of Guilt: Memories of War in Germany and Japan*. New York: Farrar, Straus and Giroux, 1994.

Butler, Judith. *Excitable Speech: A Politics of the Performative*. New York: Routledge, 1997.

Canning, Charlotte M. *On the Performance Front: U.S. Theatre and Internationalism*. London: Palgrave Macmillan, 2015.

Carayannis, Tatiana. "CAR's Southern Identity: Congo, CAR, and International Justice." In *Making Sense of the Central African Republic*, edited by Tatiana Carayannis and Louisa Lombard, 244–66. London: Zed Books, 2015.

Carlson, Marvin. "Theatrical Performance: Illustration, Translation, Fulfillment, or Supplement?" *Theatre Journal* 37, no. 1 (March 1985): 5–11.

Center for Defense Information. "Paul Newman: U.S. Delegate." *The Defense Monitor* 7, no. 7 (1978): 1–5.

Chow, Rey. *The Age of the World Target: Self-Referentiality in War, Theory, and Comparative Work*. Durham, N.C.: Duke University Press, 2006.

Churkin, Vitaly. "SC President, Vitaly I. Churkin (Russian Federation) on Central African Republic (CAR), Syria—Security Council Media Stakeout (20 March 2013)." United Nations Webcast streaming video, 17:58. March 20, 2013. http://webtv.un.org/search/sc-president-vitaly-i.-churkin-russian-federation-on-central-african-republic-car-syria-security-council-media-stakeout-20-march-2013/2240819371001.

Clark, Janine Natalya. "The First Rape Conviction at the ICC: An Analysis of the Bemba Judgment." *Journal of International Criminal Justice* 14 (2016): 667–87.

Clarke, Kamari M. *Fictions of Justice: The International Criminal Court and the Challenge of Legal Pluralism in Sub-Saharan Africa*. New York: Cambridge University Press, 2009.

Claude Jr., Inis L. *The Changing United Nations*. New York: Random House, 1967.

Cohen, Raymond. *Theatre of Power: The Art of Diplomatic Signaling*. London: Longman, 1987.

Connor, Steven. "The Help of Your Good Hands: Reports on Clapping." In *The Auditory Culture Reader*, edited by Michael Bull and Les Back, 67–76. Oxford: Berg, 2003.

Constantinou, Costas M. *On the Way to Diplomacy*. Minneapolis: University of Minnesota Press, 1996.

Corder, Mike. "Testimony of Former Congo Child Soldier Halted." *San Diego Tribune*. January 29, 2009. http://www.sandiegouniontribune.com/sdut-eu-international-court-congo-012909-2009jan29-story.html.

Cover, Robert. "Violence and the Word." In *Narrative, Violence, and the Law: The Essays of Robert Cover*, edited by Martha Minow, Michael Ryan, and Austin Sarat, 203–38. Ann Arbor: University of Michigan Press, 1993.

The Daily Show. "Dude Is Crazy." *The Daily Show with John Stewart*. February 5, 2003. Streaming video, 1:58. http://www.cc.com/video-clips/04ik13/the-daily-show-with-jon-stewart-dude-is-crazy.

Davis, Tracy C. "Theatricality and Civil Society." In *Theatricality*, edited by Tracy C. Davis and Thomas Postlewait, 127–55. New York: Cambridge University Press, 2003.

De Marinis, Marco. *The Semiotics of Performance*. Bloomington: Indiana University Press, 1993.

De Vos, Christian. "Case Note: Prosecutor v. Lubanga: 'Someone Who Comes between One Person and Another': Lubanga, Local Cooperation, and the Right to a Fair Trial." *Melbourne Journal of International Law* 12 (2011): 217–36.

Debord, Guy. *Critique de la separation*. Streaming video hosted by UbuWeb Film, 17:23. 1961. http://ubu.com/film/debord_critique.html.

———. *The Society of the Spectacle*. Translated by Donald Nicholson Smith. New York: Zone Books, 1994.

Debrix, François. *Re-Envisioning Peacekeeping: The United Nations and the Mobilization of Ideology*. Minneapolis: University of Minnesota Press, 1999.

Der Derian, James. *Virtuous War: Mapping the Military-Industrial-Media-Entertainment Network*. 2nd edition. New York: Routledge, 2009.

Derrida, Jacques. *Limited, Inc*. Translated by Samuel Weber and Jeffrey Mehlman. Evanston, Ill.: Northwestern University Press, 1988.

DJ Shadow and Run the Jewels. "DJ Shadow ft. Run the Jewels—Nobody Speak." Directed by Sam Pilling. Vimeo video, 3:46. 2016. https://vimeo.com/180016993.

Donnelly, Pat. "FTA Calls Off the Dogs Today but Nella Tempesta Storms On." MontrealGazette.com. May 25, 2013. http://blogs.montrealgazette.com/2013/05/25/fta-calls-off-the-dogs-today-but-nella-tempesta-storms-on/.

Doss, Alan. "United Nations Organization Mission in the Democratic Republic of the Congo (MONUC)." In *The Oxford Handbook of United Nations Peacekeeping Operations*, edited by Joachim A Koops, Norrie Macqueen, Thierry Tardy, and Paul D. Williams, 656–70. Oxford: Oxford University Press, 2015.

Douglas, Lawrence. *The Memory of Judgment: Making Law and History in the Trials of the Holocaust*. New Haven, Conn.: Yale University Press, 2001.

Douglas, Mary. *How Institutions Think*. Syracuse, N.Y.: Syracuse University Press, 1986.

Doyle, Leonard. "Has Colonel Gaddafi Lost His Chance to Meet Barack Obama?" *The Telegraph*. September 6, 2009. http://www.telegraph.co.uk/news/worldnews/northamerica/usa/6143761/Has-Colonel-Gaddafi-lost-his-chance-to-meet-Barack-Obama.html.

Dreysse, Miriam, and Florian Malzacher, eds. *Experts of the Everyday: The Theatre of Rimini Protokoll*. Berlin: Alexander Verlag, 2008.

Dromgoole, Dominic, Ladi Emeruwa, Miranda Foster, Rawiri Paratene, and Iona Thomas. "The Globe Theatre—Press Conference." United Nations Webcast streaming video, 30:09. August 4, 2014. http://webtv.un.org/search/the-globe-theatre-press-conference/3712745997001.

Edkins, Jenny, and Adrian Kear. Introduction to *International Politics and Performance: Critical Aesthetics and Creative Practice*, edited by Jenny Edkins and Adrian Kear, 1–15. London: Routledge, 2013.

Eliav, Pinhas. "Letter dated 13 March 1978 from the Charge d'affaires a.i. of the Permanent Mission of Israel to the United Nations addressed to the

Bibliography

Secretary-General." S/12598. March 13, 1978. http://www.un.org/en/ga/search/view_doc.asp?symbol=s/12598.
Erskine, Emmanuel A. *Mission with UNIFIL: An African Soldier's Reflections.* New York: St. Martin's Press, 1989.
Felman, Shoshana. *The Juridical Unconscious: Trials and Traumas in the Twentieth Century.* Cambridge, Mass.: Harvard University Press, 2002.
Flint, Julie, and Alex de Waal. *Darfur: A New History of a Long War.* London: Zed Books, 2008.
Foucault, Michel. *Dits et écrits II, 1976–1988.* Paris: Gallimard, 2001.
———. *Security, Territory, Population: Lectures at the Collège de France, 1977–78.* Edited by Michel Senellart, translated by Graham Burchell. New York: Palgrave Macmillan, 2007.
Friedman, Sharon. "The Gendered Terrain in Contemporary Theatre of War by Women." *Theatre Journal* 62 (2010): 593–610.
Fun Home on Broadway. "Welcome to FUN HOME at Circle in the Square Theatre." April 15, 2016. YouTube video, 1:24. https://www.youtube.com/watch?v=510IdY6xPr4.
Genius Media Group, Inc. "Nobody Speak Lyrics," Genius.com. http://genius.com/9016845.
GNRSlashLover. "Chubby Checker—Pony Time." YouTube video, 2:07. September 18, 2010. https://www.youtube.com/watch?v=JyaxcvHSyZY.
Green, Jeffrey Edward. *The Eyes of the People: Democracy in an Age of Spectatorship.* Oxford: Oxford University Press, 2010.
Haley, Nikki. (@nikkihaley). "I have always loved the Grammys, but to have artists read the Fire and Fury book killed it. Don't ruin great music with trash. Some of us love music without the politics thrown into it." Twitter, January 28, 2018, 10:12 p.m. https://twitter.com/nikkihaley/status/957813664207245313.
———. (@nikkihaley). "Loving the Americans!" Twitter. February 19, 2017, 10:43 p.m. https://twitter.com/nikkihaley/status/833522357037854720.
———. "Remarks at an Emergency UN Security Council Briefing on Iran." January 5, 2018. https://usun.state.gov/remarks/8248.
———. "Remarks at an Emergency UN Security Council Meeting on Nonproliferation in the Democratic Republic of Korea." July 5, 2017. https://usun.state.gov/remarks/7890.
———. "Remarks before a UN General Assembly Vote on Jerusalem." December 21, 2017. https://usun.state.gov/remarks/8232.
———. "Remarks to Press before the Presentation of Credentials to the UN Secretary-General." January 27, 2017. https://usun.state.gov/remarks/7659.
Hammersmith, James. "Hamlet and the Myth of Memory." *ELH* 45, no. 4 (1978): 603–4.
Hare, David. *Obedience, Struggle, and Revolt.* London: Faber and Faber, 2005.
———. *Stuff Happens.* London: Faber and Faber, 2004.
Harris, William. *Lebanon: A History 600–2011.* Oxford: Oxford University Press, 2012.
Haslam, Emily and Rod Edmunds. "Managing a New 'Partnership': 'Professionalization,' Intermediaries and the International Criminal Court." *Criminal Law Forum* 24, no. 1 (March 2013): 49–85.

Heinze, Alexander. "Some Reflections on the Bemba Appeals Chamber Judgment." Opinio Juris. June 18, 2018. http://opiniojuris.org/2018/06/18/some-reflections-on-the-bemba-appeals-chamber-judgment/.

Heller, Kevin Jon. "'Crossing Lines' Is Going to Be a Disaster . . ." Opinio Juris. May 12, 2013. http://opiniojuris.org/2013/05/12/crossing-lines-is-going-to-be-a-disaster/.

———. "The Problem with 'Crossing Lines.'" Opinio Juris. June 24, 2013. http://opiniojuris.org/2013/06/24/the-problem-with-crossing-lines/.

———. "Crossing Lines S01E04 ('Long-Haul Predators')." Opinio Juris. July 9, 2013. http://opiniojuris.org/2013/07/09/crossing-lines-s01e04-long-haul-predators/.

———. "Crossing Lines S01E07 ('Animals')." Opinio Juris. August 1, 2013. http://opiniojuris.org/2013/08/01/crossing-lines-s01e07-animals/.

———. "The Curious Timing of the Bemba Arrests." Opinio Juris. November 27, 2013. http://opiniojuris.org/2013/11/27/curious-timing-bemba-arrests/.

———. "Crossing Lines Is Back! (And Actually Better Than Ever)." Opinio Juris. October 5, 2015. http://opiniojuris.org/2015/10/05/crossing-lines-is-back-and-actually-better-than-ever/.

Hesford, Wendy. "Rhetorical Memory, Political Theater, and the Traumatic Present." *Transformations* 16, no. 2 (2005): 104–17.

———. *Spectacular Rhetorics: Human Rights Visions, Recognitions, Feminisms.* Durham, N.C.: Duke University Press, 2011.

Hibbitts, Bernard J. "'Coming to Our Senses': Communication and Legal Expression in Performance Cultures." *Emory Law Journal* 41, no. 4 (1992): 873–960.

Higate, Paul. "Peacekeepers, Masculinities, and Sexual Exploitation." *Men and Masculinities* 10, no. 1 (2007): 99–119.

Higate, Paul, and Marsha Henry. *Insecure Spaces: Peacekeeping, Power and Performance in Haiti, Kosovo and Liberia.* London: Zed Books, 2009.

Hijazi, Ihsan A. "Pro-Iranian Group Claims Abduction." *New York Times.* February 20, 1988, A1.

Hillen, John. *Blue Helmets: The Strategy of UN Military Operations.* 2nd edition. Washington, D.C.: Brassey's, 2000.

Holderness, Graham, and Bryan Loughrey. "Arabesque: Shakespeare and Globalization." *Essays and Studies* 59 (2006): 24–46.

IntlCriminalCourt. "Bemba Case: ICC Appeals Chamber Judgement, 8 June 2018." YouTube video, 48:00. June 8, 2018. https://www.youtube.com/watch?v=M_NK5nopbsM.

———. "Bemba Case: Verdict, 21 March 2016." YouTube video, 1:13:50. March 21, 2016. https://www.youtube.com/watch?v=Uy4y-pinGWY.

Jack, Homer A. *Disarmament Workbook: The U.N. Special Session and Beyond.* New York: World Conference on Religion and Peace, 1978.

Jackson, Richard L. *The Non-Aligned, the UN, and the Superpowers.* New York: Praeger, 1983.

Jakovljevic, Branislav. "From Mastermind to Body Artist: Political Performances of Slobodan Milošević." *TDR: The Drama Review* 52, no. 1 (2008): 51–74.

Katsana, Elvis. "Jean-Pierre Bemba Is Eagerly Awaited by Many in the DRC." Justice Hub. March 18, 2016. https://justicehub.org/article/jean-pierre-bemba-eagerly-awaited-drc.

Kershaw, Baz. "Oh for Unruly Audiences! or, Patterns of Participation in Twentieth-Century Theatre." *Modern Drama* 44, no. 2. (summer 2001): 135.
Knowles, Beverley. "Fierce Festival, Bennett Miller, Dachshund U.N." This Is Tomorrow. April 2, 2012. http://www.thisistomorrow.info/viewArticle.aspx?artId=1223.
Kolnai, Aurel. *On Disgust*. Edited by Barry Smith and Carolyn Korsmeyer. Chicago: Open Court, 2004.
Kovatch, Bonnie. "Sexual Exploitation and Abuse in UN Peacekeeping Missions: A Case Study of MONUC and MONUSCO." *Journal of the Middle East and Africa* 7, no. 2 (2016): 157–74.
Krasner, David. "Empathy and Theater." In *Staging Philosophy*, edited by David Krasner and David Z. Saltz, 255–77. Ann Arbor: University of Michigan Press, 2006.
Krasno, Jean E. "Founding the United Nations: An Evolutionary Process." In *The United Nations: Confronting the Challenges of a Global Society*, edited by Jean E. Krasno, 19–45. Boulder, Colo.: Lynne Rienner, 2004.
Kristeva, Julia. *Powers of Horror: An Essay on Abjection*. Translated by Leon S. Roudiez. New York: Columbia University Press, 1982.
Kron, Lisa. Foreword to *Fun Home*, music by Jeanine Tesori, book and lyrics by Lisa Kron, 7–8. Acting Edition. [New York]: Samuel French, 2015.
Lahav, Pnina. "Theater in the Courtroom: The Chicago Conspiracy Trial." *Law and Literature* 16, no. 3 (2004): 381–474.
Lennon, John. *Imagine*. Abbey Road Studios, 1971.
Lynch, Colum. "Exclusive: Russia Vetoes House of Cards." *Foreign Policy*. July 2, 2014. http://foreignpolicy.com/2014/07/02/exclusive-russia-vetoes-house-of-cards/.
Martin, Carol. "Introduction: Dramaturgy of the Real." In *Dramaturgy of the Real on the World Stage*, edited by Carol Martin, 1–14. London: Palgrave Macmillan, 2010.
Mattila, Kalle Oskari. "Selling Queerness: The Curious Case of *Fun Home*." *The Atlantic*. April 25, 2016. http://www.theatlantic.com/entertainment/archive/2016/04/branding-queerness-the-curious-case-of-fun-home/479532/.
Maupas, Stéphanie. "Jean-Pierre Bemba jugé coupable de crimes contre l'humanité en Centrafrique." *Le Monde*. March 21, 2016. http://www.lemonde.fr/afrique/article/2016/03/21/l-ancien-vice-president-congolais-juge-coupable-de-crimes-contre-l-humanite-en-centrafrique_4887192_3212.html.
Mazower, Mark. *No Enchanted Palace: The End of Empire and the Ideological Origins of the United Nations*. Princeton, N.J.: Princeton University Press, 2009.
Mbokani, Jacques B. "The Bemba Appeals Judgment: The ICC Facing the Tower of Babel?" International Justice Monitor. June 26, 2018. https://www.ijmonitor.org/2018/06/the-bemba-appeals-judgment-the-icc-facing-the-tower-of-babel/.
McCormick, Niall. *Crossing Lines*. Season 3, episode 1. "Redux." Written by Frank Spotnitz. Aired September 30, 2015, on Netflix.
———. *Crossing Lines*. Season 3, episode 2. "Whistleblower." Written by Wendy Battles. Aired September 30, 2015, on Netflix.
McCormick, Ty. "Is the U.S. Military Propping up Uganda's 'Elected' Autocrat?" *Foreign Policy*. February 18, 2016. http://foreignpolicy.com/2016/02/18/is-the-us-military-propping-up-ugandas-elected-autocrat-museveni-elections/.

McMillan, Katie. "Out of the Doghouse: Katie McMillan on Dachshund UN." *Harbourfront Centre Blog.* March 4, 2013. http://www.harbourfrontcentre.com/blog/2013/03/katie-mcmillan-discusses-dachshund-un/.

Médecins Sans Frontières. "Nothing New in Ituri: The Violence Continues." MSF Report. August 2005. http://www.msf.org/sites/msf.org/files/old-cms/source/countries/africa/drc/2005/ituri_violence_2005report.pdf.

Meloni, Chantal. *Command Responsibility in International Criminal Law.* The Hague: T.M.C. Asser, 2010.

Mobley, Jennifer-Scott. "Melodrama, Sensation, and Activism in *Ruined.*" In *A Critical Companion to Lynn Nottage*, edited by Jocelyn L. Buckner, 129–44. London: Routledge, 2016.

Mohamad, Abdalmahmood. "Media Stakeout: Informal Comments to the Media by the Permanent Representative of Sudan, H. E. Mr. Abdalmahmood Abdalhaleem Mohamad, on the Situation in Sudan." United Nations Webcast RealVideo, 10:00. June 5, 2009, http://www.un.org/webcast/2009.html.

Mooney, Alexander. "Obama Says Time to Rid World of Nuclear Weapons." *CNN.* July 16, 2008. http://www.cnn.com/2008/POLITICS/07/16/obama.speech/.

MosesTKrikey. "TEEN TIME—The Horse." YouTube video, 4:44. February 11, 2008. https://www.youtube.com/watch?v=l4XFk2VCgVc.

Mulvey, Laura. "Visual Pleasure and Narrative Cinema." In *Film Theory and Criticism: Introductory Readings*, edited by Leo Braudy and Marshall Cohen, 833–44. 5th edition. New York: Oxford University Press, 1999.

Murphy, Ray. *UN Peacekeeping in Lebanon, Somalia and Kosovo: Operational and Legal Issues in Practice.* Cambridge: Cambridge University Press, 2007.

Museveni, Yoweri. "Statement by H.E. Yoweri Kaguta Museveni, President of the Republic of Uganda, at the United Nations General Assembly." September 23, 2009. https://gadebate.un.org/sites/default/files/gastatements/64/64_UG_en.pdf.

Ndahinda, Felix Mukwiza. "The Bemba-Banyamulenge Case before the ICC: From Individual to Collective Criminal Responsibility." *International Journal of Transitional Justice* 7 (2013): 476–96.

Nesirky, Martin. "Daily Press Briefing: SG in California, Syria, Syria—UNRWA, Secretary-General's Appointments, Security Council, Darfur, DRC, Mali." UN Webcast streaming video, 15:32. January 17, 2013. http://webtv.un.org/search/daily-press-briefing-sg-in-california-syria-syria-%E2%80%93-unrwa-secretary-general%E2%80%99s-appointments-security-council-darfur-drc-mali/2101083964001/?term=2013-01-17&sort=date.

Nestruck, J. Kelly. "Why Man's Best Friend Is the Ultimate Performance Artist." *The Globe and Mail.* February 26, 2013. http://www.theglobeandmail.com/arts/theatre-and-performance/why-mans-best-friend-is-the-ultimate-performance-artist/article9094230/.

Newby, Vanessa F. *Peacekeeping in South Lebanon: Credibility and Local Cooperation.* Syracuse, N.Y.: Syracuse University Press, 2018.

Ngũgĩ Wa Thiong'o. *Penpoints, Gunpoints, and Dreams: Towards a Critical Theory of the Arts and the State in Africa.* Oxford: Clarendon, 1998.

Nichols, Michelle. "Serbian Military Song at U.N. Concert Sparks Bosnian Outcry." *Reuters.* January 17, 2013. http://www.reuters.com/article/us-serbia-bosnia-un-song-idUSBRE90G1D520130117.

Nielsen, Lara D. "Institutionalizing Ensembles: Thinking Theatre, Performance, and 'the Law.'" *Law, Culture and the Humanities* 4, no. 2 (2008): 156–78.
Nottage, Lynn. *Ruined*. New York: Theatre Communication Group, 2009.
Now Magazine (@nowtoronto). "Hey turns out the #DaschundUN is totally ineffective and has no consequent bearing on international law . . . just like the real UN! #rimshot." Twitter. March 3, 2013, 3:31 p.m. https://twitter.com/nowtoronto/status/308313724433862656.
O'Brien, Conor Cruise. *United Nations: Sacred Drama*. New York: Simon and Schuster, 1968.
Obama, Barack. "Presidential Memorandum—International Initiatives to Advance the Human Rights of Lesbian, Gay, Bisexual, and Transgender Persons." December 6, 2011. https://obamawhitehouse.archives.gov/the-press-office/2011/12/06/presidential-memorandum-international-initiatives-advance-human-rights-l.
———. "Remarks by President Barack Obama." Speech given in Prague, Czech Republic. April 5, 2009.
———. "'Responsibility for our Common Future': Address to the United Nations General Assembly." September 23, 2009. https://gadebate.un.org/sites/default/files/gastatements/64/64_US_en.pdf.
———. "United States of America, General Debate, 66th Session." September 21, 2011. United Nations Webcast streaming video, 36:31. http://www.unmultimedia.org/tv/webcast/2011/09/united-states-of-america-general-debate-66th-session.html.
Obara, Brian. "'He Will Appeal. He's Our President'—Reactions to Bemba's Sentencing." Justice Hub. June 23, 2016. https://justicehub.org/article/he-will-appeal-hes-our-president-reactions-bembas-sentencing.
Osiel, Mark. *Mass Atrocity, Collective Memory, and the Law*. New Brunswick, N.J.: Transaction, 1997.
Ostrower, Alexander. *Language, Law, and Diplomacy*. Philadelphia: University of Pennsylvania Press, 1965.
Paden, Jeff. "Renegotiating Realism: Hybridity of Form and Political Potentiality in *Ruined*." In *A Critical Companion to Lynn Nottage*, edited by Jocelyn L. Buckner, 145–60. London: Routledge, 2016.
Paris, Roland. "International Peacebuilding and the 'Mission Civilisatrice.'" *Review of International Studies* 28, no. 4 (2002): 637–56.
Peel, Quentin. "Gaddafi Offers Mere Sideshow to Main Event." *Financial Times*. September 25, 2009, 6. https://www.ft.com/content/2560cb3a-a94f-11de-9b7f-00144feabdc0.
Percival, Daniel, dir. *Crossing Lines*. "Pilot." Written by Edward Allen Bernero. Aired June 23, 2013, on NBC.
Powell, Colin. "Iraqi Weapons Compliance Debate." *C-Span*. February 5, 2003. Streaming video, 3:35:44. https://www.c-span.org/video/?174942-1/iraqi-weapons-compliance-debate.
Power, Samantha. "Remarks on 'I Know You: Making LGBTI Rights Human Rights at the UN and Abroad' at the Human Rights Campaign's Equality Convention." March 12, 2016. http://usun.state.gov/remarks/7185.
———. "Remarks on 'From Turtle Bay to Broadway: The Power of Art in American Diplomacy' at the Foundation for Art and Preservation in Embassies

(FAPE) Dinner." March 7, 2016. https://2009-2017-usun.state.gov/remarks/7178.

Power, Samantha, and Subhi Nahas. "Samantha Power (USA) and Subhi Nahas on LGBT in the Middle East—Security Council Media Stakeout, Arria formula (24 August 2015)." United Nations Webcast streaming video, 14:44. August 24, 2015. http://webtv.un.org/search/samantha-power-usa-and-subhi-nahas-on-lgbt-in-the-middle-east-security-council-media-stakeout-arria-formula-24-august-2015/4441763676001/.

Prunier, Gérard. *Africa's World War: Congo, the Rwandan Genocide, and the Making of a Continental Catastrophe*. Oxford: Oxford University Press, 2009.

Qaddafi, Muammar. "General Debate of the 64th Session (2009)." United Nations Webcast RealVideo, English translation, 1:36:00. September 23, 2009. http://www.un.org/en/ga/64/generaldebate/LY.shtml.

Rancière, Jacques. *Disagreement: Politics and Philosophy*. Translated by Julie Rose. Minneapolis: University of Minnesota Press, 1999.

———. *The Emancipated Spectator*. Translated by Gregory Elliott. London: Verso, 2009.

———. *The Politics of Aesthetics: The Distribution of the Sensible*. Translated by Gabriel Rockhill. London: Continuum, 2004.

Registry of the International Criminal Court. "Guidelines Governing the Relations between the Court and Intermediaries." March 2014, 5. http://www.icc-cpi.int/en_menus/icc/legal%20texts%20and%20tools/strategies-and-guidelines/Documents/GRCI-Eng.pdf.

Rehn, Elisabeth, and Ellen Johnson Sirleaf. *Women, War and Peace: The Independent Experts' Assessment on the Impact of Armed Conflict on Women and Women's Role in Peace-Building*. New York: United Nations Development Fund for Women, 2002.

Reid, Richard J. *A History of Modern Uganda*. Cambridge: Cambridge University Press, 2017.

Reinelt, Janelle. "The Politics of Discourse: Performativity Meets Theatricality." *SubStance* 31, no. 2/3 (2002): 201–15.

———. "Review: *Stuff Happens* by David Hare, Nick Hytner." *Theatre Journal* 57, no. 2 (2005): 303–6.

Riles, Annelise. "Infinity within the Brackets." *American Ethnologist* 25, no. 3 (1998): 378–98.

Rimini Protokoll. "WELT-KLIMAKONFERENZ (World Climate Change Conference) | Helgard Haug, Stefan Kaegi, Daniel Wetzel (with English subtitles)." Vimeo video, 54:34. 2015. https://vimeo.com/129199465.

Rivlin, Benjamin. "The UN Secretary-Generalship at Fifty." In *The United Nations in the New World Order: The World Organization at Fifty*, edited by Dimitris Bourantonis and Jarrod Weiner, 81–104. New York: St. Martin's Press, 1995.

Roberts, Rebecca. *Palestinians in Lebanon: Refugees Living with Long-Term Displacement*. London: I.B. Tauris, 2010.

Roessler, Philip, and Harry Verhoeven. *Why Comrades Go to War: Liberation Politics and the Outbreak of Africa's Deadliest Conflict*. Oxford: Oxford University Press, 2016.

Rymer, Michael, dir. *Battlestar Galactica*. "Miniseries." Written by David Eick and Ronald D. Moore. Aired December 8 and 9, 2003, on the Sci Fi Channel.

Bibliography

Sarat, Austin, Lawrence Douglas, and Martha Merrill Umphrey, eds. *Law and Performance*. Amherst and Boston, Mass.: University of Massachusetts Press, 2018.

Schechner, Richard. *Environmental Theater*. New York: Applause, 1973.

———. *Performance Theory*. New York: Routledge, 1988.

Schipper, Imanuel. Interview with author. August 2016.

Schroeder, Kent. *Politics of Gross National Happiness: Governance and Development in Bhutan*. New York: Palgrave Macmillan, 2017.

Scott, James C. *Seeing Like a State: How Certain Schemes to Improve the Human Condition Have Failed*. New Haven, Conn.: Yale University Press, 1998.

Security Council Report. "Security Council Working Methods: A Tale of Two Councils?" Special Research Report. March 25, 2014. http://www.securitycouncilreport.org/special-research-report/security-council-working-methods-a-tale-of-two-councils.php.

———. "September 2015 Monthly Forecast—Status Update." August 31, 2015. http://www.securitycouncilreport.org/monthly-forecast/2015-09/status_update_33.php.

Shakespeare, William. *Hamlet*. Edited by Harold Jenkins. London: Arden Shakespeare, 1982.

Shimakawa, Karen. *National Abjection: The Asian American Body Onstage*. Durham, N.C.: Duke University Press, 2002.

Shimazu, Naoko. "'Diplomacy as Theatre': Recasting the Bandung Conference of 1955 as Cultural History." Working Paper Series No. 164. Singapore: Asia Research Institute, 2011.

Shore Fire Media. "DJ Shadow Unveils 'Nobody Speak' Music Video Featuring Run the Jewels." Press release. August 24, 2016. http://shorefire.com/releases/entry/dj-shadow-tour-dates-nobody-speak-music-video-featuring-run-the-jewels.

Skloot, Robert. "Review Essay: Old Concerns and New Plays in the Theater of Genocide." *Genocide Studies and Prevention* 5, no. 1 (2010): 114–20.

Small, Christopher. *Musicking: The Meanings of Performing and Listening*. Middletown, Conn.: Wesleyan University Press, 1998.

Stone, Kelly. "News—Dachshunds for World Peace." Museum of Contemporary Art Australia. May 30, 2012. http://www.mca.com.au/news/2012/05/30/dachshunds-world-peace/.

Stover, Eric. *The Witnesses: War Crimes and the Promise of Justice in The Hague*. Philadelphia: University of Pennsylvania Press, 2005.

Streiff, Fritz. "The Bemba Acquittal: Checks and Balances at the International Criminal Court." International Justice Monitor. July 18, 2018. https://www.ijmonitor.org/2018/07/the-bemba-acquittal-checks-and-balances-at-the-international-criminal-court/.

Sunde, Karen. Interview with author. New York. February 2011.

———. *Plays by Karen Sunde*. New York: Broadway Play, 2001.

Tan, Marcus. "K-Contagion: Sound, Speed, and Space in 'Gangnam Style.'" *TDR: The Drama Review* 59, no. 1 (spring 2015): 83–96.

Taylor, Adam. "Worldviews: MAP: The U.S. Military Currently Has Troops in These African Countries." *Washington Post*. May 21, 2014. https://www.washingtonpost.com/news/worldviews/wp/2014/05/21/map-the-u-s-currently-has-troops-in-these-african-countries/.

Taylor, Diana. *The Archive and the Repertoire: Performing Cultural Memory in the Americas*. Durham, N.C.: Duke University Press, 2003.
Thomas, June. "Bad Theatre Happens: The Problem with David Hare's Iraq Play." Slate. April 14, 2006. http://www.slate.com/articles/news_and_politics/theater/2006/04/bad_theater_happens.html.
Time. "Jamil the Irrepressible." *Time* 98, no. 24 (December 13, 1971): 46.
Tripp, Aili Mari. *Museveni's Uganda: Paradoxes of Power in a Hybrid Regime*. Boulder, Colo.: Lynne Rienner, 2010.
Tuéni, Ghassan. "Letter Dated 15 March 1978 from the Permanent Representative of Lebanon to the United Nations Addressed to the President of the Security Council." (S/12600). March 15, 1978. http://www.un.org/en/ga/search/view_doc.asp?symbol=s/12600.
Turner, Cathy, and Synne Behrndt. *Dramaturgy and Performance*. Revised edition. New York: Palgrave Macmillan, 2016.
Turner, Victor. *From Ritual to Theatre: The Human Seriousness of Play*. New York: PAJ Publications, 1982.
———. *On the Edge of the Bush: Anthropology as Experience*. Tucson: University of Arizona Press, 1985.
UN General Assembly. Final Document of the Tenth Special Session of the General Assembly. A/S-10/2. Adopted as a resolution, June 30, 1978. http://undocs.org/en/A/S-10/2.
———. Resolution 66/281. "International Day of Happiness." A/RES/66/281. June 28, 2012. https://undocs.org/A/RES/66/281.
———. Tenth Special Session. 9th Plenary Meeting. A/S-10/PV.9. May 30, 1978. http://undocs.org/en/A/S-10/PV.9.
———. Tenth Special Session. 12th Plenary Meeting. A/S-10/PV.12. June 1, 1978. http://undocs.org/en/A/S-10/PV.12.
———. Tenth Special Session. 13th Plenary Meeting. A/S-10/PV.13. June 1, 1978. http://undocs.org/en/A/S-10/PV.13.
———. Tenth Special Session. 19th Plenary Meeting. A/S-10/PV.19. June 6, 1978. http://undocs.org/en/A/S-10/PV.19.
———. Tenth Special Session. 27th Plenary Meeting. A/S-10/PV.27. June 30, 1978. http://undocs.org/en/A/S-10/PV.27.
———. 2400th Plenary Meeting. A/PV.2400. November 10, 1975. http://undocs.org/en/A/PV.2400.
———. Verbatim Record of the 13th Meeting of the Ad Hoc Committee of the Tenth Special Session. A/S-10/AC.1/PV.13. June 23, 1978. http://undocs.org/en/A/S-10/AC.1/PV.13.
———. Verbatim Record of the 15th Meeting of the Ad Hoc Committee of the Tenth Special Session. A/S-10/AC.1/PV.15. June 28, 1978. http://undocs.org/en/A/S-10/AC.1/PV.15.
———. "Viva Vox Choir (Belgrade)—New Year's Concert of the 67th Session of the General Assembly." UN Webcast streaming video, 1:03:31. January 14, 2013. http://webtv.un.org/search/viva-vox-choir-belgrade-new-years-concert-of-the-67th-session-of-the-general-assembly/2094291812001?term=viva%20vox.
UN Secretary-General. "Report of the Secretary-General on the Implementation of Security Council Resolution 425 (1978)." (S/12611). March 19, 1978. http://unispal.un.org/UNISPAL.NSF/0/00ECA24D7952AD83852568BA0070C4B9.

———. "Report of the Secretary-General on the Implementation of Security Council Resolution 1701 (2009)." (S/2017/591). July 11, 2017. https://www.un.org/en/ga/search/view_doc.asp?symbol=S/2017/591/.

———. "Second Special Report of the Secretary-General on the United Nations Organization Mission in the Democratic Republic of the Congo." (S/2003/566). May 17, 2003. http://www.un.org/en/ga/search/view_doc.asp?symbol=S/2003/566.

———. "Third Special Report of the Secretary-General on the United Nations Organization Mission in the Democratic Republic of the Congo." (S/2004/650). August 16, 2004. http://www.un.org/en/ga/search/view_doc.asp?symbol=S/2004/650.

———. "Thirteenth Report of the Secretary-General on the United Nations Organization Mission in the Democratic Republic of the Congo." (S/2003/211). February 21, 2003. http://www.un.org/en/ga/search/view_doc.asp?symbol=S/2003/211.

———. "Thirty-First Report of the Secretary-General on the United Nations Organization Mission in the Democratic Republic of the Congo." (S/2010/164). March 30, 2010. http://www.un.org/en/ga/search/view_doc.asp?symbol=S/2010/164.

UN Security Council. Resolution 1887. "Maintenance of International Peace and Security: Nuclear Non-Proliferation and Nuclear Disarmament." S/RES/1887. September 24, 2009. http://www.un.org/Docs/sc/unsc_resolutions09.htm.

———. "Reports of the Secretary-General on the Sudan." S/PV.5125. February 16, 2005. http://www.un.org/en/sc/meetings/records/2005.shtml.

———. "Security Council [Meeting]: Maintenance of International Peace and Security—Nuclear Non-Proliferation and Nuclear Disarmament." United Nations Webcast RealVideo, English translation, 1:44:00. September 24, 2009. http://www.un.org/webcast/2009.html.

———. "The Situation between Iraq and Kuwait." S/PV.4701. February 5, 2003. http://www.un.org/Depts/dhl/resguide/scact2003.htm.

———. "The Situation between Iraq and Kuwait." S/PV.4692. January 27, 2003. http://www.un.org/Docs/journal/asp/ws.asp?m=S/PV.4692.

United Nations. Charter of the United Nations. June 26, 1945. http://www.un.org/en/documents/charter/.

———. "Growth in United Nations Membership, 1945–Present." 2018. http://www.un.org/en/sections/member-states/growth-united-nations-membership-1945-present/.

———. "International Day of Happiness Event." UN Webcast streaming video, 55:05. March 20, 2015. http://webtv.un.org/watch/international-day-of-happiness-event/4129206146001/.

———. "'Ruined': Ban Attends Theatre Play." YouTube video, 2:57. June 19, 2009. http://www.youtube.com/watch?v=Ftd0G67-ZUk.

———. Treaty on the Non-Proliferation of Nuclear Weapons. July 1, 1968. http://www.un.org/en/conf/npt/2005/npttreaty.html.

United Nations Foundation. "What We Do: Campaigns and Initiatives." 2013. http://www.unfoundation.org/what-we-do/campaigns-and-initiatives/.

Ura, Karma, Sabina Alkire, Tshoki Zangmo, and Karma Wangdi. *A Short Guide to Gross National Happiness Index*. Thimphu: Centre for Bhutan Studies, 2012.

U.S. Department of State. "Seventh Report on War Crimes in the Former Yugoslavia." *U.S. Department of State Dispatch* 4 (April 19, 1993): 257–69.

Vandewalle, Dirk. *A History of Modern Libya*. 2nd edition. Cambridge: Cambridge University Press.

van Leeuwen, Sophie. "This Is Round One, Says Bemba's Lawyer." Justice Hub. March 22, 2016. https://justicehub.org/article/round-one-says-bembas-lawyer.

Van Woudenberg, Anneke. "MONUC: A Case for Peacekeeping Reform." Human Rights Watch. February 28, 2005, https://www.hrw.org/news/2005/02/28/monuc-case-peacekeeping-reform.

Viva Vox Choir. "Choir History." 2015. http://www.vivavoxchoir.com/eng/choir-history.

Weber, Samuel. *Theatricality as Medium*. New York: Fordham University Press, 2004.

Weiss, Thomas George, Tatiana Carayannis, Louis Emmerij, and Richard Jolly. *UN Voices: The Struggle for Development and Social Justice*. Bloomington: Indiana University Press, 2005.

Weiss, Thomas George, David P. Forsythe, Roger A. Coate, and Kelly-Kate Pease. *The United Nations and Changing World Politics*. 5th edition. Boulder, Colo.: Westview, 2007.

Whiting, Alex. "Appeals Judges Turn the ICC on Its Head with Bemba Decision." Just Security. June 14, 2018. https://www.justsecurity.org/57760/appeals-judges-turn-icc-head-bemba-decision/.

Whoriskey, Kate. Introduction to *Ruined*, by Lynn Nottage, ix–xiii. New York: Theatre Communication Group, 2009.

Wickremesekera, Channa. *The Tamil Separatist War in Sri Lanka*. London: Routledge, 2016.

Williams, Ian. "An Un-Green Noggin Heads Earth Summit." *New York Observer*. May 11, 1992.

Williams, Pharrell. *GIRL*. Columbia. 2013.

Worsnip, Patrick. "Obama Debut, Gaddhafi, Ahmedinejad a Potent U.N. Brew." *Reuters*. September 6, 2009. http://www.reuters.com/article/2009/09/06/us-un-assembly-idUSTRE5850DX20090906.

Yester, Katherine. "Happy Math." *Foreign Policy*. October 14, 2009. http://foreignpolicy.com/2009/10/14/happy-math/.

INDEX

Page numbers in **boldface** refer to illustrations.

abjection, 103, 105, 106, 180n39
activism, 20, 64, 76, 155–56
aesthetics and politics, relationship between, 13–15, 34, 35
Afghanistan, 67, 144
Agasandyan, Mikael, 25
Ahmed, Sara, 95, 106, 180n45
Ahrendt, Rebekah, et al., 180n27
Akasaka, Kiyotaka, 43
al-Assad, Bashar, 6
al-Bashir, Omar, 109–10
Aluoch, Joyce, 128
Americans, The (television series), 161
Araud, Gérard, **2**, 6–7, 8
Arbour, Louise, 109
Arria-formula meetings, 29–30, 74
Autesserre, Séverine, 168n9, 171n55, 171n63, 172n67
Avdović, Erol, 101, 104, 105
Ayala-Lasso, José, 142

Ban Ki-moon, 6–7, 46, **70**, 81; International Happiness Day and, 95–96, 98; Paris Agreement and, **132**; Psy and, 91–92, 93; Viva Vox Choir and, 99–100, 101–5
Baranac, Zoran, 100, 102
Baroody, Jamil, 99, 145
Bartlett, Dan, 36–37
Battlestar Galactica (television series), 43–44, 47, 66–67, 157, 168n2
Bechdel, Alison, 71–72, 76, 78. *See also Fun Home*
Bellamy, Alex J., and Paul D. Williams, 169n16
Bemba, Liliane, 116, 129
Bemba Gombo, Jean-Pierre, 18, 57, 112–13, 116, 118, 123, 126–30, 183n14; acquittal of, 130–31, 186n66

Benito, Odio, 121
Benjamin, Walter, 84–85
Benndorf, Rosemarie, 151–52
Bensouda, Fatou, 118, 128
Bernero, Edward Allen, 157
Bhabha, Homi, 178n51
Bhutan, 95
Binički, Stanislav, "March on the Drina," 100, 101–2, 104
Blair, Tony, 35
Blix, Hans, 31–32, 37–38
Bosnia, 29, 101
Brantley, Ben, 60
Bregman, Ahron, 49
Brown, Gordon, 87, 89
Bueno, Olivia, 122
Burkina Faso, 87, 96
Bush, George H. W., 145
Bush, George W., 31, 34, 35, 38, 159
Butler, Judith, 79

Canning, Charlotte M., 165n44
Carter, Jimmy, 149
Cheney, Dick, 37, 67
China, 10, 25, 28, 87
Chow, Rey, 170n40
Churkin, Vitaly I., **2**, 6–7, 24, 25
clapping and applause, implications of, 102–4, 180n38
Claude, Inis L., 9
climate change, 20, 91, 98, 150–57
Clinton, Hillary, 85, 134
Coastal Road Massacre, 48
Cohen, Raymond, 145
colonialism, 57, 63, 82, 110, 173n94, 178n51
consensus: diplomatic goal of, 17, 46, 77, 88, 92, 102, 105, 146, 148–49; in theater, 149. *See also* dissensus

205

Congo, Democratic Republic of the (DRC), 10, 17, 23, 47, 56–62, 63, 112–16, 118, 122, 127, 138; Autesserre on, 171n55, 171n63, 172n67
Congress of North American Bosniaks, 101, 103
Connor, Steven, 102, 103
Cotte, Bruno, 137–41
Cousteau, Philippe, 96
Cover, Robert, 119
Crossing Lines (television program), 18, 123–29

Daniel, Louis, 124–25
Darfur. *See* Sudan
Davis, Tracy C., 14, 83
Debord, Guy, 71, 75, 79, 80
Debrix, François, 50
devised theater, 51, 137, 188n10
DiCaprio, Leonardo, 156–57
diplomacy, etymology of, 136, 187n7
diplomacy and performance (diplomatic theater), 4–5, 7, 8, 13, 15, 16–19, 30, 73–75, 78–79, 81–82, 89, 129–30, 161; Broadway comparisons, 71, 79; history of, 26–27; motivations for, 19–20
diplomacy and texts, 18, 26, 135–58; brackets in, 146–48, 151–52; Herzog performance of, 144; Powell performance of, 31–33, 35–36, 167n19; Qaddafi performance of, 81–84
"diplomatic performatives," 5, 73–75, 79, 83–86, 88, 95; definition of, 175n9
dissensus, 83, 88, 103, 141, 143, 149, 188n21
documentary theater, 33, 34–35, 166n18
Douglas, Mary, 28
dramaturgy defined, 12–13, 15, 17, 18
Dromgoole, Dominic, 23, 26, 166n7

Earle, Sylvia, 96
Eban, Abba, 145
Eboe-Osuji, Chile, 130
Edkins, Jenny, 15
Edmunds, Rod, 121
Egypt, 10, 63

Eick, David, 43, 67
ElBaradei, Mohamed, 32
Eliav, Pinhas, 48
El-P, 134, 135, 187n2
empathy, 47, 60–61, 78, 173n81; "critical empathy," 61, 68; as policy tool, 73, 157
emplacement, 14–18, 20, 49, 89, 97, 99, 104, 111, 115
equine dance crazes, 92–93
Erskine, Emmanuel A., 50–52, 64, 170n37, 173n94

Farrow, Mia, 110, 111
Fernando, B. J., 148–49
Fichtner, William, 124, 127
Fofé, Jean-Pierre, 138–39
Foucault, Michel, 64–65, 174n96
France, 6–7, 37
Friedman, Sharon, 61
Fulford, Adrian, 119, 122
Fun Home (Broadway musical), 17, 71–78, 80, 87, 88, 104, 157

Garcia, Lucio, 138, 139, 141
Gbandi, Kenneth, 152
gender-based violence and exploitation, 23, 47, 58–59, 64, 65, 102; Bemba trial and, 112, 113–15, 131
Goldberg, Whoopi, 43–45
Goulding, Marrack, 62–63
governmentality, 18, 64–65, 68, 91, 95, 96–97, 104, 106, 126, 174n96; Foucault on, 64–65
Green, Jeffrey Edward, 15, 177n40
Gross National Happiness metric, 95, 96–97, 105
Guterres, António, 159

Haley, Nikki, **158**, 159–61
Hammarskjöld, Dag, 10, 99, 104
Hammersmith, James, 29
Hannig, Ute, 156, 157
happiness and harmony, institutional attempts at, 95–99, 105
Happy Party website, 97–98
Happy Planet Index, 96
Hare, David, *Stuff Happens*, 17, 34–40, 104, 177n42
harmony metaphor, 100, 180n27

Index

Haslam, Emily, 121
Haynes, Peter, 115, 129, 130
Heller, Kevin Jon, 123–28
Helms, Ed, 33, 34
Henry, Marsha, 50
Herzog, Chaim, 99, 144
Hesford, Wendy, 61
Hezbollah, 46, 49, 53
Hezel, Bernd, 152
Higate, Paul, 50, 59
Higgins, William R., 46, 52, 170n37
Hillen, John, 169n25
Hofmański, Piotr, 130
Holderness, Graham, 26
Hooper, David, 138–39
House of Cards (television program), 25
Howe, Dave, 43, 46
human rights, 3, 20, 44, 47, 65, 74, 87, 117, 160. *See also* UN Human Rights Council

India, 10
institutional memory, 28, 41
"insurrectionary speech," 79–80, 89
International Atomic Energy Agency, 11, 32, 89
International Criminal Court (ICC), 5, 6, 11, 12, 16, 18, 19–21, 109–31, 137, 155; African view of, 116, 183n14; founding and function of, 181n5, 183n13; intermediaries at, 119–21; transcripts at, 138–41, 183n8; Victims and Witnesses Unit (VWU) of, 115, 183n13
International Happiness Day, 95–97
interposition, 49, 50, 56
Iran, 89, 160
Iraq, 10, 23, 31–40, 67, 74, 144
Israel, 30, 48–49, 51–52, 63, 144, 145, 160
Iverson, Eric, 113–15

Jaroszek, Henryk, 146
Jeremić, Vuk, 100, 101, 102, 105

Kabila, Joseph, 57, 116
Kabila, Laurent-Désiré, 57
Katanga, Germain, 138, 140, 141, 188n11
Kear, Adrian, 15

Kershaw, Baz, 180n38
Khrushchev, Nikita, 99
Killer Mike, 134, 135, 187n2
Klee, Paul, 84–85
Kolnai, Aurel, 105, 106
Kony, Joseph, 88
Krasner, David, 173n81
Kristeva, Julia, 180n39
Krogh, Per, 84
Kron, Lisa, 71, 75–76, 77–78

Lavigne, Bernard, 119
League of Nations, 8, 9, 36
Lebanon, 17, **42**, 47–55, 63
Lee, Matthew, 26
Lennon, John, "Imagine," 101
LGBTI rights, 72, 74–75, 77, 88, 175n3
Libya, 81–82, 84, 144
liveness, 36, 53, 142
Lorin, Jasmina, 100
Loughrey, Bryan, 26
Lubango Dyilo, Thomas, 18, 118–22
Lyall Grant, Mark, 24–25

Mabille, Catherine, 119, 122
MacDonald, Eric, 140, 141
male gaze, 172n71
Martin, Carol, 166n18
Mazower, Mark, 164n16, 177n36
McDonnell, Mary, 43, 66–68
Médecins Sans Frontières, 58, 127
Mexico, 67
Miller, Bennett, *Dachshund UN*, 3–5, 6, 155, 157
Mobuto Sese Seko, 57
Mohamad, Abdalmahmood Abdalhaleem, **108**, 109–11
Monageng, Sanji, 130
moral disgust, grounds for, 105
Moreno Ocampo, Luis, **108**, 109–11, 128; *Crossing Lines* and, 124–25
Morrison, Howard, 130
multilateralism, 21, 25, 85
Muppet Show, The (television series), 82
Museveni, Yoweri, 17, 80, 87–89, 178n48
music events staged by UN, 17, 91–106, 159
"musicking," 93–94, 103–4

Nahas, Subhi, 74
Nasser, Maher, 98
Ndahinda, Felix Mukwiza, 183n11
Newby, Vanessa S., 169n22
Newman, Paul, 149, 152
Ngudjolo Chui, Mathieu, 138, 188n11
Ngũgĩ wa Thiong'o, 34
Nguyen Phuong Nga, 72
9/11 attacks, 34, 35, 54
Nixon, Cynthia, 71, 76
North Korea, 10, 160
Nottage, Lynn, *Ruined*, 17, 47, 56–64, 65, 104, 157
nuclear energy, 87–88
nuclear weapons and disarmament, 9, 19, 81, 84–89, 142–49
Nuseibeh, Hazem, 147–48

Obama, Barack, 7, 17, 88, 159; at UN, 71, 74, 80, 85, 89
Obia, Akurotho, 138, 141
O'Brien, Conor Cruise, 104
Olmos, Edward James, 43–46, 51, 66–68
Organization for the Prohibition of Chemical Weapons (OPCW), 7, 11
Ostrower, Alexander, 136, 187n7
Ozaki, Kuniko, 128

Pakistan, 10
Palestine, 26, 30
Palestine Liberation Organization (PLO), 48–49
Paratene, Rawiri, 27, 30–31, 34, 73
Paris, Roland, 173n94
Patassé, Ange-Félix, 112
Patten, Lauren, 73
peacekeeping. *See under* spectatorship; United Nations
Peel, Quentin, 81–82
performance. *See* diplomacy and performance; "diplomatic performatives"; *and under* power; theater
performance as epistemology, 44, 45, 68, 168n3
performance space: expectations of, 99, 179n24; peacekeeping and, 49–51

performance studies, 14, 20, 44, 121
Pharrell (Williams), 17, **90**, 96–99, 102, 157
Pillay, Navi, 47
postdramatic theater, 135, 137, 138
Powell, Colin, 17, **22**, 31–40, 104, 167n19
power: performance and, 19–20, 40–41, 79, 83, 130, 137; "soft power," 26, 72, 97, 166n7, 175n5; spectatorship and, 14–15, 17, 47, 95
Power, Samantha, 17, 71, 73–78, 80, 87, 159, 160
Probst, Leonard, 149
Psy (Park-Jae Sang), 17, 91–92, 93, 157

Qaddafi, Muammar, 17, **70**, 80–85, 87–88, 89, 155; death of, 176n31

race, 44–45
Rajapaksa, Mahinda, 117
Rancière, Jacques, 14, 143, 154, 155
rap and hip-hop, words and violence in, 133–35
Reinelt, Janelle, 39, 188n17
Rice, Condoleezza, 38
Rice, Susan, 85
Riles, Annelise, 146
Rimini Protokoll, 137; model proposed by, 153–54; *World Climate Conference*, 150–57
Rome Statute, 117, 124–27, 181n5, 183n13
Rumsfeld, Donald, 38
Run the Jewels. *See* Shadow, DJ
Russia, 9–10, 23, 25, 28, 72, 144, 170n37
Rwanda, 10, 23, 57

Sanders, Bernie, 134
Sarkozy, Nicolas, 89
Saudi Arabia, 144, 145, 156
Schechner, Richard, 14, 137
Schipper, Imanuel, 150–51, 152–54, 156–57
Serbia, 99–103
Shaaban, Muhammad, 70
Shadow, DJ, and Run the Jewels, "Nobody Speak," 133–35, 145, 157

Index

Shakespeare, William: Globe Theatre and, 29, 157, 166n7; *Hamlet*, 17, 23–27, 29–30, 33–34, 39, 104;
Skloot, Robert, 60
Small, Christopher, 93–94, 179n24
South Africa, 144, 145, 177n36
South Korea, 10, 91
Soviet Union. *See* Russia
spectatorship, 14–15, 46, 91, 103–4, 111, 165n42, 177n40; action and, 41, 61, 79; dance and, 92–93; global political, 5, 6, 12, 13, 15, 16, 20–21; ICC and, 111, 112, 118–19; governmentalizing force of, 65; peacekeeping and, 49, 50–53, 56, 61, 65, 68; power and, 14–15, 17, 47; in *Ruined*, 59–60; in *Stuff Happens*, 37–38; violence and, 59–60, 64, 65
speech acts, 45, 47, 79–80, 135, 146, 175n9
Sri Lanka, 117
Stand and Deliver (film), 45
Stavropolous, Constantin, 145
Steiner, Sylvia, 114, 115–16, 128–29
Straw, Jack, 36
Sudan, 109–11
Sunde, Karen, *In a Kingdom by the Sea*, 17, 46, 47, 52–56, 62–64, 66, 104, 157, 170n45
Sutherland, Donald, 124–25, 127
Syria, 6–8, 25, 63, 74, 144

Tan, Marcus, 92
Taylor, Diana, 168n3, 184n31, 185n35
Tesori, Jeanine, 71, 76, 77, 78, 94
theater: definitions of, 12, 78–79, 111, 136; text vs. performance of, 136–37
theatricality: definitions of, 12, 83, 89; skepticism of, 82–83; spectatorship and, 14–15, 83, 89
Thomas, June, 33
time: cyclical, 80, 89; irreversible, 80, 85, 89; teleological, 140
transcripts: archival use of, 16; Hare's use of, 34–35; performative functions of, 135–41; Powell's use of, 28, 31, 33–35; sources of, 167n19
Treki, Ali Abdussalam, **70**, 81
Trump, Donald, 21, 134, 159, 160

Tuéni, Ghassan, 48
Turner, Ted, 96
Turner, Victor, 14, 165n32

Uganda, 63, 88
Ukraine, 23
"unfolding present," 75–80, 83, 89, 144
United Kingdom, 6–7, 24–25, 87, 133–34
United Nations: Economic and Social Council (ESOSOC) Chamber of, 23, 25, 29, 39, 43, 45, 66; founding and charter of, 8–11, 82–84, 91, 141–42, 164n16; General Assembly role in, 11; organization of, 9–12, 164n26; peacekeeping operations of, 10, 11, 17, 46, 47, 49, 57–59, 64–65; penholders at, 28; Right of Reply at, 145; Secretariat role in, 11; secretary-general role in, 10, 91, 104
United Nations Development Fund for Women, 58
United Nations Disengagement Observer Force (UNDOF), 63
United Nations Foundation, 96, 98
United Nations Framework Convention on Climate Change (UNFCCC), 150–57, 189n46
United Nations Human Rights Council, 3, 72, 74
United Nations Interim Force in Lebanon (UNIFIL), 17, **42**, 46, 48–56, 63, 64, 169n22
United Nations Monitoring, Verification, and Inspection Committee, 32
United Nations Organization Mission in the Democratic Republic of the Congo (MONUC), 17, 57–59, 62, 64, 174nn95–96
United Nations Resolutions: General Assembly, no. 65/309, 95; no. 66/281, 95; no. 3379, 144; S-10/2, 143; Security Council, nos. 425 and 426, 49–50; no. 1325, 23; no. 1593, 109; no. 1887, 85–87; no. 2118, 7;
United Nations Security Council: location and decor of, 84–85; permanent members of, 9, 10–11, 28, 82–83; role of, 11, 17, 27–28; Rules of Procedure at, 27–28; veto power of, 9, 164n15

United Nations Truce Supervision Organization (UNTSO), 10, 63, 169n25, 170n37
United States Mission to the United Nations (US–UN), 72, 159–60, 175n5

Van den Wyngaert, Christine, 130–31
Van Woudenberg, Anneke, 65
Villepin, Dominique de, 37
violence. *See* gender-based violence; rap and hip-hop; spectatorship
Viva Vox Choir, 17, 99–102, 105, 157

Waldheim, Kurt, 51
Walters, Barbara, 38
war, performances justifying, 31
Weber, Samuel, 14–15
Whoriskey, Kate, 63–64
Wilder, Thornton, 75
Wolff, Michael, *Fire and Fury*, 161, 190n7

YouTube, 91, 128; UN's channel on, 47

Zimbabwe, 154–55